Dedication

I dedicate this book to Nancy Kerr, my best friend and frequent mountain companion for all the years that this guide was in development. Much of the time, she would rather have been in other places, doing other things—I thank her, for sticking it out.

EMIGRANT WILDERNESS

AND NORTHWESTERN YOSEMITE

Ben Schifrin

Wilderness Press
Berkeley

FIRST EDITION February 1990
Second printing May 1992

Copyright © 1990 by Ben Schifrin
Photos by the author except as indicated
Cover photo: Maxwell Lake © 1990 by Thomas Winnett
Maps revised by Larry Van Dyke, Jeffrey P. Schaffer and Barbara Jackson
Design by Thomas Winnett
Library of Congress Card Catalog Number 89-40027
International Standard Book Number 0-89997-103-2
Manufactured in the United States of America
Published by Wilderness Press
              2440 Bancroft Way
              Berkeley, CA 94704
              (510) 843-8080

Write for free catalog

Library of Congress Cataloging-in-Publication Data

Schifrin, Ben.
    Emigrant Wilderness and northwestern Yosemite / Ben Schifrin.
        p.   cm.
    ISBN 0-89997-103-2
    1. Hiking--California--Emigrant Wilderness--Guide-books.
    2. Outdoor recreation--California--Emigrant Wilderness--Guidebooks.
    3. Natural history--California--Emigrant Wilderness.   4. Emigrant
    Wilderness (Calif.)--Guidebooks.   I. Title.
    GV199.42.C22E476   1990
    917.94'47--dc20   89-40027
                                                        CIP
                                                        r89

CONTENTS

Acknowledgements

Thomas Winnett and Jeff Schaffer of Wilderness Press have patiently allowed this book project to drag out for years. In addition, they have kindly allowed me to use prose and trail maps from previous works. I thank Jeff Schaffer, cartographer *extraordinaire,* for his map and description of the Pacific Crest Trail in the Tower Peak quadrangle—this guide's Route YP-2.

My grandfather, Elmo W. Adams, introduced me to the joys of camping and natural history in general, and the delights of the Sierra Nevada in particular. Without his direction, I doubt that I'd have ever written this trail guide.

Todd Fitzgibbon supplied companionship on Emigrant Basin forays by foot, ski, mountain bike and airplane, too numerous to count. I also appreciate his sage advice on all things geological—he is a keen observer and explained many mysteries.

Blaine Rodgers, a pre-eminent Sierran botanist and professor of biology at Columbia College, gave me notes on the evolution of the Sierran alpine flora which contributed to my chapter on mountain ecology.

Ch. 1: The Hospitable Wilderness
An Introduction to the Emigrant Basin and The Yosemite North Country

Near Sonora Pass, the Sierra Nevada's two personalities meet. To the north, born of volcanic fire, rolling hillsides and heavily forested canyons predominate. To the south, the ice-carved High Sierra is wild, raw and bare. In the huge wilderness covered by this guidebook, fire and ice meet, creating a land of startling contrasts and variety.

The Emigrant Wilderness may be the best-kept secret of the High Sierra. While hordes of backpackers, fishermen and mountaineers throng to the alpine lakes and crags of national parks and wildernesses in the southern Sierra, the Emigrant Wilderness and the adjacent north boundary country of Yosemite National Park have mile upon mile of sweeping granite ridges, spectacular vistas, and a lifetime of fishing possibilities in literally hundreds of sparkling mountain lakes. While families and day hikers trample the Lake Tahoe region in search of easy trails, away from unpredictable high-country weather, the 118,000-acre Emigrant Wilderness offers hike after easy hike in quiet, middle-mountain forest, reaching dozens of safe, pretty campsites. And crowds are the exception, rather than the rule.

Anyone can find fun, relaxation, and solitude in the Emigrant Wilderness at any time of year. The trout fishing is legendary (yet many lakes are still lightly fished), and this guidebook describes most of the fishable waters. Most wilderness visitors are hikers and backpackers, and, for them, much of this hospitable land is available most of the year. Since the lowest trails, near Pinecrest Lake, Cherry Reservoir and Hetch Hetchy are usually snow-free by early May, and even the highest elevations are accessible by late June, the wilderness season begins a month earlier than in the higher southern Sierra. For your summer pleasure, this guide describes every mile of trail, and most of the good cross-country routes in this hiker's paradise.

The high country stays open well into October, until snow blankets the region. When winter comes, wilderness enthusiasts don't need to look to overcrowded, expensive ski areas to enjoy the snow, for this guidebook describes cross-country ski tours that traverse the wilderness.

Using this guidebook is easy. If you know where you want to go, just find the appropriate trail in the route descriptions, and take off, guided by the prose and the updated topographic map inside this book's back cover. If you don't know where you want to go—browse through the introductions for some hikes, until you find one of appealing length and character. Alternatively, scan the topo map for a nice-looking spot. The topo map is keyed to the route chapters, so that you will immediately know which trail description to look up, to describe a particular path.

To enjoy your stay in the backcountry even more, spend your lunch hour educating yourself about the origins of its landforms, the patterns of its ecosystems and its human history as explained in the chapters that follow. You will gain a deeper appreciation of its value—and you will want to return again.

Finally, there are alternatives to walking to enjoy the Northern Yosemite-Emigrant Basin high country. Check out the chapters on horse packing, cross-country skiing, mountain biking and rock climbing to gain new perspectives for enjoyment of John Muir's Range of Light—the most hospitable mountains in America.

Ch. 2: The Lay of the Land
Evolution of the Emigrant Basin Landscape

The Sierra Nevada:
A Short Biography:

The Sierra of today, which appears to be a range in comparative infancy, was born over 200 million years ago! Back then, the Pacific Ocean lapped against what is now the Sierra's foothills. While dinosaurs battled above, vast quantities of molten rock, called magma, migrated up through the earth's crust under eastern California in giant liquid irregular-shaped columns. Some of the magma reached the surface, erupted, and constructed volcanoes, but most of it cooled several miles below the earth's surface, solidifying into discrete bodies, called plutons. In each pluton the minerals slowly crystallized from the mixture to form one or another kind of granitic rock. Plutons were created from about 210 to about 80 million years ago, and they compose collectively the Sierra Nevada batholith. (This originally extended unbroken, eastward into western Nevada.) The granitic intrusions buckled the overlying strata, and the pressure and heat to which the overlying rocks were subjected altered their crystalline structure—that is, the pressure and heat **metamorphosed** the rocks. This was not the first time these overlying rocks had been metamorphosed. Indeed, some of the older rocks, which originally may have been sandstone, shale, limestone and volcanic rocks, had been metamorphosed as many as five times by major compressive forces in the earth's crust. Each episode of metamorphism was likely accompanied by mountain building. The Sierra Nevada may have been a substantial range throughout its lengthy period of plutonism, which ended about 80 million years ago.

The lofty Sierra Nevada, shedding prodigious sediments for millions of years, had forced the Pacific Ocean westward until it was just west of the present-day Great Valley. Gradually, the Sierra's volcanic and metamorphic rocks were gnawed away by the erosive action of wind, sun, frost and rain. By some 50 million years ago, most of the overlying layers had been removed from the now low range, baring the granitic batholith. The climate during the erosive period was quite tropical, with much rain and lush vegetation. During this time, a thick, bright-red soil was formed by weathering of the rocks to clay and iron oxides (rust). One special mineral, however, was resistant to the weathering process—gold. This very heavy element, collected in veins found in the upper batholith and the metamorphic rocks, was eroded from them and washed downstream to be redeposited at the base of the range. These rich alluvial deposits, called placers, would draw fortune seekers from around the world in the Gold Rush of 1849.

About 30 million years ago, this erosive period was replaced by one of renewed volcanic activity and uplift. This phase was marked by two types of eruptive products: rapid, glowing avalanches and slower lava flows. The period opened, no doubt, with a bang. From vents near and east of what is now the Sierra crest, many cubic miles of hot volcanic ash cascaded over the Sierra, burying most of the previous landscape. Ash eruptions were followed by eruptions of denser volcanic rocks which, saturated with water and mixed with sediments, were transformed into voluminous mudflows. Man's major interest in these ancient volcanic activities—remnants of which blanket the Emigrant Basin—is that they buried the river channels that contained placer gold. These volcanic flows now form mountains that overlie old granitic river beds—a process called "topographic inversion." A classic example is East Flange Rock and the Three Chimneys, as seen from the Night Cap Trail—the granite trough filled with extrusive debris is obvious. The Dardanelles, just north of our area, are another example.

Well into the phase of volcanism, the Sierra began to tilt. Certainly by 10 million years ago, the present-day Sierra and some land to its east, began to rotate upon an axis somewhere in the Great Valley. By about 3 million years ago, mammoth cracks, or faults, developed along the top of the arched Sierra, and eastern lands dropped to form Mono Basin, Owens Valley and other fault-formed eastside depressions.

The final chapter of the Sierra's evolution to date is primarily a cosmetic one: about 2½ million years ago a world-wide Ice Age began, and glaciers covered the latitudinal extremes and the mountainous regions of the earth. In the Sierra Nevada, glaciers were so extensive that they coalesced into an octopuslike ice cap which, in northern Yosemite and the Emigrant Basin, covered almost the entire area above 8000 feet. Glaciers waxed and waned, and they were responsible for the deep U-shaped valleys, the sparkling lakes and waterfalls, and the glacier-transported debris, or till—a loose mix of boulders, sand and pebbles—now found throughout the Sierran backcountry.

The Rocks:

One will find three types of rocks in the Emigrant Wilderness: intrusive, extrusive, and metamorphic. The intrusive rocks, usually granites, and the extrusive rocks, which are the products of volcanic eruptions, belong to the igneous rock family, which encompasses all rocks formed from magma. The metamorphic rocks we see used to be another kind of rock, but heat and pressure altered them to their present states.

Intrusive Rocks—Taken for Granite:

The intrusive rocks are of greatest interest to the Sierra traveler, for they make up most of the High Sierra. Molten magma, because of its relative lightness, rises to near the earth's surface, or, as extrusive rock, bursts upon it. As this superheated fluid cools, its rate of cooling and its chemical makeup determine what kind of igneous rock will form. Some minerals solidify at higher temperatures than others. In igneous rocks, the minerals that do are rich in iron, calcium and magnesium. These minerals are usually darker and always denser than those that form at lower temperatures, such as quartz, which is the last mineral to form in granitic rocks. The presence of both heavier, dark minerals, called **mafic** because of their high **ma**gnesium and iron (**Fe**) content, plus the light-weight, light-colored **felsic** minerals (high in **fel**dspar and **si**lica) result in the usual salt-and-pepper coloration and pattern of most Sierran intrusive rocks.

A colorful variety of intrusive rocks is seen in the Sierra, due to varying combinations of mafic and felsic minerals. Granite and quartz monzonite are examples of felsic (high-quartz) rocks. True granite is uncommon in the Sierra, but much quartz monzonite is found. In the intermediate range lies granodiorite, quite common in the Emigrant Basin, while the darker mafic rocks (little or no quartz) are diorite, gabbro and peridotite, outcrops of which are scattered throughout the area, particularly at the edges of contacts with metamorphic rocks. See them near Whitesides Meadow, Toejam Lake, Studhorse Meadow, the Bond Pass High Trail, or the path between Black Bear Lake and Twin Lakes. Formed under conditions of higher temperature and pressure than felsic rocks, mafic rocks are more unstable at the low temperatures and pressures found at the earth's surface. This makes them weather more easily than the granites and granodiorites, as can be seen near Whitesides Meadow, or at 5600 feet in Cherry Creek canyon. Here, as in other places throughout the region, granodiorite stands obdurate against the elements while, close by, gabbroic rock crumbles to sand.

Usually, the texture of intrusive rocks is rather uniform and granular. However, in many spots across the Yosemite Sierra, the rock seems to be made of white cubes, up to 2 inches on a side, imbedded in a smaller-grained matrix. These light cubes are crystals of potassium feldspar which formed early in the cooling phase. The textured rock they form is called a granitic porphyry.

Dikes and xenoliths will be commonly seen in association with the intrusive rocks. A dike is formed when new magmatic material, usually of a different composition, flows into a fissure in either a cooling pluton or an intruded rock. Two types are seen: Aplite dikes, composed of sugary-textured light minerals, are quite common, while pegmatite dikes, marked by large, coarse crystalline structure, are more rare. In pegmatites many valuable mineral deposits, such as gold or, in the Emigrant Basin, tungsten, are found.

Xenoliths are pockets of minerals (usually dark) found in the lighter granitic pluton. They have two origins. 1) As a pluton intrudes the overlying rock (called country rock) most of that rock melts and is assimilated into the pluton. Often, however, some chunks of country rock are too big to be completely melted—this leaves chunks of country rock, usually metamorphosed by the heat, imbedded in the pluton. 2) A second, more common type of xenolith forms when convection currents in the cooling magma swirl newly formed dark mafic minerals into eddies. When the pluton finishes crystallizing, these accumulations appear as oval lenses, generally with their longer dimension pointing in the direction of the ancient convection current. Examples of these xenolith swarms are seen near 7600 feet in North Fork Cherry Creek and near Waterhouse Lake. We can tell that the xenoliths at Waterhouse Lake are of the convection-eddy variety because they have some cubic feldspar crystals mixed with them, and these also occur in the surrounding porphyritic rock. If these xenoliths had been chunks of country rock, no minerals from the pluton would be found in them.

Breaking It All Down—How Granites Crumble:

An observant traveler in the Emigrant Basin will note that many major features of the landscape—cliffs, outcrops and valleys—are predetermined in their shape by one of two kinds of fracturing of the rock. The

Right-angle joints in granite bedrock (from summit of Mercur Peak)

Exfoliation of a granite dome in Emigrant Wilderness

effects of the first kind, jointing, can be determined merely by looking at the region's topo map. Note how all the major canyons and their attendant ridges trend northeast/southwest, while most tributaries are at right angles to them. These large-scale features are controlled by granite's tendency to fracture along three planes, all at right angles to one another, forming solid rectangles.

The second type of fracturing, responsible more for smaller features—generally domes and cliffs—is called exfoliation sheeting. Exfoliation can be likened to the peeling of an onion, layer by layer. Huge, curved sheets of granitic rock, from only inches to tens of feet thick, separate from the parent rock, and their departure gradually rounds it to form the numerous domes, large and small, and the sweeping cliffs that abound in Emigrant Wilderness. The mechanism behind exfoliation is thought to involve the original crystal structure of the rock as it cooled many miles beneath the surface. The crystals were so arranged to withstand the incredible pressure at this great depth. Then, as erosion removed the overlying soil, the crystal structure, which was "pushing up" to support its burden, no longer had so much weight above. The internal pressure then fractured the rock roughly along the profile of the ground surface above it. Hence, exfoliation sheets that develop along a canyon's walls are roughly parallel to the walls, while those that form under a flat area are essentially horizontal.

Rivers of Ice—Sculptors of Granite:

The remaining features of intrusive rocks that we see today were added by the Ice Age, which temporarily ended about 10,000 years ago. Massive tongues of ice emanated from **cirques,** which are ice-carved mountain hollows where snow accumulation exceeds melting. Cirques abound in the area: Kirkwood and Beartrap lakes, the Cascade Creek Basin, Leavitt Lake's bowl, the basin of Upper Peninsula Lake and the trough in which Many Island Lake rests are examples of cirques. Glaciers had three tools with which to sculpt the landscape: rock debris, weight and freezing. As the glacier moved, it picked up and carried with it loose rock fragments, ranging in size from sand grains to rocks the size of Greyhound buses. These rocks, embedded in the moving ice, chiseled, gouged, scratched and polished the underlying rocks. Long, parallel grooves, called **striae** and found throughout our area, indicate the direction of a glacier's flow. Where sand could do its work, the rock below was given a mirrorlike finish. Often, jointing or exfoliation features were so aligned that a glacier could tear off massive blocks or flakes. Frozen firmly into the glacier, the rock was "plucked" from the bedrock. Plucking is responsible for the staircase alternation of steep faces and smooth flats that one sees while walking up any valley in the Emigrant Wilderness. Where rock was massive and resistant, the glacier could get no purchase, and its effort was expended in smoothing the surface. Wherever the glacier could grip an edge, however, it ripped up large chunks of rock. The French term **roche moutonnée** is used for glacially scoured outcrops that show this action: smooth and gentle on the upstream side; rough, broken and steep-faced downstream. *Roches moutonnées* are found throughout the northern Yosemite Sierra.

"Erratic" glacial boulder

Extrusives: Hot Rocks in a Land of Ice:

The ruddy-brown ridge stretching from Cooper Peak to East Flange Rock, Relief Peak and Leavitt Peak is a remnant of a thick blanket of extrusive rocks that once completely covered today's primarily granitic landscape.

Extrusive igneous rocks, like the intrusives, were formed from a chemical soup called magma. One difference between an extrusive rock and the corresponding intrusive rock is that the extrusive one, being exposed to the air, cooled much more quickly and had very little time for crystals to grow in it. Hence, most extrusive rocks are more fine-grained than intrusive rocks are. Silicon-rich quartz latite will be seen when you climb the 7200-foot ridge separating the Bell and Lily Creek waters on the Bell Meadow Trail, while iron-rich andesite, a much more commonly seen porous volcanic rock of a gray-to-red-brown color, is found throughout the Basin's volcanic outcrops. Most of the andesite is seen as a jumble of textures and colors mixed willy-nilly throughout a cementing matrix, the result of volcanic mudflows, called **lahars.** As andesite was ejected from vents near the Sierra crest (near Relief Peak in our region), it mixed with water to flow as far as the Central Valley. This rock is called mudflow **breccia** (meaning made of fragments) or **agglomerate.** Castle Rock, the Three Chimneys and Big Sam are remnants of volcanic mudflows.

Less commonly seen is a very fine-grained gray rock, which upon close examination seems to have bits of glass scattered in it. This is **tuff,** the remnant of glowing-hot avalanches of volcanic ash. The Pacific Crest Trail crosses such rocks on the shoulder of Leavitt Peak.

A final point of interest in Sierran volcanic rocks is the presence underneath them of uranium-bearing minerals in the Niagara and Eagle Creek drainages. The largest uranium mine in California, the Juniper Mine, discovered in 1955, is located south of Sardine Meadow. Here, worked from a large open pit, uranium-bearing minerals named autunite, torbernite and uraninite are found in a black alluvium resting on granite. In association with these minerals, many pieces of petrified wood can be found, a reminder of the dense vegetation that prevailed there at the time volcanos were erupting.

That's Gneiss—It Must Be Metamorphic:

Metamorphic rocks are not common in the Yosemite region. However, they are interesting in part because they contain the only economically important minerals yet found deep in the wilderness.

The major metamorphic feature of the western Emigrant Basin is the Toms Canyon **septum,** which runs discontinuously south from Whitesides Meadow to near Studhorse Meadow. A septum, in the geologic sense, is a remnant of a metamorphic formation. In Toms Canyon all but scattered outcrops of the original metamorphic rock, surrounded by the plutonic rocks which melted the rest of it, have been eroded away. What remains consists of compactly folded rock ranging from dark colored schist (a fine-grained metamorphic rock that easily fractures along

the old sedimentary layers to light-colored gneiss (a coarse-grained previously granitic rock that has been compressed into layers). Mixed in and cutting through all these rocks are numerous dikes of very dark, coarse-grained ultramafic intrusive rock, called gabbro.

The major metamorphic feature of the eastern Emigrant Wilderness is the Bigelow Peak roof pendant, sitting astride the Yosemite Park boundary from Twin Lakes to Bond Pass, with a smaller pendant stretching across the ridge north from Dorothy Lake to just west of Cinko Lake. These are large remnants of the now-metamorphosed sea-bottom alluvial rocks into which the Sierran granites intruded. The Bigelow Peak roof pendant consists of tortured, twisted layers of marble (metamorphosed limestone), gneiss, schist and quartzite (metamorphosed sand). Near contact zones with the surrounding granitic rocks, deposits, called tactites, of tungsten-rich scheelite ore were discovered in 1941. These have been prospected extensively, and mined briefly, but the quantities of this valuable steel-hardening mineral have thankfully been too small to justify full-scale mining in the Emigrant Basin.

Toms Canyon septum

Ch. 3: What Grows Where
Patterns of Plants and Wildlife in the High Sierra

Life Zones—The Master Plan:

In 1898 naturalist C. Hart Merriam divided North America into seven broad ecosystems, which he called Life Zones. These zones corresponded roughly with latitude, from the Tropical Zone, which stretches from Florida across Mexico, to the Arctic Zone, which includes the polar regions. Hart noted that an increase in elevation has the same effect on life zones as movement toward a pole. In fact, rising 100 feet in the Northern Hemisphere is roughly the same as heading north for 17 miles on the level. Climbing a high mountain could be similar to walking to Alaska, in terms of the resulting changes in flora and fauna. Hence in the Sierra Nevada, one will, by climbing east to the crest from the foothills, traverse five life zones in less than 10,000 feet of elevation gain.

The life zones are defined, for convenience, mostly by plant species, since plants don't migrate and are therefore more indicative of the climatic conditions to which they have adapted. The four life zones found in the Emigrant-Yosemite Sierra are as follows:

Transition Zone (Yellow Pine Belt). The main timber region of the Sierra lies in this zone, above the Foothill (Upper Sonoran) Zone. It has pleasant summers but also receives the greatest amount of annual precipitation—up to 80 inches, much of it as winter snows. In some cooler canyons, such as the Stanislaus' deep gorge, this zone extends down to the 2000-foot elevation, but generally it starts near 3500 feet. It usually gives way to the Lodgepole/Red Fir Belt above 6500 feet. Good examples of Transition Zone forest are seen along Highway 108 from Twain Harte for most of the way to Kennedy Meadows and on Highway 120 near Buck Meadow. Some of this book's lowest trails start in the Yellow Pine Belt— notably the Pinecrest Lake Loop and the first few miles of trail above Kennedy Meadows, Bell Meadow, Cherry Reservoir and Hetch Hetchy.

Canadian Zone (Lodgepole/Red Fir Belt). Most of Emigrant Wilderness and the backcountry of Yosemite National Park lies in this high-mountain belt of lakes and glaciated granite. Here, above 6500 feet, snows linger late into summer, a boon for the winter-sports enthusiast but a hindrance to plant growth—the growing season lasts only for the summer months. Interestingly, most Canadian Zone forests are a uniform growth of a single conifer, either red fir (on deeper soils, such as in canyon bottoms) or lodgepole pine (as throughout most of the rocky, thin-soiled high country). The two species rarely intermix to a significant degree, in contrast to patterns in the Yellow Pine Belt, where mixed pine and fir forests are the rule. In northern Yosemite, this belt begins to intergrade with the Hudsonian zone close to the 8800-foot contour.

Hudsonian Zone (Subalpine Belt). Bracing air in all seasons and the nodding tips of mountain hemlocks herald our passage into this ecosystem. Here the yearly precipitation is much less than in the lower zones, but nearly all of it is snow. The eastern Emigrant Basin, the uppermost Walker River Basin, and the higher lakes and ridges in Yosemite exemplify the Hudsonian Zone.

Arctic Zone (Alpine Belt). As the Hudsonian forest thins due to exposure to thinner air, shrill winds and killing ice, its plants shrink to lilliputian dimensions and, prostrate, find the shelter of protective boulders or the lee of a ridge. Higher still, even these plants, and the animals that live with them, cannot cope with the intense cold, the frozen ground and the short summer growth period. This is the realm of the specialists in winter survival. Arctic-Alpine conditions are found only in the highest extremes of the Emigrant Basin and northern Yosemite. Granite Dome and the volcanic eminences around Cooper Peak and East Flange Rock thrust above timberline into the Alpine Belt, as do Leavitt Peak and the Tower Peak environs. The easiest trails on which to sample the arctic environment are the Pacific Crest Trail south of Sonora Pass, the old Horse Meadow "road" atop Big Sam, and the pass above Tower Lake. Although many other places in the region are similarly barren, lack of vegetation in them is usually due to the massive nature of the granitic bedrock, which fails to afford a toehold for plants.

Communities—The Complex Mosaic:

Hikers in the Emigrant Yosemite backcountry will quickly note that the plants and animals in a life zone are not distributed uniformly. Some plants and animals are always found together, and some live together in only one set of circumstances; others can be found all over *except* in one situation. Patterns soon become apparent, and these patterns are the basis for the subdivision of life zones into biotic communities.

A biotic community is a unique combination of plants, animals, soil and environmental factors different from all other combinations found in the same life zone. For example, the Transition Zone is made up of a patchwork quilt of the following biotic communities: marsh; ponderosa forest; chaparral; mixed coniferous forest; lakes; meadow; and streamside communities.

Each biotic community has one or two or a handful of species which set it apart from all others. To illustrate: each of the four life zones found in Emigrant Wilderness has meadow communities, and they superficially resemble one another, but the meadows differ in many respects. In the Transition Zone, meadows are moist and dense, characterized by lush grasses with some sedges, and a myriad of colorful annual herbs. Hudsonian meadows are much less robust, although they share many species with Transition Zone meadows. Alpine meadows are generally mats of tough, drought-resistant perennial shrubs and willows, with only a few tufts of hardy sedges. High mountain meadows can also be distinguished from their lower counterparts by the presence of fewer species and a sparser ground-cover. In a dry alpine meadow, less than half the surface may be vegetated; the rest is barren soil.

Some plants, and many animals, overlap in either zonal or community affiliations. For example, Brewers blackbirds range from low elevations to alpine climes, but are seen only in meadows. Robins are less particular about whether they feed in meadow or in forest, but they always remain below the colder high country. Cocky Steller jays prefer the Transition Zone, but will forage anywhere in it. Filling essentially the Steller jay's niche, but restricted to alpine country, we find the Clark nutcracker. Many predatory animals roam throughout the Sierra, without respect for life-zone boundaries—for example, hawks, ravens and coyotes—but some predators are restricted, such as the small red fox, which patrols only the high country. Other animals, like the playful

Oregon junco, will be seen anytime, anywhere.

In the plant world, some genera are represented throughout the Emigrant-Yosemite Sierra, but in different places by different, though similar-looking, species that reflect subtle ecological differences—shooting-star and manzanita are good examples.

An Imaginary Walk to View the Whole:

Let's look at the homes and habits of a sampling of typical Sierran flora and fauna along an imaginary hike up the South Fork Stanislaus River which, in a 3900-foot ascent from 5621-foot Pinecrest Lake, touches all four life zones in our area.

The Transition Zone—Moving up in the World: Pinecrest Lake sits squarely in classical Transition Zone Mixed Coniferous Forest. Our elevation here is just below the zone of maximum precipitation, which averages some 55 inches annually. The combination of heavy precipitation and warm summers has created an ideal climate for a host of evergreens, which make up the bulk of the community. Ponderosa pine and white fir are the key species, but they are usually found in combination with incense-cedar, sugar pine, black oak and some Jeffrey pines. This mixture of tall conifers creates a high, open canopy that lets dappled light filter down to the mat of dead pine needles which covers the forest floor. An interesting group of plants finds a home in the detrital layer's deep shade. Called saprophytes, they live solely on decaying vegetation and don't need chlorophyll to produce food. These bizarre plants all have red coloration caused by anthocyanin pigments, which convert light energy into heat. Their extra heat allows them to sprout soon after the snows have melted. Snow plant, the most common saprophyte, has the appearance of a squat crimson asparagus tip. Pine drops, a cousin of snow plant, has a thin, dull-red stalk reaching 3 feet in height, from which hang globular flowers resembling Christmas ornaments on a sickly tree. If you come across

Snow plant (*Sarcodes sanguinea*)

sugar-stick, you can count yourself very lucky: this gaudy specimen resembles nothing so much as a flowery candy-cane!

Animal life abounds in the mixed-coniferous forest. The Beechey ground squirrel fulfills the role of scavenger-at-large throughout the Transition Zone. This large rodent is quite conspicuous in a hoary coat of gray, a white shoulder cape and a long, bushy tail. Being of catholic tastes, the Beechey squirrel strays frequently from a squirrel's usual fare of pine nuts, black-oak acorns and manzanita berries to dine on insects, small snakes, birds, other rodents, and anything at all from your picnic basket.

But it is in the forest's vertical world that a visitor will see most of the Transition Zone's life. Hundreds of species of birds and a number of mammals make their homes almost exclusively in the forest canopy. In the birds, in particular, one will note specializations that keep species from competing with one another. Clownlike chickadees—tiny birds with tinier voices and black burglar's masks—frolic in groups only near the ends of branches, obtaining insect dinners by means of gravity-defying acrobatics.

On the tree trunks, feeding is even more specialized. Brown creepers—homely birds with long, curving beaks—walk *up* the tree to find meals, while red-breasted nuthatches, with slaty-blue backs, black caps and white underpinnings, search for insects only while heading *down* the trunk!

General custodian and trouble-maker of the Transition Zone avian world is the jaunty Steller jay, which flits about in a pelage of bright blue and a charcoal-crested cowl. This jay roams throughout the Transition Zone, from forest to meadow to chaparral, but confines itself to that altitude; it's replaced by scrub jays lower down and Clark nutcrackers higher up.

Chickarees, small squirrels resplendent in neat coats of grizzled brown above and tan below, separated by a flashy black racing-stripe, are the mammalian farmers of the Transition forest. A true denizen of the high canopy, a chickaree will seldom leave the trees except to retrieve and bury the pine cones that it harvests. Some of the cones are stripped and eaten just after cutting, leaving "cone cobs" and piles of empty scales lying at a conifer's base. Not hibernators like ground squirrels, these furry dynamos are active on most any winter's day. Chickarees are not very sociable. Upon an invasion of its small aerial fiefdom, real or imagined, a chickaree will scuttle down a trunk to engage in a long-winded tirade of apoplectic coughs and staccato cries. It will maintain this uproar until the intruder departs, whereupon it may lapse into less convulsive mutterings, often lasting long after the incident!

Flying squirrels are the chickaree's nighttime counterparts. Once thought to be rare, these soft gray rodents are probably quite numerous. Flying squirrels can't "fly" in the sense of birds or bats, but can glide quite a distance by means of furry membranes extending between their legs. When they finish exploring the upper reaches of one tree, they throw themselves into the air and glide to the base of another bole. Their big, dark eyes, necessary for nocturnal feeding, help them search out cones, fungi, insects, meat and bird's eggs. Dawn finds flying squirrels, which live and feed in family groups, safely re-ensconced in their arboreal nests, which, like the homes of other tree squirrels and many owls, are appropriated from woodpeckers.

While walking around Pinecrest Lake, one cannot help but notice that the north shore is more brushy and open than the south shore, which is almost uniformly clad in forest. The vegetational differences between the north and south sides of the entire Stanislaus River canyon are due to differing amounts of sunshine. On Pinecrest Lake's north shore, sunlight and its attendant heating and drying affects are almost too much to allow a growth of conifers—only drought-tolerant Jeffrey pines are found sparsely dotting the slopes. But the hillside is far from bare. Its hot exposure is the ideal situation for chaparral, which in the Transition Zone is made up of huckleberry, black and gold-cup oaks, manzanita, chinquapin and deerbrush whitethorn. This impenetrable thicket is an entirely different environment from the forest, due to its dry, sandy soil, temperature and terrain. Birds suited to long glides in an open forest can't navigate in these brushy confines, so green-tailed towhees and fox sparrows, which have stubbier wings and ground-feeding habits, take their place.

Climbing Higher—The Calendar Reverses Itself: Moving up through the meadows above Pinecrest Lake, we note more and more Jeffrey pines and an occasional lodgepole pine, sure indications that we're entering the Canadian Zone. As we climb, we notice that species of flowers which have bloomed and died below are either still blooming or not even opened up yet. This phenomenon is an example of another precept of the Life Zone principle: not only does life differ with elevation and latitude, but it differs also with time of year. Winter comes first to higher elevations and thaws set in first at lower elevations. In general, seasonal change—as in time of flowering or insect hatch—follows this rule: one day equals 100 feet in elevation. So if corn-lilies flower May 30 at Pinecrest, they will flower about June 17 at Waterhouse Lake, 1800 feet higher. So

At 6200′ on S. Fork Stanislaus River

as we climb, we go back to earlier in the season, from an ecological viewpoint.

First Forest, at 6200 feet, provides our first look at a Canadian Zone flora. We'll note, coming into it, that this Canadian Zone community is like a finger pointing down the Stanislaus River canyon, surrounded by Transition Zone life. The boundaries of life zones and communities are never distinct, because a change in environmental conditions is rarely abrupt. Where warm slopes prevail at a higher altitude than normal, a "lower" community will be found next to life that more accurately reflects the elevation. Inversely, as at First Forest, in river canyons or on north-facing slopes "higher" life can take advantage of cooler conditions to extend into lower altitudes.

The Canadian Zone is exemplified by two very different floral and faunal combinations. The Lodgepole Pine Forest, which we'll see upcanyon, is the commoner of the two. In Second Forest, we are in the Red Fir community, a valuable lumbering community. Here, the fir's dark canopy screens out

so much light, and the litter of broken tree limbs is so dense, that the only plants able to grow are saprophytes, like coral-root, in the shadows, and bracken fern, along the tree stand's margins. Where no plants grow, there are no animals. In a Red Fir Forest, animal life is restricted primarily to the overstory.

As we walk along the South Fork, it's obvious that communities in the canyon don't come right down to the water's edge. Instead, another community parallels the streamside. It has many of the plants found in adjoining communities—e.g., willows, grasses, spiraea and ferns—but the dominant species—quaking aspen, cottonwood and alder—occur only near water. Certain animals are quite at home in this interface of water and land, such as yellow-legged frogs, the most common Sierran amphibians, which hunt for stream-dwelling insects. Strangely enough, these frogs' competition comes from a bird. Though related to thrushes, the water ouzel, or dipper, shares few of its ancestors' habits—this little slate-gray bird is completely at home *under* the water! Using a pair of oversize feet and unique waterproof feathers, the ouzel walks right into cascades in search of its favorite food, the caddis-fly nymph. Final proof of this bird's overwhelming affinity for water is its choice of nesting sites—right behind a waterfall, where the spray keeps its moss-lined nest damp!

Lodgepole Pines—The Pre-eminent High Sierra Conifer: By the time we reach Waterhouse Lake, the second basic community making up the Lodgepole/Red Fir Belt has become dominant. Lodgepole pines are the order of the day, almost to the exclusion of other species. The biotic composition of this community is determined primarily by the density of its lodgepole pines. Where the trees are sparse and soil is relatively lacking, as on slabby granitic bedrock, only streptanthus, pussy-paws or mouse-tailed ivesia grows sparingly. On the other hand, on a deep soil with plenty of moisture, there might be a nearly impenetrable stand of young trees. Numerous shrubs, such as spiraea, rose and mat manzanita, will be found in these dense forests. Corn-lily is the most common annual, with yarrow, yellow violets and false-Solomon's-seal in accompaniment. Corn-lily will be seen ringing almost every meadow in the Canadian Zone, intermingled with clumps of young lodgepole pines. This classical progression of meadow encroachment is hastened by overgrazing by cattle or pack stock, which are frequently thoughtlessly and illegally picketed in these delicate grasslands.

The most frequent inhabitant of any meadowed patch in the Canadian Zone is the little gray-brown Belding ground squirrel, or "picketpin". These colonial rodents, each about rat-size, dwell in labyrinthine tunnels, their entrances usually concealed by overhanging grasses. A Belding first responds to the approach of a hiker, or any assumed predator, to its home by adopting an upright "picketpin" stance, and then by sounding a shrill whistle that sends its fellows scurrying for their holes. Studies conducted in Yosemite have shown that the squirrel that warns the group—usually an elderly female—is much more likely to be caught and eaten—an interesting example of altruism among these matrilocal animals. Along with meadow mice, picketpins are low on the food-chain totem pole, and hawks, snakes, weasels, martens, coyotes and badgers assure the average picketpin a short life span. Additionally, predation of infant squirrels by unrelated adult squirrels and a high mortality rate during winter hibernation add to turnover in their communities.

When we reach Cooper Meadow, we note a change in the character of the meadow growth. The most obvious difference in this meadow is that its soil is primarily volcanic alluvium, washed down from the mud-flow battlements of Castle Rock and the Three Chimneys. Both soil texture and type of plants differ between granitic-soil and volcanic-soil meadows. In granite soil, the grass cover is nearly uniform and thick, forming a turf of grasses, sedges and moisture-loving annuals like buttercup, gentian, violet, shooting star and aster. Volcanic meadows, however, have an appearance of anemia, much bare earth showing between tufts of vegetation. No doubt the hundreds of pocket gophers that call these meadows home are a contributing factor, for mounds of earth marking the entrances to their tunnels and criss-crossing "gopher ropes" (cylindrical cores of soil deposited by the gophers where they tunneled through winter snows) are found throughout these grasslands.

Leaving Cooper Meadow on our way to Cooper Pocket, note the curious horizontal rows of pits in the bark of some lodgepole pines. These are the work of Williamson's sapsuckers, specialists among woodpeckers who drink the trees' sap as well as the odd ant caught in the sticky liquid.

Moving up into the Hudsonian Zone: Our encounter with Hudsonian Zone species in the South Fork Stanislaus River is a short one. This zone fingers down into Cooper Pocket almost to 8600 feet, and ends at timberline near 9400 feet. It is typified by one tree in the Emigrant-Yosemite Sierra—mountain hemlock. Preferring colder north slopes, this tree sometimes grows tall in barren-floored forest and sometimes in a more stunted form on isolated rock perches. Characteristic of this species are (1) branches

Gopher ropes near Wilson Meadow

down the trunk almost to the ground, (2) numerous immature trees forming a bower (excellent for camping) around a larger hemlock's base, and (3) extremely flexible branches, which can bend under heavy snows without breaking.

Flitting among the hemlocks will be a raucous, assertive bird called Clark nutcracker, a large relative of jays and crows. It is, like its kin, catholic in tastes and an adept plunderer, but its specialty is cracking hard green pine cones, for which it has developed a strong, sharp, black beak.

As mountain hemlock exemplifies the Hudsonian Zone's conifers, the typical ground cover of the zone consists of two similar shrubs—red heather and white heather. These wiry perennials, which form foot-high mats wherever soil and moisture permit, have among the prettiest flowers to be seen at high altitudes. Their bell-shaped blossoms attract rufous and calliope hummingbirds, both of which visit these altitudes in summer. A close relation of heather is bog kalmia, which inhabits wet meadows in the Hudsonian Zone. This pink-flowered shrub has developed an unusual mechanism to ensure that its pollen is spread to others of its kind: In its flower, the pollen-producing stamens are bent back and hooked, like miniature catapults, in recesses in each petal. When an unsuspecting insect lands on a blossom, its jostling releases the stamens, which spray its undersides with pollen.

Our climb out of Cooper Pocket witnesses a thinning of the hemlock overstory, until only scattered specimens dot a jumble of broken granite and brown volcanic slope wash. The rock piles are a favored home of the Sierra's largest rodent, the yellow-bellied marmot. About the size of an overfed domestic cat, with the carriage of a badger, a marmot suns its grizzled yellow-brown coat while perched on protected rock viewpoints. Sometimes hibernating for almost nine months out of the year, marmots emerge in early summer and quickly make up for lost feeding time. By the end of summer most marmots have taken on a decided Churchillian bearing, and some can't even

keep their yellow stomachs from dragging on the ground between their stubby legs! When alarmed, these soporific creatures rouse themselves onto their haunches and let forth a shrill warning whistle before plunging into a den among the talus.

A Land Above the Trees: Finally, we emerge on the volcanic ridge southeast of Cooper Pocket, at an elevation of over 9450 feet. Here we stand on the lower margin of the highest Sierran life zone, the Alpine zone. The few trees scattered about are mostly hardy whitebark pines. The plants that survive here are of two types: perennials that find acceptable sheltered microclimates that keep the elements' full intensity from afflicting them; and delicate annuals that dare to sprout only in the few weeks of summer when the weather is least inhospitable.

All the plants here owe their existence to a much smaller organism found crusting the rocks in splashes of green, gray, black, red, orange, chartreuse or lemon-yellow. Called lichens, they are actually two separate plants growing in a mutual-benefit relationship. The main body is a fungus, and imbedded in it are algae cells, which through their possession of food-producing chlorophyll produce food for

Marmot

both. The fungus provides the algae with minerals from the rock and water from the air. Although lichens work and grow with painful slowness, they inexorably decompose the rock surfaces they cling to and thus gradually develop a soil suitable for plant growth. Almost impervious to cold, rain and solar radiation, these minute crusts here coat everything from autobrecciated boulders down to tiny pebbles in a blaze of yellows and fiery reds to trumpet their eventual domination of even this most hostile landscape.

The Arctic Zone is often called the Alpine Desert, for it receives little precipitation, most of it snow, which is quickly evaporated to the cold, dry air by shrieking winds. But, as in the hot deserts, plants and animals in the Alpine Desert have made special adaptations for survival. Plants waste little energy on yearly growth or elaborate flowers that might be killed in a sudden frost. Like desert species, some plants here have developed waxy coatings and smaller leaves to minimize water loss. Other plants, like hulsea, ivesia and sky pilot, have gone another route, by developing highly dissected, feathery leaves so that the copious evaporation of water from the leaves forcibly "pulls" water up through their roots. Generally, all plants get smaller, hunched to the wind and the cold. Sagebrush and mule ears are the largest species, though much smaller than their cousins lower down. Fireweed, which grew to 6 feet near Pinecrest, can't live at this altitude, but a diminutive member of the same genus, rockfringe, puts out its beautiful pink flowers in the protection of rock niches. Nearby, we could find an extreme example of adaptation to this austere environment—an alpine willow, scarcely 4 inches tall, yet the cousin of 60-foot specimens in the Sierra foothills!

Only the smaller rodents make this place home. Most of them hibernate through the bitter winter, coming out when flowers put forth a brief, colorful flurry of blossoms and seeds. The short summer attracts numerous seed-eating birds, notably sparrows, and mule deer, which come up from winter stayovers in lower climes to sample the sweet grasses.

Down the East Side—The Life Zones Compress: If we were to continue our imaginary journey eastward, perhaps descending to the Sierra's eastern foot via the West Walker Basin, we would note that, as we lost altitude, we would encounter the same plant communities we'd seen on the trip up, but in reverse order. On closer inspection, however, some important differences could be seen. Life zones of the Sierran east slope are literally compressed into smaller spaces, and hence have a greater tendency to overlap. Whereas the gentle west slope may extend 40 miles from foothills to crest, the east side is much more abrupt—only 5–10 miles may separate top and bottom. On the east side, too, summer's heat is hotter and winter's chill colder than on the west, due to the Great Basin's continental climatic influence. Also, far less precipitation falls at any elevation east of the crest, since most Pacific storms have dropped most of their moisture on the western Sierra. This combination of factors serves to bring the high desert sagebrush steppe well up into the High Sierra. Indeed, on some exposed ridgetops, desert-dwelling sagebrush, rabbitbrush and even cacti are the commonest species. In all, life zones in the eastern Sierra are muddled by comparison to those on the west slope, with hot-dry climate species extending up high, and cold-climate plants ranging low. In some canyons, entire zones, such as the yellow-pine belt, may be omitted completely, or mixed uncharacteristically with species of other zones. The unusual blend of Jeffrey pines, lodgepoles and red and white firs found near Leavitt Meadow is a good example of such mixing.

Another Fish to Fry:

No discussion of the Emigrant Basin's natural history could be concluded without mention of the fishes that inhabit its waters. Actually, fish in the Emigrant Basin are part of *un*-natural history, for no trout are native to this area. Before Fred Leighton's construction of stream-flow-maintenance dams in the

Cherry and Lily Creek drainages, not enough water ran in late season to allow migration of trout up these streams, so the area was barren of fish except for those few lakes where planted trout could survive. Once the dams had been built, the state Department of Fish and Game planted trout in almost all waters, using this rough formula: Golden trout in the alpine waters, like Lewis and Sardella lakes; brook trout in the warm lakes, where they surface-feed and are easily caught on flies; and rainbows in all the colder waters. Now, almost any lake or larger stream in the basin will afford good fishing.

Freshly caught brook trout

Ch. 4: Red Man, White Man, Fisherman
Man and the Emigrant Basin

The First Inhabitants

The Sierran Miwok Indians were the first men to view the pristine upper reaches of the Stanislaus and Tuolumne rivers, but, visiting for business, not pleasure, they never lingered long. The names of both rivers commemorate the Miwoks. Captain Gabriel Moraga, leading a Spanish expedition to establish inland missions, was the first European to see the Stanislaus, which he named "Rio de Nuestra Señora de Guadalupe". The Stanislaus received its present name after 1827, when a Miwok, forced by the Spaniards to work in peonage at Mission San Jose, ran away and fomented a general uprising among his relatives in the Central Valley. Named Stanislaus (in honor of a Russian saint) by the missionaries, he and his followers battled the Spanish on the river that now bears his name.

Moraga's Spanish explorers also named the Tuolumne River, calling it, "Rio de Nuestra Señora de Dolores". The tribe of Miwoks living on its lower reaches called themselves "Tu-ah-LUM'-ne" possible derived from "Telala"—a soup made of the Miwok staple, ground acorns.

Most of the Miwoks in the region around the Emigrant-Yosemite Sierra lived in the Upper Sonoran Life Zone, which is the biotic zone of the Sierran foothills up to almost 4000 feet elevation. Because they couldn't store enough food to last the winter months in higher elevations, the Miwoks were not able to live permanently in higher regions. Few permanent villages were higher than Twain Harte, at 3700 feet, or Hetch Hetchy Valley, 3600 feet, and most were around 2000 feet, like the large village at Tuolumne. But Miwoks did venture into the High Sierra, especially in the summer and the fall, when their lower homes became hot, and acorns were ripe and hunting prosperous in the upper hills. In summer, too, the Miwoks traded with their eastern neighbors, the Monos (also called Piutes) for obsidian, used for arrowheads, giving acorns and food in return. While encamped in these high-country meadows, the Miwoks also bartered for a great delicacy collected by the Monos— dried fly pupae from Mono Lake. Once-meadowed Strawberry Flat, the lake bed of today's Pinecrest Lake, was an often-used meeting point and summer camp for Miwok and Mono trading parties. One of their Pinecrest campsites has been recreated as the "Shadow of the Miwok" trail, a ¼-mile long self-guiding walking tour, across the street from Summit Ranger Station. Proof that conflict was nothing new to California's natives comes from an incident that occurred at Strawberry Flat, not long before the coming of white men: a party of Miwoks massacred a camp of Monos here one night. The next year, Monos struck back, killing a summer party of Miwoks encamped near present-day Little Sweden.

The Miwoks had relatively mild living conditions, but survival necessitated daily

17

toil nevertheless. Most of their time was spent in the laborious gathering of grain staples. The nuts of Digger pines were one dietary mainstay. A foothill tree, its name is rooted in the white man's epithet "Digger" for the Miwoks, conferred because they spent much time scratching meadow areas with sharp sticks, foraging for bulbs of mariposa lilies and brodiaea. In late summer they also harvested the nuts of Transition Zone sugar pines and collected black-oak acorns and manzanita berries.

The Miwoks also hunted here, stalking mule deer, snaring ground squirrels, and netting fish. It is interesting to note that the Indians, like most game, traveled on ridges, avoiding the clammy, brush-choked canyons in which white men build their trails.

The Mono Indian culture of the eastern Sierra was very different from that of the Miwoks. Related by language to Shoshoni cultures of the Great Basin, the Monos were adapted to the harsh climate and the scarce food supply of the sagebrush desert. They lived in small parties, and moved frequently to follow game or to seasonally harvest pinyon-pine nuts. Like the Miwoks, they would ascend high into the Sierra with the retreat of winter's snow, to hunt and fish. Additionally, they supplemented their less diverse foodstuffs by trading for Miwoks' dried meat, elderberries, acorns and manzanita berries, giving, in return, their valuable obsidian and magnificent, tightly woven basketry. There is little doubt that the Monos knew the High Sierra region covered by this guide very well, for their arrowheads have been found throughout the region, including near the summit of Tower Peak! Routes of both the Emigrant Pass wagon road and today's Tioga Pass Highway 120 approximate Mono trading trails that were used for centuries before the advent of European man.

The decline and fall of all Sierran native cultures was swift. Except for a few incursions by Spanish missionaries, the Sierran Miwoks had little to do with Europeans until a man named Woods found gold in the stream that now bears his name near James-town. The great Gold Rush of 1849 ensued, sending droves of miners to the heart of the Miwoks' domain. The 49ers, bringing with them callousness, greed, racism and disease, quickly eliminated the Miwoks. Effective destruction of the Mono peoples came soon afterward, with the influx of gold-seekers to the eastern Sierra, bound for mining camps at Dogtown, Mono Diggings and Bodie.

Mountain Men and Early Discoveries

The Gold Rush also brought an upsurge of interest in the northern Sierra. Gold was the motive for this period of exploration. People entering the high country were either looking for it, traveling over the Sierra to reach the places it was found, or building dams to allow hydraulic mining downstream.

Long before the 49ers' arrival, however, the northern Sierra had fallen under the tread of white men and their horses. Legendary mountain-man Jedediah Smith was the first to cross the Sierra—surprisingly enough, from west to east. He had gained California overland by a southern route, arriving near present-day Los Angeles. The local Spaniards, jealous to guard their isolation, ordered his band to retrace their steps. Instead, Smith turned north through the Central Valley (as yet uninhabited by Spanish), and attempted to cross the Sierra, which he called Mount Joseph. But he started up too early in the season, and was twice rebuffed by heavy snow and loss of pack animals, during attempts via first the Kings River and later the American River drainage. Backtracking a bit to the Appelamminy River (Smith's name for the Stanislaus) they struck east on May 20, 1827, and finally succeeded by crossing in the vicinity of Ebbetts Pass (a few miles north of the area covered in this guide). They required only eight days for the traverse.

The next trans-Sierran expedition passed, historians believe, directly through northern Yosemite. In 1833, as demand for beaver pelts was reaching a peak, 35-year-old Joseph Reddeford Walker led a band of more than 70 trappers southwest from their Green River rendezvous to find a route to as-yetuntrapped fur grounds along the Pacific Coast. After striking the Sierra's east scarp at the Carson Valley, Walker's band probed south to find a gap in its defenses. They led their horses up, probably from the East Walker River, into late October snows, and travelled for five days across the rocky upper reaches of the Tuolumne River in northern Yosemite. Zenas Leonard, a member of the group, wrote, "Here we began to encounter in our path, many small streams which would shoot out from under these high snow-banks, and after running a short distance in deep chasms which they have through ages cut in the rocks, precipitate themselves from one lofty precipice to another, until they are exhausted in rain below. Some of these precipices appeared to us to be more than a mile high." Walker's contingent was thus the first party of Caucasians to view from the north rim, the incomparable Yosemite Valley. Pushing on, they made a second discovery, of a grove of Sierra Big Trees, before they escaped the Sierra for the comforts of Monterey.

An Avalanche of Gold-seekers

Jed Smith and Joseph Walker were experienced woodsmen. Following them, however, came a trickle and then a tide of inexperienced emigrants bound for California gold. Actually, the first emigrants to cross the Emigrant Yosemite Sierra were the Bartleson/Bidwell Party of 1841, well before the discovery of gold. California had other enchanting attractions, and a wagon train left Missouri in 1841 bound for this promised land. In October, having been forced to leave their wagons behind, they ascended the West Walker River basin and crossed the Sierra crest in the vicinity of Emigrant Pass. With great difficulty, 60 members of the Bartleson/Bidwell group marched west through the northern reaches of today's Emigrant Wilderness to the Great Valley, but not before Indians had stolen their horses and young Bidwell had stumbled upon the South Grove of Calaveras Big Trees.

Members of their intrepid band went on to leave their marks on California. Soon a wealthy rancher, and the founder of Chico, California, John Bidwell eventually ran for the Presidency against Grover Cleveland on the Prohibition ticket in 1896. Josiah Belden became mayor of San Jose; Charles Weber founded Stockton. As related in *Gateways to California,* "Another Bartleson-Bidwell Party member was Talbot H. Green, for whom Green Street in San Francisco is named. Green was a young man who was popular with the rest of the emigrants despite his one idiosyncrasy: he insisted on lugging a large chunk of what appeared to be lead with him until he was finally forced to bury it when the wagons were abandoned. Soon after the party's safe arrival, Green returned to the desert for his cache, which events showed was not mere lead. He returned to San Francisco where he spent money freely, got married, and, in 1851, ran for mayor." But "He was suddenly confronted by a Philadelphia lady who exclaimed, 'Paul Geddes, I know you!' It turned out that Paul Geddes had plundered a bank and vanished, leaving a wife and children. The popular 'Talbot H. Green' hastily took ship for the East, again leaving a family behind him."

The next group of pioneers to attempt the Sonora Trail, as the Emigrant Pass route was called, was the Clark/Skidmore Party in 1852. This group of men, 75-strong, managed to work their wagons far up the east slope of the Sierra, but an early snowstorm engulfed the wagons and forced their abandonment. Able to push on only a bit farther, the group descended to a sheltered spot in a small valley. From there a few men kept going, reached a ranch sear Soulsbyville and brought back a rescue party. From that day on the bivouac site was known as Relief Valley.

By the next year, 1853, Sonora was a growing boom town. The citizens sent Mayor George Washington Patrick to Humboldt, Nevada, the staging area for trans-Sierran emigrant trains, to tap some of that never-ending human stream for the Sonora Trail. Possessing the artful tongue of his namesake, but little of that founding father's legendary truthfulness, the good mayor proceeded to regale travelers with the virtues of Emigrant Pass and the deathly dangers of all other passes. He found takers in the combined Duckwall and Trahern parties. The Duckwall group had only 2 wagons and 11 members (6 of them children), but the party of Cherokee Indians led by George Washington Trahern was much larger. They brought with them 500 head of cattle. To surmount Emigrant Pass, these hardy pioneers had to construct their own grade, for only the most rudimentary path existed. Gorges had to be filled with rocks, trees felled, and steep bluffs ascended before they emerged on the comparatively easy slopes around Emigrant Pass. But the worst was yet to come. Descending the canyon of Summit Creek their way was blocked by domes and precipices which threatened destruction of their wagons and their worldly possessions. By hitching oxen behind their wagons to hold them back, the Duckwall Party finally negotiated this treacherous canyon to reach Upper Relief Valley on September 27, 1853. The Trahern Party, after losing two wagons on the steep descent, reached this grassland the following day. Once again snow fell prematurely, and the band had to send word to Sonora for help. Like previous parties, they then proceeded to Whitesides Meadow and generally along the volcanic-capped ridge just south of the South Fork Stanislaus' headwaters, paralleling Route PC-3 in this guide. Past Lake Valley, where a later group was stranded by snow, and Burst Rock (which is a corruption of "Birth Rock," given in commemoration of a baby born in its shelter to a pioneer woman) the Duckwall/Trahern Party descended Dodge Ridge to Sonora and safety.

That this route was dangerous and hardships were severe is attested to by the gravesite located just above Saucer Meadow (see Route KM-1.) There, Bahi A. Hubbs, one of the 1853 emigrants, lies, just a few days short of the gold fields that he had travelled all year to reach. At about the same time, Major John Ebbetts passed west-east along the Sonora Trail route, scouting a potential route for the Atlantic and Pacific Company's planned San Francisco-to-Las Vegas railroad line. He noted that the way was littered with dead oxen, destroyed wagons and broken wheels, and recommended ". . . I would advise none to undertake it hereafter." Even today, evidences of the old wagon road remain—ruts across Leavitt Meadow; trenching at the outlet of Fremont Lake, where pioneers actually lowered the natural lake level to allow passage of their wagons around its western edge; iron spikes driven in a smooth rock slope near Chain of Lakes; and a wheel rim bolted to a boulder at the head of Lower Relief Valley.

In all, about 485 persons, 135 wagons, and 3000 cattle undertook the arduous Emigrant Pass route between 1851 and 1853, but even so, it was apparent to Sonorans that a better route had to be found. But little was done in that respect until after a minor gold rush to Dogtown and Mono Diggings, near Mono Lake, in 1857. Pack trains from Sonora made a two-week round trip to supply these short-lived camps. When major finds at Bodie and Aurora caused a mass exodus eastward, mostly via more-northern trails, the people of Tuolumne County stirred themselves to find a better path. Initially, the road was routed up Clark Fork (now in Carson-Iceberg Wilderness) and over St. Marys Pass before descending to Leavitt Meadow. By 1864, however, J. D. Patterson had finished construction of the current route of Highway 108, which lies some 8 miles north of Emigrant Pass.

Miners find water—the high country's treasure

During this time much mining was still going on in the region just west of Emigrant Wilderness. Confidence, Tuolumne and Groveland were prosperous communities boasting numerous hard-rock gold mines. But the miners' main interest in the high country was not so much gold, which was rare in these upper reaches where most of the gold-bearing quartz had been stripped away by weathering, but in the copious water, which was used to mine the gold flakes that had been washed from the high country and subsequently deposited in the foothills, near Sonora and Columbia. These elusive specks of "color" were mixed with many feet of alluvium, so miners sprayed powerful streams of water on the soil, then allowed the heavier gold to settle in the bottoms of mesh sluices, where it was easily collected. In 1852 the Tuolumne County Water Company was formed to supply water to these hydraulic mines, and it tapped the North Fork Tuolumne River for that purpose. But miners objected that the water's price was too high, and that the water ceased to flow in late summer. So, by 1858, a miners' collective had built a series of flumes and ditches to Donnell's Flat, now the site of Donnells Reservoir, to utilize the Middle Fork Stanislaus River as a water supply. At the same time, they dug a tunnel from the South Fork to the Middle Fork so that the former's waters might also be tapped. To ensure an adequate flow year-around, they then built three storage reservoirs near the South Fork's headwaters. The lowest of these stood where Pinecrest Lake now lies, and was called Edna Lake. Just above it was a smaller lake called Eleanor Lake. Some 1800' higher, at 7350', was the largest impoundment, called Gertrude Lake or Big Dam. The Big Dam was big. It was almost 450 feet long, and it held water to a depth of 62 feet, making it the largest all-wood dam in the world. All three dams were built by Chinese labor entirely of massive timbers cut on the site. Big Dam burned down in the '20s, but a few timbers can still be seen in the creek, and spikes driven into the rock nearby indicate its dimensions.

The dam at Eleanor Lake is in much better repair. Some stonework and one complete segment of the dam still remain, as indicated in Route PC-2. Scattered around in the general area one will find spikes and eyelets driven into the granite, plus cable and rusted hulks of machinery. They are the remnants of steam-donkeys, powerful steam-driven winches which could literally pull themselves up a mountain. These engines were used to haul and set timbers and boulders for the dams.

"Hooved Locusts" and California's first national park

Gold-seekers were not the only early visitors to the Emigrant Basin and the Yosemite North Country. Central Valley cattlemen and sheep owners quickly recognized the superior forage available in the subalpine meadows. Beginning in the 1860s, great herds of cattle and sheep were driven to summer pastures deep in this pristine wilderness. The destruction of fragile subalpine grasses was quickly evident. In fact, denudation by sheep of Yosemite's great meadows was a primary motive for John Muir and other to call for establishing a national reserve in Yosemite. With the creation of Yosemite National Park in 1890 came the U.S. Army Fourth Cavalry to police its borders. One of their most difficult tasks was the eviction of sheepherders from the Yosemite North Country. To facilitate their patrols, the park was mapped for the first time, and most of the park's current trails were laid out. T and H blazes, chopped in pine trees by the Cavalry, can still be found along much of the Pacific Crest Trail in northern Yosemite and around Tilden Lake. And the names of many of the protagonists in the drama of hide-and-seek between sheepherders and Army are commemorated in northern Yosemite—over 25 lakes and peaks are named for military figures of the times, and some of the major canyon names, including Jack Main, Kerrick, Thompson and Stubblefield, honor early sheepmen.

As mentioned, cattlemen were also present in the High Sierra. A man named Cooper first ran cattle into the upper South Fork Stanislaus in 1861. He built the cabins now standing in Cooper Meadow. Another, named Rosasco, ran cattle in Piute Meadow and built a cabin there around 1880. Later, a young Sonoran named Fred Leighton helped to herd cattle which grazed much of Emigrant Wilderness from Piute Meadow to Long and Emigrant lakes. In 1896 he helped

Rosasco build a crude cabin at a granitoid tarn now called Yellowhammer Lake. Leighton noticed that few fish could be found in the basin. Most of the streams dried up soon after the snows melted each year because there was little soil to hold the moisture. In 1916 Leighton built another cabin at Yellowhammer Lake and erected small rock-and-concrete dams at Yellowhammer, Leighton, and Red Can lakes to hold back water to be slowly released later in the season. These dams kept the streams below running year-round. In 1931 Leighton raised money to pay for five more dams, on Bigelow, Emigrant Meadow, Emigrant, Lower Buck and Long lakes, so that all forks of Cherry Creek would flow throughout the summer, allowing trout to be planted in waters that were once barren.

In all, 16 check dams have been constructed in Emigrant Wilderness, and they ensure not only running water in the later part of summer, but excellent angling in over 80 named lakes.

Cherry Creek Mine

SMALL DAMS NEAR HERE SAVE SPRING SNOW WATER FOR RELEASE IN DRY MONTHS. A DOZEN GREEN MEADOWS, FISHING STREAMS AND LAKES BENEFIT US WITH FISH LIFE AND CLEAR WATER. FRED LEIGHTON AND OTHER CONSERVATIONISTS PIONEERED THE FIRST 3 DAMS IN 1920-25 FOR THEIR VISION AND LABORS THEY HAVE EARNED OUR DEEPEST THANKS.

Tungsten Mining—An Arrow in the Heart of a Wilderness

Surprisingly, one of the latest chapters in the history of the Emigrant Basin was again concerned with mining. World War II spurred a search throughout western America for strategic minerals. Prospectors along the Yosemite Park-Emigrant Basin Primitive Area boundary discovered a small band of tungsten deposits. Tungsten is vital for the hardening of steel, and few deposits were known within the United States. Hence, a rough and dangerous jeep road was gouged along the Sierra Crest, snaking south from Leavitt Lake to the Montezuma Mine, near Snow Lake, and to the Cherry Creek Mine, below Horse Meadow, to allow transport of tungsten ore. Mining continued after the war, and over 12 tons of tungsten were packed out by mules in 1951, and a small crushing-concentrating mill was constructed at the Cherry Creek Mine in 1967. However, it was soon destroyed by winter avalanches, and meaningful production of tungsten has ceased. Unfortunately, the main legacy of the tungsten mines is their service road (see Route SP-2), whose presence, as a man-made feature, for many years prevented the addition of this scenic strip of High Sierra to Emigrant Wilderness.

In 1975 the Wilderness Act finally gave protection to most of the Emigrant Basin. In 1984, 6100 acres—the tungsten-mining strip along the Yosemite Park border—was added to the Wilderness. The fate of the West Walker River Basin is still in doubt. It is part of the 49,200-acre Hoover Wilderness Addition Study Area, which has repeatedly failed to obtain wilderness designation by Congress. Protection of that scenic and historic basin for future generations should be the final act in the saga of man's exploration of the north-central Sierra.

Ch. 5: Stop and Think
A Wilderness Ethic

Freedom and wilderness are America's most vital treasures, and the freedom of the wilderness, like our citizenship, entails certain responsibilities. Yosemite National Park, Emigrant Wilderness and the Hoover Wilderness Addition Area were set aside *primarily* to protect the land from the hand of man, *not* to protect it as our playground. It is the responsibility of every wilderness user to respect and protect this land and its plants and animals.

Summer backcountry visitors to Emigrant Wilderness now number about 20,000—whereas *millions* enjoy Yosemite yearly! To protect the land from being literally loved to death, the following common-sense regulations have been established by the U.S. Forest Service and National Park Service. Obey them because they will preserve the wilderness for future generations:

1. Overnight visitors to Emigrant Wilderness and Yosemite National Park backcountry areas, or the Hoover Wilderness Addition Area must possess a valid wilderness permit, available at any ranger station (see the list at chapter's end).

2. Maximum group size is 15 persons, with no more than 20 stock animals.

3. Campsites must be at least 100 feet from lakes, streams and trails to protect water-edge habitat, scenic values and privacy. Don't construct new campsites—any place worth camping in already has one!

4. Dispose of body waste, wash water, and fish entrails at least 100 feet from all water—dig deep and bury it.

5. If you pack it in, pack it out—all litter, from cans to bottles to foil and tampons—must be carried out of the backcountry.

6. Don't use *any* kind of soap in lakes or streams! It might not make *you* sick, but it will surely kill the fish!

7. Don't hack up trees—live or dead. Snags have a higher value, as animal homes and as scenic resources, than to be carved up for firewood or to record the names of passers-by.

8. Shortcutting trails is damaging, dangerous, and *slower* than staying on-route! (If you want to be a trailblazer, try reaching your destination *completely* cross-country!)

9. Construction of rockwalls, fireplaces, beds and tables is prohibited. Wilderness is no place to build the comforts of home.

10. Machines, from mountain bikes to carts and chainsaws, are prohibited in all wilderness and national-park backcountry.

11. Hunting *AND* carrying firearms on Yosemite Park trails are strictly prohibited. In the Emigrant Wilderness and Hoover Wilderness Addition Area, firearms are permitted only for hunting, in accordance with California regulations.

12. No pets of any kind are permitted in the Yosemite backcountry. In USFS wilderness, pets must be controlled—squirrels and marmots do not exist to be Rover's playthings!

13. Pack-stock grazing is prohibited before July 1 at Kennedy Lake and Relief Valley, and before July 15 in higher areas of the Emigrant Wilderness, to protect delicate meadows.

14. Holding stock within 100 feet of any water source is impermissible, and threatens wilderness water quality.

15. Campfires are prohibited above 9000 feet elevation throughout Emigrant Wilderness. In Yosemite Park, campfires are legal up to 9600 feet. But in any case don't build one—they deplete carbon needed to replenish forest soil, create ugly black scars on rocks, and are unsafe and inconvenient. Instead, carry a lightweight gas stove. You'll spend more of your time enjoying the backcountry and less time hassling with a smoky fire.

16. Anglers over age sixteen must possess a valid California fishing license. Part of your fee goes to pay for stocking trout in high-country lakes and streams.

This guide is not intended to be a treatise on hiking, backpacking, nordic skiing or mountain biking. Perfect these skills elsewhere. Novice mountain travellers will do well by reading Thomas Winnett's excellent *Backpacking Basics* as a start. Some comments are in order, however, on some particular problems that may be encountered in the Emigrant-Yosemite Sierra:

The easiest way to get badly injured, or worse, in this area is to be swept away in a swift-moving early-season stream, when it is swollen with icy snowmelt. When fording, look high and low for the *widest,* shallowest place to cross. Undo the waist band of your pack before crossing, so that the pack can be jettisoned in the event of a swim. Use a sturdy stick (or a friend, crossing in tandem), as a "third leg" on your upstream side.

Bears are a frequent nighttime nuisance.

A group at Benson Lake—pre-wilderness ethic

Learn to "bearbag" your food from a tree limb. Loud shouts, waved flashlights or a well-aimed rock will usually send them scurrying.

Far more ferocious (and ubiquitous) than bears are early summer clouds of mosquitos, which thrive in the Emigrant Basin just after snowbanks melt. If you choose to travel then (and fishing is at its best, early!), bring long-sleeved clothes, a hat, a tent, and copious mosquito repellent. Otherwise, your trip will be hell!

Forest Service and National Park Service rangers can answer all of your questions, and more, at the following ranger stations. They will also issue wilderness travel permits, sometimes by mail:

For trailheads near Highway 108, west of Sonora Pass: The Summit Ranger District (Stanislaus National Forest) station is located at the Pinecrest **Y**, 30.1 miles above Sonora. The address is: Star Route, Box 1295, Sonora, CA 95370. Telephone (209) 965-3434. They have a night pick-up box for prearranged permits.

For trailheads at Cherry Lake, a permit may be obtained from either the Forest Service or the National Park Service. The USFS Groveland Ranger District Station is on Highway 120 in Buck Meadow, 7.8 miles east of downtown Groveland (15.7 miles west of Yosemite Park's Big Oak Flat Entrance Station). The address is Star Route, Box 75G, Groveland, CA 95321. Telephone (209) 962-7825.

Travel from Hetch Hetchy, in Yosemite National Park, requires a permit from the Hodgdon Meadow Ranger Station, located a few yards from the Park's Big Oak Flat Entrance Station on Highway 120. By mail, any park wilderness permit may be reserved by writing (February through May *only*):

> Yosemite National Park
> Back Country Office
> P.O. Box 577
> Yosemite, CA 95389
> (209) 372-4461

In Tuolumne Meadows, the start of Route YP-2, the Park Service issues permits at an information station in the backcountry parking area just west of Tuolumne Meadows High Sierra Camp. Mail reservations may be made, as noted above.

Trailheads leading into the Hoover Wilderness (for Route YP-1) and Hoover Wilderness Addition from Leavitt Meadow are served by Toiyabe National Forest's Bridgeport Ranger District. The office is on the east side of Highway 395, almost ½ mile south of Bridgeport. Some summer permit reservations are available, by writing:

> P.O. Box 595
> Bridgeport, CA 93517
> (619) 932-7070

A self-service permit station is in place, in front of the office. At times, Leavitt Meadow Pack Station will issue permits for Leavitt Meadow trailheads.

Ch. 6: Let's Go
Choosing Your Trail

The 62 trail and cross-country routes described in this guide are grouped in 9 chapters. Each chapter clusters together trails that leave from or are most easily reached by trails from one trailhead or a particular access road. Each chapter is named for a central feature of its region of coverage, and all the routes in the chapter are encoded with two letters, such as "KM" for Kennedy Meadows, that match the chapter heading. The same codes are marked on the topo map.

For those who may be new to Emigrant Wilderness, and northern Yosemite, the following chapter summaries may aid in selecting a first expedition.

Chapter 7: *Pinecrest.* This western access to the Emigrant Basin offers two of the three most popular trails into the wilderness—the Burst Rock and Crabtree trails. No one camping in the environs of Pinecrest should leave the area without taking three hours to hike the start of the Burst Rock Trail, up to wonderful vistas atop Burst Rock, then on to lovely Powell Lake, 3.6 miles roundtrip. Although the long trails from Pinecrest penetrate about 12 miles into an incredibly dense cluster of lakes, all with excellent fishing, most visitors fish only on populous Pinecrest Lake, which is circumnavigated by the 4-mile Pinecrest Lakeshore Loop Trail. If you're camped in the large campgrounds in the Pinecrest Recreation Area, take it for an exhilarating morning jogging path.

Chapter 8: *Herring Creek.* Three routes leave Herring Creek Road, a much-less-visited thoroughfare just north of the over-crowded Pinecrest Recreation Area. Many horsemen use the Cooper Meadow Trail as rapid access to the western Emigrant Basin. It has little elevation gain or loss, and hence is quite easy. The Pinecrest Peak Trail *should* be more popular—it's fast, all downhill, and has great views—but you'll likely have it to yourself.

Chapter 9: *Eagle Meadow.* Four little-used routes penetrate the northwestern Emigrant Basin from long, interesting Eagle Meadow Road. Absolutely the fastest way into the wilderness' heart is via Silver Mine Creek. Even if you don't hike, this region is fine for mountain biking. Don't leave without visiting the incomparable Bennett Juniper and the Juniper Uranium Mine—each is just moments from the well-graded road.

Chapter 10: *Kennedy Meadows.* These routes are the principal northern accesses to the Emigrant Basin. Kennedy Meadows Resort, at the start of these hikes, is the hub of horsepacking activities for the Emigrant-Yosemite country. Most hikers take only the first 3 or 4 miles of the Huckleberry Trail up to Relief Reservoir. A far more scenic day hike or overnighter is the Night Cap Trail. Immense Emigrant Lake is the crown jewel of the Emigrant Basin. Reached in 2 easy days via Route KM-1, it is the jumping-off point for explorations of the higher eastern Emigrant Basin. If you have just one long weekend to visit the area, go there. If you have another day to spend, link together a loop among Snow, Bigelow, Black Bear and Twin lakes, via Route KM-3.

Chapter 11: *Sonora Pass.* The apex of

Sonora Pass Highway 108 spawns the finest alpine hiking in the entire Northern Sierra. Indeed, the first 8 miles of Pacific Crest Trail, south of Sonora Pass may be the finest alpine day-hiking path in the entire Northern Sierra. If you have only one day along Highway 108, take this walk—better yet, make a loop trip, with return via Blue Canyon, or Latopie and Koenig Lakes. The more adventuresome should hike the strenuous Horse Meadow Road, Route SP-2, an amazing crest-top mining access road that climbs to a fantastic 360-degree panorama atop 10824-foot Big Sam before dropping into the eastern Emigrant Basin's subalpine fishing grounds.

Chapter 12: *Walker Basin.* Immense Leavitt Meadow is the jumping-off point for long trails into the West Walker River Basin. Numerous small lakes with prime angling are scattered throughout. Roosevelt and Lane Lakes are the most frequented, by dayhikers or as an easy weekender. Far nicer are lakes at the valley's head—the Cascade Creek basin's lakes are justifiably popular. They lie near Dorothy Lake Pass, Yosemite's northern gateway. Tilden Lake is the loveliest in northern Yosemite in my opinion—a delightful 5-day backpack loop would reach it via Route WB-1, then exit Yosemite via Dorothy Lake Pass and the Pacific Crest Trail.

Chapter 13: *Yosemite Park.* Superlatives are completely insufficient to describe the well-known splendors of Yosemite. But few travelers know the more subdued but equally delightful North Boundary Country. All the trails here are relatively long. The Pacific Crest Trail is the best of them, and you'll leave behind most other hikers after the first 6 miles. All but one of the other trails begin at Hetch Hetchy, Yosemite Valley's reservoir-drowned and all-but forgotten counterpart chasm. This roadend gets a lot of automobile tourist traffic, but thankfully almost no hikers except on peak summer weekends. Most backpackers venture no farther than Rancheria Falls—an inspirational, almost level overnighter. Considerably more work is involved to reach Tilden Lake, or surprising, intimate Bear Valley— but both will more than compensate for the effort.

Chapter 14: *Cherry Lake.* The southern access to Emigrant Wilderness, Cherry Lake is popular because its lower elevation makes it accessible early in summer. Nine out of ten backpackers here will head for Kibbie Lake on a short weekend sojourn. But both Boundary Lake and Flora Lake are prettier and less crowded, offer more options for side trips, and take little more effort to reach than Kibbie Lake. Possibly the ruggedest and wildest trip in the region is a cross-country descent of remote Cherry Creek Canyon—do it in early summer to see the cataracts at their most tumultuous.

Chapter 15: *Bourland Creek.* Three little-used trails each wind a few miles to Chain Lakes. Neither the trails themselves nor Chain Lakes are particularly inspiring, but if you want to be alone, these hikes might be for you.

Most of the trips in this book are shown in their entirety on the large foldout map that comes with the book. But some trips are shown in whole or in part on separate pages at the end of the book. The maps for these trips, in the order needed, are listed at the beginning of the trips that need them. (The term "main" refers to the large, foldout map in the back of the book.)

Ch. 7: Pinecrest

PC-1

Pinecrest Lakeshore Loop Trail

Distances
1.4 miles to South Fork-Cleo's Bath Trail
3.8 miles to South Shore Roadend

Introduction
The Pinecrest Lakeshore Trail, though a tame thoroughfare by wilderness standards, provides a nice afternoon for those with only enough time to sample the flavor of the Sonora Pass country. For a more extensive discussion of the lake's flora and fauna, see Chapter 3, "What Grows Where." The author recommends a counter-clockwise route.

Trailhead
Pinecrest Lake is reached by paved Dodge Ridge Road, which leaves Highway 108 at Summit Ranger Station (30 miles from Sonora), where wilderness permits are issued. Parking is available in large public lots across from the shopping complex. The northshore trail follows the dirt-road terminus of Pinecrest Avenue past the public marina (at the extreme west end of Pinecrest Lake), while the south-shore trail is reached by walking east-southeast along Pinecrest Lake Road or by taking a paved bicycle path, which goes through the Pinecrest Picnic Area and along the shoreline. At road's end, the path takes over. Please note that bicycles are not allowed.

Description
5621-foot-high Pinecrest Lake, a Pacific Gas and Electric Co. impoundment created in 1916, covered an old meadow and a smaller lake resting behind the terminal moraine of the glacier that once filled South Fork Stanislaus River's valley. This moraine is seen today as the sandy beach and hummocky terrain that bound the southwest end of the lake. As the level of Pinecrest Lake drops (the water is used for power and irrigation in the Central Valley), the lake bed becomes a show-piece of glacial erosion as numerous glacially grooved *roches moutonees,* plucked surfaces, polish, chatter marks, spectacular erratics, and concentric recessional moraines emerge from the warm water. Also in evidence is the bouldery till that is smeared high along the south shore—a lateral moraine. Our path along the south shore starts in front of one of the many lakefront summer homes built here under Forest Service lease. Anyone may use the trail or the beaches, but please respect this private property.

Proceeding levelly on packed-sand trail under windows and balconies in the classical Transition Zone forest of Jeffrey and sugar pine, incense-cedar, white fir, black oak and some aspen, we gradually leave behind the campground roar and most of its populace. The churn of motorboats, some trolling for kokanee salmon or rainbow or brown trout to 15", is soon forgotten as we concentrate on the surprising array of wildlife which tolerates the intruding hordes. Kingfishers, gulls, mallards, grebes, coots and mergansers are commonly seen on the water, while tanagers, robins, grosbeaks, juncos and, of course, cocky Steller jays inhabit the forest's avian niches. Their mammalian counterparts are California ground squirrels, chickarees, flying squirrels and chipmunks. Larger mammals, seen only at night, are raccoons, porcupines, deer and an occasional wandering black bear.

Uneventfully rounding the south shore, we then, upon hitting the east shore, turn northwest over outcrops of gray-lichened granodiorite and soon descend into a debris-strewn flat that was the Boy Scouts' Camp Bob MacBride. Only trash and broken concrete remain. Our route here turns northeast up a jeep trail beside a meadow of Queen Anne's-lace, brodiaea, saxifrage, farewell-to-spring, lotus, bistort and other middle-mountain flowers. After a few yards we leave the rocky jeep trail for a prominent trail (although its often-vandalized trail sign is usually gone) that branches left (north). Next we climb slightly over bedrock to arrive at South Fork Stanislaus River, which plunges through a narrow joint chute. Our way over it is eased by a sturdy bridge, which lets us off on the north bank for a much rockier hike over broken slabs and less-shady forest cover around the north shore of Pinecrest Lake. Look for ducks and trail signs showing the way.

Passing through another group of cabins, we meet a junction with the Catfish Lake/Pinecrest Peak Trail (Route HC-3), then climb along steep granodiorite slopes above the dam. Past a quarry, we make a sandy switchback down to the concrete-faced dam's top, which is built of granitic boulders blasted from the canyon walls. Before this dam was built, an all-wood structure, built by a now-defunct power company supplying water to Sonora-area gold mines, stood near this site, impounding Edna Lake. In the meadows above Camp MacBride was another reservoir, called Eleanor Lake. At the dam's north end we find an unsigned trail to Strawberry, ½ mile west. Across the dam, our route is a trail that, like an adjacent rough dirt road, heads south over to the Pinecrest Marina.

PC-2

South Fork Stanislaus River from Pinecrest Lake to Upper Relief Valley (cross-country route)

Distances
1.2 miles to Cleo's Bath
4.9 miles to Waterhouse Lake
10.7 miles to Cooper Meadow
14.2 miles to Upper Relief Trail

Introduction
This long route follows the sparkling South Fork Stanislaus River from Pinecrest Lake, at 5621 feet in the Transition Zone, all the way to its headwaters, at 9460 feet, at timberline on the border between the Hudsonian and the Arctic-Alpine life zones. Hence this exciting trip, already diverse geologically, passes through four different life zones as well. Most hikers won't traverse its length in one trip; combining its scenic lower part with a hike to Waterhouse Lake (see Route HC-2) makes a nice day hike.

Trailhead
Same as the Route PC-1 trailhead.

Description
Follow Route PC-1, the Pinecrest Lakeshore Loop Trail, more or less levelly east to the head of Pinecrest Lake. At the east end of Pinecrest Lake, we find the Cleo's Bath Trail, which guides us for the first leg of our journey along South Fork Stanislaus River, in a meadowed glade of black oak and incense-cedar. Here a jeep road climbs gently northeast through the forest. This road is now our trail, and we walk along it, ignoring a MAIN TRAIL sign which indicates the Pinecrest Lakeshore Loop Trail (Route PC-1).

As we continue gently up, with some short pitches where the tread was ruthlessly blasted from the gray-lichened granodiorite, the forest peters out in favor of open slabs with manzanita, Jeffrey pine and some junipers scattered about. History buffs will note red-rusted scraps of riveted metal, cable and spikes beside the trail. These are remnants of steam-driven "donkey engines" which helped to build the dams that impounded water here for downstream gold-mining activities before the turn of the century.

Past the boiler of one of these engines, we emerge on a flat nose where the interested hiker can traverse at 300° to the remains of one of these dams, the lake behind which was called Eleanor. We can clearly see the waterline of this reservoir preserved on the rocks and on old snags in the empty lake bed, now choked with willows and immature pines. From this rock rib we follow painted arrows down to the sagebrush-floored meadow. Traversing behind willows that all but prevent access to the South Fork, we wind levelly through fields of wild-flowers. In a few minutes we come alongside the stream, then re-enter shrubbery at a sharp turn in the sand-cleft stream bed. A red-fir grove on the right provides good camping. Beyond it we walk on slabs above alder-lined banks to the abrupt talus-footed headwall that marks the end of our defined trail.

Just past a spring-muddied tunnel in a high thicket where mountain kingsnakes, the almost-look-alikes for coral snakes, are sometimes seen, we find a duck marking the beginning of a scrambling ascent over mossy ledges and under the branches of gold-cup oaks to Cleo's Bath. The ducks lead us, panting, to a sand flat on the rib just above Cleo's Bath, where heavily littered campsites are found under some junipers and Jeffrey pines.

Cleo's Bath, a shallow, sand-bottomed, willow-lined pool situated below a series of sparkling cascades and whirlpools, is a favorite destination of weekend sun-worshippers. At times, upwards of thirty people can be seen broiling on nearby slabs or partaking of the brisk waters.

The ducks we've been following end at the campsites, so we push on beside the rock-bound river as it flows over rock plates or pauses to circle in deep green tubs. For the next ⅓ mile, while gazing at a succession of clean climbing walls across the canyon, we negotiate slippery exfoliation features, sometimes climbing well above the stream to avoid difficulties. At 6200 feet we come to First Forest, a pleasant mixture of fir, cedar, and pines, plus an occasional black oak, cottonwood or aspen. Here it is advantageous to hop boulders to the Stanislaus' north side. The forest's thick duff floor has numerous good campsites to lunch at, before we push on, back to open slabs and a more raucous stream.

Cleo's Bath

Above a small series of falls we cross back to the south bank to traverse a slick exfoliation surface past house-sized erratics. Denizens of the foaming waters likely to be seen here are the drab brown water ouzel, a bird as at home under water as it is above, and yellow-legged frogs. Entering Second Forest, a rare stand of mature mixed conifers, we pass an excellent camp beside the South Fork, which pools deeply between banks of bracken and willow. We're forced to veer uphill momentarily, away from the Stanislaus, but soon return to traverse forest-floor litter and bracken to another series of open, step-laddered cascades.

Nearing the influx, from the south, of a minor tributary (6720') we cross the South Fork once again and then climb moderately past beautifully water-sculptured, brown-patinated granite down which the Stanislaus leaps. Huckleberry oak, red-ossier dogwood, willow, shrubby spiraea, manzanita and bittercherry are the woody species that flank the stream as we near Third Forest, situated on the branch stream coming steeply down from the north. The way around the Stanislaus' north bank is made impassable by an under-aspen tangle of alders, so we're forced to ford once again, then traverse a thigh-high ground cover of fern, twinberry and thimbleberry to a good camp on the south bank. As soon as possible after passing Third Forest we recross the river.

Those who want to take the recommended detour to Waterhouse Lake should bear at about 35° from this crossing, breaking free from the vegetated canyon bottom to open slabs. Heading along the small, sliding creek that is Waterhouse Lake's drain, we climb easy slopes to the densely forested west shore of Waterhouse Lake. The best campsites around the lake are found here.

To resume our trek up the Stanislaus we skirt Waterhouse Lake's south shore, then climb east from its inlet, avoiding aspens and mosquitoes by keeping above them to the south. Passing just north of Adele Lake, a dinky affair of interest only to the most rabid angler, we cut southeast over the shoulder of the knob to the south, soon topping out at an overlook amid lodgepoles. Sighting south over the oak scrub and slabs by which it is reached, we see an immense meadow of saw grass and willows which used to be Gertrude Lake. Like its sisters down-canyon, this reservoir was impounded by an all-wood dam, the remains of which can be seen at 7350 feet. Across the canyon we can see the cliffs on Burst Rock's north face.

Dropping down into the grassland, we turn east to wind through head-high jungles of cow parsnip, self-heal, Queen Anne's-lace and paintbrush to the Stanislaus, which bends north here. When possible, ford to its south bank, then wind over many fallen logs. Where the river turns south, ford again and keep almost 0.2 mile from the creekside to avoid entanglement in horrendous thickets of alder and willow. Soon the Horse and Cow Meadow tributary of the Stanislaus is crossed, and we climb east along a mafic ridge. This hot traverse leads to a shrub-dominated meadow, where we branch northeast along the Stanislaus' Cooper Meadow fork. This stream canyon is conspicuously marked by boulders of brecciated volcanic material, heralding our ascent into the volcanic rocks which mantle the summit reaches of the Sierra.

Presently the climb levels out along a wide, deep stream in a quiet lodgepole forest. Color is in the air, in the form of finches, warblers and juncoes. Castle Rock and the Three Chimneys swing into view, standing above naked hillsides of more friable debris. A bifurcating cowpath leads us into Cooper Meadow, and, cutting across the grassland with its cinquefoil, pentstemon and little elephant's heads, we reach two cabins, owned by the Sanguinetti Cattle Company. These two buildings, the first built in 1865 and the "youngest" in 1875 by Mr. Cooper, for whom this meadow is named, have been used for cattle operations ever since. From the second gate we can follow either a wide path going northeast or the meadow's fence line, trending more eastward, to the trail from Coyote Meadows Roadend (Route HC-1)

Cooper Meadow, Three Chimneys, Sanguinetti cow camp

and its junction with the Eagle Pass Trail (Route EM-1).

To continue into Cooper Pocket and thence to Upper Relief Valley, we leave these trails behind and stroll east over the clumpy remains of Cooper Meadow and into a moderate forest. After easily leaping the infant Stanislaus, we trace an intermittent use-trail through patches of meadow that have representatives of almost all herbaceous species found in the upper Canadian Zone. Above us, the Three Chimneys' south face looms forbiddingly, a study in reds and brown.

Our route up the Cooper Pocket headwall leads along the north bank of a branch stream that curves south of volcanic Peak 9189. Our steep ascent under western white pine, hemlock and red fir passes a meadow at the 8800-foot level, then climbs in earnest toward the ridgetop in the southeast. Hemlock forest fades as we climb the clayish volcanic soil, pantingly gaining the ridge at 9460 feet. Here one wants to drink deeply of the clean, cool air and the exhilarating vistas of the volcanic peaks ringing the upper South Fork Stanislaus River. This ridgetop, right at timberline, bears stunted, wind-beaten lodgepole and white-bark pines that find a meager subsistence on the cobbly volcanic soil, while more ephemeral herbs soften the moonscape with pastel shades. Green gentian, dwarf lupine, mule ears, buckwheat, mouse-tailed ivesia and rockfringe are among the species that seasonally grace these slopes.

From this rest spot we contour southeast to a second arm of the ridge, from which verdant Upper Relief Valley and the Relief lakes are seen below. Scrambling down on a treacherous volcanic hardpan, we angle southeast toward South Relief Lake. A much more diverse assortment of wildflowers is seen on this descent, which might be accomplished under the watchful eyes of a soaring red-tailed hawk or sparrow hawk. Bottoming out, we penetrate a shallow fringe of sagebrush and lodgepole before reaching the Relief Valley Trail (Route KM-6) just west of South Relief Lake.

PC-3

Burst Rock Trail: Gianelli Cabin to Deer Lake, Powell Lake, Whitesides Meadow, Starvation Lake and Long Lake

Distances

1.8 miles to Powell Lake
3.1 miles to Lake Valley
5.7 miles to Whitesides Meadow
9.4 miles to Wire Lakes Trail
11.1 miles to Deer Lake

Introduction

This historic path is the west end of the difficult Emigrant Pass wagon trail, which brought gold seekers to the Sonora mines over 100 years ago. Today, it is by far the most pleasant and scenic west-side avenue into the Emigrant Basin's heart. While winding over a succession of viewful granitic ridgetops and dipping into flower-decked meadows, the way passes a succession of small lakes, each teeming with brook trout. The trail's destination, Deer Lake, possibly has more good fishing within a two-hour walk than any other spot in the entire Sierra.

Trailhead

Crabtree Road 4N26.1 leaves State Highway 108 just 0.8 mile east of Cold Springs (2.0 miles west of the Pinecrest Y). Follow its two paved lanes 6.5 miles to Aspen Meadow, passing paved road 4N06Y, which is a cutoff to Dodge Ridge Road. Here beside Sardella's Pack Station our road becomes dirt. Continue on 4N26 2.6 miles farther to well-signed Crabtree Camp spur road 4N26, from where we continue straight ahead on larger Gianelli Road 4N47. 4.0 miles distant, park at the signed Burst Rock Trail parking area, near Gianelli's cabin.

Description

The Burst Rock trailhead stands in a 8560-foot-high meadow amid moderate-to-dense lodgepole pines and a smattering of mountain hemlocks and red firs. Our trek begins as we amble south 200 yards to cross a miniature upper branch of Bell Creek, where we find what now remains of A. E. Gianelli's turn-of-the-century hunting cabin—four tiers of lodgepole logs in a 15-foot square. As we "lower our gears" for the predominantly steep 600-foot ascent to come, we note that, unfortunately, even though our route lies on a boulder-strewn slope heavily clothed in timber, 4-wheel-drive and dirt-bike owners can also adjust their machine's gearing to cope with the grueling ascent. They have blazed two breakneck "trails," both cut deeply into the rich duff earth, which obscure or render useless the hiker's path. Not inclined to further the wanton destruction, we stick to one of these routes, and emerge, panting, on the sandy, pine-dotted plateau called Burst Rock, humbled but happy in the knowledge that the worst climb on the entire trail is now behind.

Our level trail heads east under the high point of Burst Rock to the signed Emigrant Wilderness boundary, but lensmen will first climb that summit to capture vistas north across the deep gorge of South Fork Stanislaus River. Volcanic mountains from Cooper Peak east to Leavitt Peak can be seen to advantage, while cerulean skies and lofty cumulonimbus clouds may backdrop Tower Peak, the Saurian Crest, and Mount Lyell and the Clark Range far to the southeast. Burst Rock's name is a corruption of "Birth Rock," so called because a Mrs Wilson, a member of an overland wagon train using the punishing Emigrant Pass trans-Sierra route, gave birth to a girl here, using a natural cave for protection from the elements.

The headwaters of Bell Creek are our next objective, and the trail leads east below the slabby summit ridge. A shallow tarn's meadowed outlet stream is skirted before the

Gianelli cabin

descent ends at a saddle and a junction with a short spur trail north to Powell Lake. This delightful granite-bound lakelet has two rock reefs extending into its shallow, humus-bottomed waters, which interrupt reflections of Cooper Peak and Castle Rock in the north and of mountain hemlocks fringing the lake. Nice but heavily used camps are nestled on the west and northeast shores. Fishing for small brookies (to 8″) is very good any time but midwinter.

Beyond the Powell Lake junction a dividing ridge causes the trail to ascend 300 feet before it levels out on the sandy ridge. Then, sidehilling down northeast, the path reaches a granitic outcrop from where excellent views encompass the entirety of Yosemite, Mount Lyell and Volunteer Peak being quite prominent, and the meandering path of Lily Creek below in Lake Valley, a boulder-pocked grassland in which Chewing Gum Lake lies. Thereafter our way becomes knee-jarringly steep down volcanic slopes cloaked in sagebrush and senecio, but we soon enough level out at the Chewing Gum Lake Trail (Route PC-5). A party of California-bound gold-seekers was once trapped here in an autumn snow storm (it would seem that most Sierra crossings were ill-timed). They cut fire wood from lodgepole pines near this point—but 10 feet above the ground, indicating the snow pack's depth! Some of the truncated trees still stand.

Once again a volcanic-topped ridge stands in the way of our eastward progress, but the moderateness of the ascent leaves some energy for gazing at the Emigrant Basin north-country or pondering the difficulties one would have had 140 years ago, nursing a family and heirloom-laden wagons over this route. Atop the ridge, slopes of pussy paws and locoweed give way to mixed conifers, but still allow us to scan the southern horizon for the prominent glacier between Mounts Lyell and Maclure, or swing our gaze east and north to Tower and Leavitt peaks. Soft-spoken white-headed woodpeckers might also be seen, but more commonly the white pate one sees will be possessed by the smaller white-crowned sparrow. Descending, we leave behind the views to switchback occasionally before striking the Y Meadow Lake Trail (Route PC-6).

The next leg of the route leads over nearly level lodgepole-covered terrain on generally sandy, sometimes muddy trail to Whitesides Meadow. We swing near South Fork Stanislaus River and a broken check dam that once held back enough water to completely inundate Whitesides Meadow. The Cooper Meadow Trail junction (Route HC-1) is reached when our route finishes rounding Whitesides Meadow's south side.

A short distance later is the Relief Valley Cutoff Trail (Route KM-6) and just yards later we top the Lily Creek-Cherry Creek divide. Dropping steeply, then more moderately, we emerge from lodgepole forest to bisect a summer-dry volcanic meadow inhabited by pocket gophers and blackbirds. A few feet beyond this sloping flat is the

Toejam Lake Trail (Route PC-7), leaving due south. Uneventful walking in viewless lodgepole groves leads down to level trail near our second linkage with the Relief Valley Trail (Route KM-6). Here we turn south and arc down through bouldery forest to the banks of West Fork Cherry Creek in Salt Lick Meadow. The water here runs 20 feet wide in spring runoff, but poses less difficulty later on. Across the stream, we track beside the old trail rut, which is cut deeper each year by running water and offers mute argument for the re-routing of all trails around fragile areas.

Climbing away from Salt Lick Meadow, a southward-bearing, steep, rock-dusty trail leads to a crossing and then a quick recrossing of an early-season creek, after which the angle of ascent lessens. Soon we wind levelly through a predominantly lodgepole forest speckled with grassy tarns and white boulders fringed by dwarf bilberry and cheerful-looking red heather. Later, one passes a good camp just before stepping onto the edge of

Casting for big rainbow trout at Deer Lake

Spring Meadow. True to its name, Spring Meadow is lush and wet, to the point of having a cluster of boggy ponds south of the trail. Cinquefoil, lupine and penstemon live on its verdant surface, while corn-lily, meadow rue and spiraea grow along the fringes. The ford of Spring Creek is a sandy 12 feet in early season. Across it, our path begins to veer southeast from the creekside, but the trail for a few hundred yards would seem to have been designed to do double duty as both creek bed and footpath, it is so muddy and eroded. One can avoid this wet stretch, and try for trout at the same time, by here leaving the trail and veering levelly east to small, meadowed Starvation Lake, tucked in a bowl under an attractive dome. Just 5 minutes from the trail, it is nonetheless little-fished—a boon to those who do stop, since it supports a good fishery of brook trout.

The remainder of the ascent to the signed Wire Lakes Trail (Route PC-8) isn't much better than the path in Post Corral Canyon, but we do have as many as four ruts to choose from in places! Later, beyond a pocket meadow, we pass a cairn-marked trail that leads east to Long Lake's open, rocky

north end, another little-visited spot with fine camps and fishing for large rainbow trout. Soon after, we climb over a pine-timbered saddle, where red-breasted nuthatches and Williamson's sapsuckers are often seen, then undertake a delightful descent through meadows and past tarns to Deer Lake. Late in the afternoon, these ponds' surfaces become glassy-still, reflecting lodgepole snags and rose-hued granite boulders. The lowest tarn of the group, rimmed by red heather, dwarf bilberry and bog kalmia, is actually a nicer camping spot than any of the larger, named lakes in this vicinity. From it, the path leads gently-to-moderately down-canyon, crossing the unnamed creek twice before leveling out in sandy lodgepole flats north of Deer Lake. Then we cross the creek once more before striking the Crabtree Trail (Route PC-4) beside a damp meadow. Deer Lake has been subjected to severe camping pressure, far too many campsites having been constructed in the past, and much erosion of the surrounding meadows having occurred. Please abide by the posted camping regulations, and camp only in designated sites.

PC-4

Crabtree Trail: Crabtree Camp to Emigrant Meadow Lake, via Camp, Piute, Gem, Jewelry, Deer, Buck, Emigrant and Middle Emigrant lakes

Distances

2.8 miles to Bear Lake Trail
6.4 miles to Piute meadow
9.5 miles to Gem Lake
11.3 miles to Deer Lake
12.9 miles to Upper Buck Lake
15.8 miles to Emigrant Lake (West End)
18.1 miles to Blackbird Lakes
19.5 miles to Middle Emigrant Lake
20.8 miles to Emigrant Meadow Lake (at Brown Bear Pass Trail)

Introduction

If you're a fisherman, this long trail is for you. Cutting directly across the entire

Emigrant Basin, hardly a mile along this easy route fails to present the angler with a lake or a stream stocked with fighting, delectable trout. On the way, you'll climb gradually from the forested, rolling hillsides of the western Emigrant Wilderness, through its bare, granitic, lake-speckled heart, to the high, open meadows of its east side, sampling the best each has to offer.

Trailhead

Follow Crabtree Road 4N26.1 east from Highway 108, just 0.8 mile east of Cold Springs, as described in the Route PC-3 trailhead. Follow it 9.1 miles to its signed junction with Road 4N47, then turn right (east) still on 4N26, 0.6 mile down to Crabtree Camp roadend. Parking is ample, beside trickling Bell Creek.

Description

Leaving the moderately forested red-fir-and-lodgepole flats of Crabtree Camp, we hop Bell Creek, making sure our canteens are full for the waterless climb to Camp Lake, and quickly come to a junction with the Chewing Gum Lake Trail (Route PC-5) on a sandy bench. Our route ascends dustily, then contours south to reach a segment of older trail. We now assault a steep, much-abused path, fortunately well-shaded, which levels out under aspen and lodgepole at the junction with a lateral to Pine Valley. This route, described now, provides a good loop-trip linkage for trips begun at Bell Meadow.

Fifty paces south we emerge on the rim of Pine Valley and are treated to a panorama, across its dark green expanse, of the jumble of white domes around Chain Lakes. Then we begin switchbacking moderately down over the treacherous "ball-bearing" volcanic hillside, where clumps of showy penstemon, mariposa lilies and eriogonum relieve the drabness of this hot slope. Gradually, our way becomes more shaded under Jeffrey pine, aspen, black oak, and the rare combination of both white and red firs. Instead of making a junction atop the ridge dividing Bell and Lily creeks, as one might prefer, our route carves along the east slope of this ridge, descending moderately to reach the Bell Meadow Trail (Route PC-10) at 7050 feet.

Back on the Crabtree Trail, open stands of mature Jeffrey pine, red fir and Sierra juniper allow a viewful traverse above deeply forested Pine Valley. Trees close in as we track a red-fir corridor around a grassy pond and gently ascend a herbaceous gully to the signed Emigrant Wilderness boundary. One hundred yards farther is the west end of shallow, green Camp Lake. This sparsely forested, sorely trampled small lake supports a harried population of brook trout. Campsites are found as we climb rockily around

the south shore, and at the east end as well.

Across a saddle just past Camp Lake, we reach a spur trail to Bear Lake, a recommended detour: A well-beaten path skirts north of a large brown pond through shady lodgepoles. A short ascent over a sandy granitic knob brings us to a muddy stream at the south end of two meadows. Ascending, we soon reach Lily Creek under high, broken slopes cloaked with huckleberry oak. Past a tepid pond, we sight the stream-flow-maintenance dam impounding Bear Lake, and soon view this pretty but often overpopulated lake from camps beside its rocky outlet. The trail terminates a few yards later, at a large cluster of fire rings on Bear Lake's west shore. Fishing is usually fair, for medium-sized rainbow trout.

After retracing our steps to the Crabtree Trail, we turn east again and switchback down on deep sand flanked by dense manzanita and ceanothus to an easy ford of Lily Creek. Swinging southeast through a meadow sporting corn-lilies, lungwort and senecio, our path soon comes to a granite headwall and makes a steep, rocky ascent. A parade of switchbacks leads to a lengthy traverse that passes through meadows south of black-streaked granite outcrops, and we soon reach a pretty lakelet, much larger than shown on the topo map, speckled with Indian pond lilies and backdropped by dancing aspens and lichen-dappled granite. Its clear, shallow waters support a thriving population of yellow-legged frogs.

After a short climb east of this tarn, we survey dome-guarded Toms Canyon in the northeast, Groundhog Meadow below in the southeast, and, on the eastern horizon, Bigelow Peak and the jutting prominence of Tower Peak. Bone-jarring dynamited switchbacks, esthetically ameliorated by a profusion of wildflowers in early season, lead down to a sidehill traverse in glacial boulders west of Piute Meadow. Keeping to the trees south of the willowed west arm of Piute Meadow, we cross Piute Creek at a large campsite. Only yards after Piute Creek the Groundhog Meadow spur trail comes in from the south. It can be followed for ten minutes, down over sandy benches and slabs, to a signed junction with the Bell Meadow Trail (PC-10) in ¾-acre Groundhog Meadow. The dry slabs and lodgepole pines demarcating the lower margin of Piute Meadow are left behind when our path bends upward on switchbacks, thrusting rockily up the east slope of Piute Creek Canyon to a broad saddle southwest of Piute Lake. Seen from this pass and from other points as we drop moderately down to the meadowed west end of Piute Lake are the rock-climbing possibilities on 400–500-foot-high faces of well-broken, aplite-diked granite on the wall north of Piute Lake. The lake itself is small and grass-fringed, except where forested with lodgepoles, and its shallow, greenish waters support rainbow trout.

We skirt the lake's north shore before climbing gently and then dropping through lushly vegetated meadow to a ford of West Fork Cherry Creek. Interesting flowers seen in the jungle of flora preceding this crossing are orange-and-maroon tiger lily, fragrant purple onion, palmate-leaved yellow cinquefoil, and stalked white rein orchid. East Flange Rock, a volcanic precipice to the north, and the upper reaches of Cherry Creek swing into prominence as we climb along a steep, forested slope on switchbacks heading for Gem Lake. Heavy pack-animal use, inconsiderate short-cutting hikers, and water runoff have reduced the trail to a shambles of ruts and cobbles. We level out on a wooded saddle, then drop to the north shore of pretty Gem Lake, which sits on the edge of a glaciated granite bench. A thin strip of lodgepoles surrounds most of Gem Lake's rocky margin, and a striking wall of orange-rusted granite, offering good climbing, lies to the north. The best camping at this shallow, warmish lake is on the north shore, which our path parallels.

After passing an unmarked spur to the Bell Meadow Trail (Route PC-10) this route switchbacks up onto sunny, glaciated slabs, speckled with sunflowers, pussy paws, buckwheat and stonecrop. An east-trending gully leads us to humus-bottomed Jewelry Lake,

A calm day at Jewelry Lake

which is rapidly being meadowed in at its inlet. The gravels and shallow lagoons at the lake's head do, however, provide good spawning for the rainbow trout that live here. The dominant feature of the Jewelry Lake area, visible for miles around, is the 600-foot-high overhanging dome north of the lake, which would provide particularly challenging technical climbing.

Tracking north of Jewelry Lake's swampy east end, we climb gently. The path turns northeast for a moment, marking the best departure point for those making a cross-country visit to Wire Lakes (see Route PC-8), then back southeast to climb a slabby ravine shaded occasionally by mountain hemlocks. Atop the gully, the wooded outlet of Deer Lake is but a few strides ahead. Frequently the open north shore gives way to willow-choked meadow pockets and lodgepole groves. Proceeding on sandy loam around the north shore of Deer Lake, which has an ample fishery of rainbow trout, we pass the Burst Rock Trail (Route PC-3), then turn east to a rock-hop ford of Long Lake creek and a junction with the Long Lake Trail.

Long Lake, one of the largest lakes in Emigrant Wilderness, is the destination of this half-mile spur trail. Bearing northeast, we amble on sandy tread into a moderately timbered grove of lodgepole and western white pines. Then, the way becomes ducked to lead us onto a steep hillside of exfoliation sheeting. This ascent levels out about 50 feet below the 8700-foot lake level, winding among willows and boulders in a lodgepole-encroached subalpine meadow. The three short sections of concrete-and-stone check dam, built in 1939, are reached shortly thereafter. Long Lake is typically granite-bound, and dotted with numerous islands, some of which, if one is equipped with a raft for access, have trees and sandy nooks suitable for camping. Most of the lake's margin is poorly suited to camping, being girdled by granitic bluffs with only enough level ground to accommodate a fringe of meadow or labrador tea, red heather and willows. From our vista point at Long Lake's impound-

ment, we see the bulk of Granite Dome looming up-canyon. Sunbathing and diving are also attractions of this spot, as are hopes of capturing some of Long Lake's large rainbow trout.

When you've finished enjoying Long Lake, descend back to Deer Lake and resume the march east on the Crabtree Trail. Zigzagging up through talus, slabs and pocket meadows, the path leaves Deer Lake behind, passes the Wood Lake Lateral Trail (described in Route PC-10), and ascends moderately to a granitic gap. Then, descending east, our way leads past two early-season tarns which, with melt-off from snow drifts along the route, ensure June and July hikers an ample supply of mosquitos. We leap to the north side of a trickling creek that drains the steep canyon our path follows, dropping past huge talus blocks and a profusion of wildflowers, to a trail junction in a forest fringe on the southwest shore of Upper Buck Lake.

Before continuing north toward Emigrant Lake, consider a scenic detour south on a 1½-mile lateral around Lower Buck Lake to the Bell Meadow–Huckleberry Lake Trail, described here: Turn south along partly rockbound Upper Buck Lake. A fine campsite sits at the southwest edge of its clear, 55-foot-deep blue waters, which hold large (to 18") rainbow trout. A sometimes tricky crossing of the creek draining Upper Buck Lake on the narrow granitic isthmus between it and the lower lake brings us to a camp in an idyllic lodgepole and mat manzanita stand, near an unfinished log cabin built by a now-defunct power company. We then traverse along the east side of Lower Buck Lake. A streamflow-maintenance dam impounds the trout-abundant waters, and is responsible for the few burnished silver snags which stand reflected in the yellow early-morning light. Our path is usually covered with duff, under a canopy of hemlock or lodgepole, but occasionally we tread on polished slabs. From Lower Buck Lake's south margin we undulate over broken granite and sand past two pinhead tarns to a signed saddle where we intersect the Bell Meadow Trail (Route PC-10), which can be followed right (west) for

Islands in Upper Buck Lake

just a few minutes to Wood Lake, or east down a steep hillside to Cow Meadow Lake.

If we neglect the Lower Buck Lake Trail, we turn north on the trail that traverses Upper Buck Lake's west shore and descend quickly to a large campsite. From here more pleasant packer camps are seen, in meadow-floored lodgepole groves, but little of the lake itself, due to a screen of high willows that is populated by clacking blackbirds and starlings. Above, clean 600-foot-tall cliffs of virgin granodiorite might catch the eye of would-be rock climbers. Eventually, we swing into damp Buck Meadow and, under the silent gaze of Domes 9497 and 9482, up-canyon, we undertake a 10-foot horse ford of cool Buck Meadow Creek. Now climb the path as it makes a well-graded assault on the morainal tills smeared over the east canyon wall. Mountain hemlocks here provide welcome coolness but prevent any vistas that we might anticipate over Buck Lakes. Almost before we realize it, 600 feet of elevation gain fall under our steps and we emerge on a sunny saddle of white granite. The final leg to Emigrant Lake now winds down through pockets of meadow to a small step-across streamlet just short of the northwest shore of that immense reservoir. A sign here proclaims that campfires are prohibited within ¼ mile of the lakeshore. Campers at this popular lake have seriously depleted the downed wood that is needed to regenerate forest soil. Here, too, the faint North Fork Cherry Creek Trail (Route CL-5) branches west across a muddy meadow.

Now the Crabtree Trail turns along Emigrant Lake's rocky northern shore. At 230 acres, it is the largest natural body of water in Emigrant Wilderness or Yosemite. It's rather hard to fish without a raft, but its shallow, grassy inlet and rocky outlet consistently produce lunker rainbow trout, to 28 inches, especially for anglers who use a spincast-lure rig. Many good campsites lie in handsful of pines in tiny pockets that dot the north shore; between them, the connecting trail wends through talus and over small ledges. We march toward the twin summits of dark Grizzly Peak, eventually reaching a larger conifer stand and a cluster of enormous, overused horsepacker camps beyond the lake's head. Rock climbers will go no farther—a particularly striking white dome sweeps 500 feet above this campground on the north canyon wall.

After a highly recommended layover in this vicinity, reshoulder your pack and proceed east momentarily to intersect the Huckleberry Trail (Route KM-1) which climbs north to Mosquito Pass and south to Blackbird Lakes. Our way merges with the southbound path as far as Blackbird Lakes. The first task is to get across wide North Fork Cherry Creek: horses wade in mid-meadow; humans can walk farther east on a use-trail to find some rocks to hop over on. Once back on track, march up an easy chain of switchbacks, then traverse to the north edge of tiny, shallow Blackbird Lakes. No trail sign marks our departure from the southbound Huckleberry Trail, so look carefully for a north-descending path that, in a moment, steps across Blackbird Lakes' seasonal outflow creek. Beyond, a brief ascent is forced north by a low *roche moutonee* to find an easy line close beside rollicking North Fork Cherry Creek. After a few minute's meanderings in thigh-high gardens of hairy lupine and senecio, the path forces a rock-hop to the creek's north bank. The pace of ascent quickens now, leading to a spongy bog of adhesive muck where trail tread is lost, and, if your shoes aren't well-tied, you might lose a boot as well! Circumvent this mudhole, then continue directly up hill. Soon the climb yields to find treeless, meadow-fringed Middle Emigrant Lake. Its expanse is usually much larger than indicated on the topo, and flycasting for rainbows is often excellent; but camping is poor and I recommend camping at Blackbird or Emigrant Lake, instead.

Imposing granitic cliffs come almost down to Middle Emigrant Lake's northwest shore, and the Crabtree Trail muddily traverses these banks, then crashes through willows to a horse ford of North Fork Cherry Creek. Now on a drier footing, wind northeast, away from the creekside, over a dry stepladder of shorthair-sedge meadowlets. These give way to a talus of recessional moraine bounding the south shore of trout-packed Emigrant Meadow Lake. Skirt the east shore, close beside water's edge, on faint, wet trail that barely indents a delightful fell field of Lemmons paintbrush, cinquefoil, Brewers lupine, single-flowered senecio and Sierra penstemon. Farther north, we drift away from the east shore, heading north to strike the much more obvious Brown Bear Pass Trail (Route KM-2) at a 2½-foot-high lodgepole post planted in the meadow verge.

Large Emigrant Lake

PC-5

Chewing Gum Lake Trail: Lake Valley to Crabtree Camp

Distances
0.8 mile to Chewing Gum Lake
5.0 miles to Crabtree Roadend

Introduction
Winding from verdant Lake Valley past Chewing Gum Lake, a favorite of week-enders, then 1900 feet down through virgin timber to Crabtree Camp, this lateral, described from north to south, provides a fine finish for a loop trip emanating from Crabtree Roadend. It makes a nice day hike, too, with a short car shuttle.

Trailhead
Same as the Route PC-3 trailhead (for the trip's start) or Route PC-4 trailhead (for the finish).

Description
Starting at the 8730-foot-high dandelion-meadowed trail junction in beautiful upper Lake Valley, 3.1 miles from Gianelli Cabin, the Chewing Gum Lake Trail leaves the Burst Rock Trail (Route PC-3) to wander over thick subalpine turf, with the precipitous north face of Peak 9040+, east of Bear Lake,

as a guiding beacon. The route, sometimes without tread on the spongy green peat, passes south through a succession of pinched-off meadows; lodgepoles under-storied by hairy lupine do the pinching. After a brief climb, we pass through a forested draw, and soon find ourselves standing on the shallow, grassy northwest arm of Chewing Gum Lake, beside which, in a fine lodgepole grove, is a very good camp complex.

Chewing Gum is a pleasant subalpine lake surrounded by porphyritic slabs that, due to weathering, prominently display their large feldspar crystals. The lake's 21-foot-deep, humus-bottomed waters' green highlights are augmented by willows, labrador tea, and lupine which crowd the shore, and these same shrubs offer camouflage for the brook-trout flycaster.

Continuing south toward Crabtree Camp, we leave the west shore along a bluff, then

Evening comes to Chewing Gum Lake

cut south through a shrubby meadow. At the glen's south end we follow ducks steeply and rockily up to a level traverse in mixed conifers, then descend a rotting gully amid myriad varieties of wildflowers. Leaving the gully, we take a ducked route across a flat and then some slabs, avoiding a ducked but hardly used route that drops steeply south to Bear Lake. Instead we switchback west into mixed-conifer forest. Beyond, we make a moderate side-hilling traverse that finally becomes steep, to the top of a bouldery morainal ridge with an open fir-pine cover.

After a pause for breath atop this 8980-foot rib, we begin the 1900-foot plunge to Crabtree Camp. This knee-jarring journey's first leg takes one moderately down through duff-floored red-fir groves to a volcanic meadow that grows willows, corn lilies, Sitka valerian, paintbrush, lupine and senecio. Across this pasture we gently descend a sandy, less homogeneous forest to a nose. Here our path turns south and steeply descends a rocky gully to a seasonal stream, running west. A well-shaded traverse keeps near the stream for one mile, and then we cross to another southward descent, this time through a tangle of huckleberry oak growing on dusty morainal till. Presently we re-enter red-fir forest, now more open, with some Jeffrey pines to reflect the lower altitude. This sandy segment leads moderately down to a signed junction with the Crabtree Trail (Route PC-4), just ½ minute south of Crabtree Camp, across Bell Creek.

PC-6

Upper Lily Creek: Y Meadow Lake Cross-Country to Granite and Bear Lakes

Distances
0.6 mile to Y Meadow Lake
1.6 miles to Granite Lake
3.9 miles to Bear Lake
5.0 miles to Crabtree Trail (near Camp Lake)

Introduction
Bear Lake is a favorite of weekenders out from Crabtree roadend, and Y Meadow Lake and Granite Lake are frequent first-night stops for trail-pounders on the Burst Rock Trail. They can be linked together by an easy, interesting, cross-country descent of Lily Creek, thereby opening up new combinations of loops and day hikes in the western Emigrant Wilderness.

Trailhead
Same as the Route PC-3 trailhead.

Description
A steeply descending cobbly ridge at the head of a volcanic meadow marks the well-signed intersection of the Y Meadow Lake Trail and the Burst Rock Trail (Route PC-3) 4.7 miles east of the Gianelli Cabin trailhead. Our route leads a few feet south to a rib dividing the Stanislaus and the Tuolumne River drainages, then drops moderately to a gopher-roped meadow with dandelions, hairy lupines and tufted sedges. Winding southwest down this discontinuously meadowed canyon, which has exposures of marbled intrusive rocks, we soon glimpse Y Meadow Lake. Soon, we arrive at slabs demarcating its northern shore. The most desirable camp on artificial Y Meadow Lake, which is held back by an 18-foot dam, is on the northwest shore in a pocket of conifers. Around the lake's east side, the porphyritic quartz monzonite which here forms gentle slabs has taken on a rosy tint, quite picturesque in the low yellow light of late afternoon. Nodding-topped mountain hemlocks shade a smattering of sand flats along this shore. About two thirds of the way south along its length, we might pick up a line of ducks indicating the route to Granite Lake.

A side trip to Granite Lake is worth the minimal effort. This secluded natural tarn has, unlike sterile Y Meadow Lake, a self-sustained population of large brook trout. To reach it, one should proceed south from Y Meadow Lake to the pair of tarns indicated on the topo. Here ducks will be found to lead up to a third pond. From its heather-rimmed shores, amble southwest past innumerable smaller puddles to the divide west of a prominent *roche moutonnee*. Down a slabby slope beyond this divide you will find Granite Lake, moderately forested with a mixture of Hudsonian Zone species. Lensmen as well as anglers will appreciate this deep, blue lake, which has, standing away from its shrubbery-lined shores, pretty islets that are reflected in the calm of morning. To continue down Lily Creek canyon without backtracking to Y Meadow Lake, follow ducks around the west shore, passing the best camp en route, and then descending west in a forested ravine to a fair-sized meadow on Lily Creek.

If we choose to disregard the joys of Granite Lake, our walk along Y Meadow Lake will soon find its dammed outlet, which empties into a willowed meadow. Continuing down the east side of Lily Creek, we leave the stream-side to scramble over a pile of house- and car-sized talus blocks. Presently cliffs force us across the stream, to traverse the north bank into a fine meadow where the route from Granite Lake is joined.

Fording back to the south bank, we wind through a forest to the top of an open, stepped slope. Dropping below the limits of mountain-hemlock growth, we move farther away from the stream-side, sticking to a ducked route on a generally shrubbery-free rib south of Lily Creek. Bear Lake, with Bell Mountain as its backdrop, soon presents itself down-canyon, as we leave open rock and Sierra junipers behind to cross the lushly forested stream that parallels Lily Creek on the south. Minutes later, the ducks guide us moderately down to Lily Creek at the influx of the Chewing Gum Lake stream. Past a little-used camp, we pass under red firs and lodgepoles to 7760 feet, where ducks indicate that a creek crossing is in order. Many species of shade- and dampness-tolerant plants—such as twinberry, currant, spiraea, larkspur, and false- Solomon's-seal—are left on the south banks when we change to sandy-floored lodgepole groves near the northeast end of Bear Lake.

Campsites herald Bear Lake's log-littered inlet, where one will discern a faint use-path cutting through spring-fed jungles of corn-lily, lungwort and fern to a camping complex on the north shore. At the next group of fire-rings we find the Bear Lake Trail. This path leads us past Bear Lake's rocky outlet, after which we skirt a small meadow and a tepid mosquito pond. We veer west from Lily Creek to drop down through two corn-lily-and-willow-throttled meadows, being encroached upon, in the normal pattern, by lodgepole pines. Across a muddy stream draining the south end of the last of these, we pass over a granitic knob. A short drop brings us to shady lodgepoles on the north side of a large brown pond. Rounding west along it, we reach the Crabtree Trail (Route PC-4). Camp Lake is only a minute's walk to the west.

PC-7

Toejam Lake Trail: Cross-Country to Leopold Lake and Piute Meadow via Toms Canyon

Distances
1.4 miles to Toejam Lake
2.5 miles to Leopold Lake
5.0 miles to Crabtree Trail in Piute Meadow

Leopold Lake. Three Chimneys just barely visible.

Introduction

Few hikers visit Toejam Lake. Even fewer take the few extra minutes to reach lovely Leopold Lake. And almost no one descends Toms Canyon to Piute Meadow. Their ignorance will be your bliss—both lakes are delightful, intimate and fishable. Toms Canyon holds a beautiful, unspoiled meadow and affords a nice shortcut to reach the Crabtree Trail from the north.

Trailhead

Same as the Route PC-3 trailhead.

Description

The unsigned Toejam Lake Trail is found a few feet after the Burst Rock Trail (Route PC-3) leaves a gopher-roped meadow at about 8840 feet, 0.7 mile east of Whitesides Meadow, and 6.4 miles east of Gianelli Cabin trailhead. The path can be seen to ascend gently south on sandy lodgepole duff. Soon it drops, with some steep sections, over a forested till slope. On a southwestward traverse in thick forest it soon reaches the final climb to Toejam Lake: a hillside of rotting, varicolored granitic rock. Ending in a pretty

meadow that gives way to a sandy flat on Toejam Lake's north shore, this climb has good over-the-shoulder vistas north to East Flange Rock and Night Cap Peak. Toejam Lake is situated in a granitic bowl and rimmed with the typical subalpine combination of sedges, red heather, dwarf bilberry and Brewers lupine with some senecio in the damper spots. While fishing for brookies in its shallow waters (20 feet) one has views northeast to Granite Dome. Very good, though exposed, campsites are found on Toejam's west shore.

Heading south to Leopold Lake, a trip which should take some 20 minutes, we climb slightly through erratic-speckled sand flats colored by lupine, huckleberry, sedges, onions and mixed conifers. Photographically induced halts to capture likenesses of the northern landscape, including the Cooper Peak-Three Chimneys divide, which shows up as a line of black crags against autumn snows, are well-rewarded. The north end of shallow, islanded Leopold Lake is reached in an open forest of mixed conifers. Mafic granitic rocks, tussocks of red heather, and bunched grasses edge its shoreline, which, though not affording exceptional camping possibilities, invites a stay because of the superb views across its wind-dimpled surface of Granite Dome, the Saurian Crest, and Bigelow, Tower and Forsythe peaks.

To continue on to Piute Meadow, our route from Leopold Lake turns west to an overlook of Toms Canyon. Now we can see our next objective: small Piute Creek, meandering lazily in a meadow in Toms Canyon's floor, 600 feet below. Pick out a line down the slope—probably using a shallow gully with some forest cover, interspersed with a bit of bitter-cherry bushwhacking and some talus-hopping. Soon enough, you'll find the canyon floor and its pretty meadow.

Hop Piute Creek and wend south along

it. In about ⅓ mile the meadow ends where a dome pinches off the canyon. Here we turn west, winding past flat exposures of white granite and spiry mountain hemlocks to a string of tarns. At the largest, westernmost of these we find a nice campsite, then turn south down a gully. One hundred feet below, we cut back under an imposing bluff, to walk abreast of Piute Creek. Picture-perfect views of Piute Meadow and Kibbie Ridge accompany us down pinkish, feldspar-cubed slabs, with occasional lodgepoles, junipers and, lower down, huckleberry-oak thickets, along Piute Creek's west side. Soon we reach an outwash of multitextured boulders that heralds Piute Meadow, and wend through meadow-floored forest, possibly hearing the queer barking of a red fox, to the Crabtree Trail (Route PC-4) near its ford of Piute Creek.

PC-8

Wire Lakes

Distances

0.6 mile to West Shore Upper Wire Lake
1.6 miles to East Shore Lower Wire Lake
2.3 miles to Crabtree Trail near Deer Lake

Introduction

Lower Wire Lake is my favorite subalpine camp in the western Emigrant Basin. Its sister lakes are worth a visit too. Although all three are only a few minutes from the Burst Rock Trail, most visitors will find that Wire Lakes' bench will give hours of solitude, good views and rewarding fishing.

Trailhead

Same as the Route PC-3 trailhead.

Description

The signed Wire Lakes Trail branches west from the Burst Rock Trail (Route PC-3) in pleasant lodgepole-hemlock forest on the morainal ridge south of Post Corral Canyon, about 9.4 miles east of the Gianelli Cabin roadend. Climbing gently, the path leads north of a cluster of small mosquito tarns. After bending south, we pass over a bouldery ridge to find upper Wire Lake. Along its

northwest shore, we see excellent campsites in meadowy turf. Upper Wire Lake has, like its sisters to the south, a good population of planted brook trout. Rounding peninsula-partitioned embayments and passing an excellent packer camp on the southwest end of upper Wire Lake, we turn south down the shallow outlet ravine to the rocky shores of Banana Lake, the middle Wire Lake. This shallow lakelet affords only poor camping, so one will most likely prefer to walk on to lower Wire Lake, just south of Banana Lake's midsection. Lower Wire Lake, most beautiful of the group, is set off from the granite basin in which it sits by a delicate rim of mixed conifers. Under the trees, bilberry, red and white heather, sedges, and delicate bud saxifrage form a thick, rolling felt in the places where smooth granite outcrops don't rise from the cobalt-blue waters. Reflected in the lake are the high peaks forming the Emigrant Basin's northern boundary. The sum of lower Wire Lake's picturesque parts is a sublime subalpine ambiance, and there are campsites to match along the east and south shores. For excellent panoramas, scramble south to a low dome—it caps a stupendous cliff overlooking Jewelry Lake to the south. From the east shoulder of this dome, one could continue easily down a broad, exfoliating basin, skirting the huge orange cliff, to meet the Crabtree Trail (Route PC-4) just a few minutes' amble west of Deer Lake.

Upper Wire Lake

PC-9

Granite Dome and Wilson Meadow Lake via Post Corral Canyon; Return via Pinto Lakes

Distances
1.7 miles to Wilson Meadow Lake
3.0 miles to Granite Dome Summit
3.9 miles to Pinto Lakes
5.9 miles to Burst Rock Trail near Salt Lick Meadow

Introduction
Used only by diehard cross-country enthusiasts, this loop visits two alpine lakes at the headwaters of Cherry Creek, linking them by an easy but exhilarating ascent of Granite Dome, an exceptional viewpoint which is not to be omitted from the itineraries of those who would claim intimacy with Emigrant Wilderness.

Trailhead
Same as the Route PC-3 trailhead.

Description

Our route begins in Spring Meadow, just before the Burst Rock Trail (Route PC-3) begins to swing southeast to the Wire Lakes environs. Here we leave the trail, heading up Post Corral Canyon along Spring Creek. On the stream's north side, pick up a faint trail. Rosy-tinted boulders, dandelion and shooting star dot the rolling swale, which we leave for steeper slopes at about 8800 feet. At 8900 feet, we find another large meadow, terminated on the east by an impressive wall of 500-foot-high cliffs. This pristine grassland would make an outstanding base camp for rock-climbers or privacy-seekers.

Turning northeast along Spring Creek, we climb through groves of mixed conifers, to find a stepped series of tufted meadows. To reach Wilson Meadow Lake from here, note the prominent spurred dome with a highly polished, west face that stands just to our north, then count two notches south along the ridge from its summit. Head for that notch, over steep talus just south of the little stream that cascades down from Wilson Meadow Lake. Many yellow-bellied marmots are present to supervise our ascent, which ends almost 500 feet above on all-but-barren slabs. Pausing for a rarified breath, we look back southwest over Wire Lakes and the Hyatt Lake region. A minute east, over gravelly sand composed of weathered feldspar crystals, we come upon willow-dotted Wilson Meadow and its small alpine tarn. Devoid of fish due to its shallowness, Wilson Meadow Lake is a crystalline mirror reflecting fleecy cumuli, the south slopes of Granite Dome and a fine unnamed summit at the meadow's head.

For those who demand only the highest possible pinnacle for attaining their vistas, an ascent of Granite Dome, 10322', is in order. Begin just north of Wilson Meadow Lake, where we clamber over orange-stained slabs to a broken chute that takes us north, up along the eastern headwall of Post Corral

Wilson Meadow Lake

Canyon's cirque. Above, we assault the final rotting granite slopes, which show thin exfoliation leaves on the bluffs that herald the summit. Atop the bluffs are Granite Dome's solution-pocketed apex, a cairn and a register and, hopefully, windless clear skies to allow a luxurious sunbath. The views were worth the effort. Starting from the west, our 360° panorama takes in Burst Rock, the canyon of South Fork Stanislaus River, Cooper Peak, the Three Chimneys, Upper and Lower Relief valleys with East Flange Rock overlooking them, the Dardanelles, and the Carson-Iceberg Wilderness, backdropped by Round Top and Mokelumne Peak on the northern horizon. Just below us to the north are Ridge, Sardella and Lewis lakes, home of large golden trout, while farther east we see the massive volcanic eminences of Relief and Grizzly peaks. Swinging our gaze more southward, we note the high points of Yosemite National Park—Tower and Forsythe peaks near Bond Pass, Mts. Dana, Lyell and Florence in the Cathedral Range south of Tuolumne Meadows, and Haystack, Michie and Kendrick peaks near the Park's border. We can also see Long and Coolidge Meadow lakes as well as Wilson Meadow Lake, plus Wire and Toejam lakes.

Leaving this eyrie, our descent, bound for Pinto Lakes, begins with a steep zigzag scramble down to a gray slope of volcanic debris which belies its distant appearance of sterility by being alive with ivesia, wallflower, lupine, blue flax and other flowers. Dropping southwest, we soon can see Pinto Lakes below us. Alpine chipmunks and pikas are irate at being chased from lushly vegetated slopes as we near the conifers fringing the larger, northern Pinto Lake. A wet meadow is gradually choking off the lake, and it is now too shallow to support golden trout as it once did. Heading back to more civilized terrain near the Burst Rock Trail, we drop along Pinto Lakes' outlet creek—a long walk in bouldery meadows and stands of timber where there is an on-and-off ducked route. If you want to drop clear to Salt Lick Meadow, just stick to this stream; otherwise, at about 8750 feet, where the route swings away from the creek, you can cut due south to the ridge separating Salt Lick and Spring meadows. Here, find the Burst Rock Trail (Route PC-3) only about a mile northwest of where we left it in Spring Meadow.

PC-10

Bell Meadow Trail to Wood Lake, Cow Meadow Lake and Huckleberry Lake

Distances
4.7 miles to Grouse Lake
8.2 miles to Louse Canyon
12.0 miles to Wood Lake
14.3 miles to Cow Meadow Lake (North Fork Trail)
17.5 miles to Huckleberry Lake (South End)

Introduction
This low-elevation route penetrates straight as an arrow into the western Emigrant Basin, traversing a succession of beautiful, ice-scoured glacial valleys to reach Wood Lake, the center of an explosion of subalpine lakes, each teeming with trout. We can then continue to Huckleberry Lake—longest in Emigrant Wilderness—via paths that meet both its northern and its southern shores.

Trailhead
From Sonora Pass Highway 108, just 0.8 mile east of Cold Springs, turn right (east) onto signed, paved Crabtree Road 4N26.1. Follow it 6.4 miles to signed Dodge Ridge Road 4N25, just 100 yards short of Sardella's Pack Station. Turn right (south) on

this one-lane, poorly paved road to dirt Road 4N20Y, reached in 0.4 mile, signed BELL MEADOW TRAILHEAD. Turn left (south) on this road, which curves down to the large Bell Meadow Trailhead parking area, 1.8 miles from Dodge Ridge Road.

Description

From the signed trailhead information billboard, follow the obvious trail sandily east, keeping close alongside a barbed-wire stock fence, which keeps a small herd of cattle and horses confined to the brushy meadow. Keep south of granitic outcrops and north of Bell Meadow's edge. Level going then brings you to two gorges that are deeply incised by Bell Creek. Through dark, coniferous timber you get infrequent glimpses of massive Bell Mountain, to the south, as the route first climbs gently and then undulates to a good campsite north of the trail at a step-across ford of East Fork Bell Creek. Tank up here, for a hot, exposed climb ensues.

Climbing steeply in a gully notable for some large ponderosa pines, we soon arrive at a junction with the old Mud Lake Trail, which climbs south through thick volcanic dust. Our way veers north to steeply ascend a cobbly nose, then alters to a fairly consistent moderate grade. In the welcome shade of Jeffrey pines and white firs atop this 7200-foot divide we lower our gears for a hot, knee-numbing, switchbacking drop on nearly barren volcanic conglomerate to a lateral to Crabtree Camp, described in Route PC-4. Dropping gently east into well-named Pine Valley—almost all lodgepoles—we come very soon to another trail south to Mud Lake (Route BC-1). From this junction we ascend imperceptibly through open forest to cross the Bear Lake fork of Lily Creek.

Entering Emigrant Wilderness, we come into more-open terrain. Reaching Grouse Lake, our route bisects a large camping complex on its north shore. Amateur naturalists who brave the hordes here—people and mosquitos—will find numerous plant and animal species, including an occasional bear, plus rainbow and brook trout. The conspicuous rings of small holes in the bark of aspen trees in this area are caused by yellow-bellied sapsuckers; those in lodgepole pines are the work of Williamson's sapsuckers.

At the head of Grouse Lake we cross to the south bank of Lily Creek and resume the gentle eastward ascent, now in an ever-narrowing canyon. The higher we climb up this granitic cleft, the steeper and taller the cliffs become, and the rougher and rockier the path grows. Finally, close under a 500-foot-high face that looms in the south, we are forced to tread gray talus blocks, and the ascent becomes steep, hot, and monotonous except for the surprising array of shrubs—huckleberry oak, manzanita, ceanothus, twinberry, ocean spray, currant, bitter cherry, serviceberry, willow, shrubby spiraea and gooseberry. Our climb does become gentler past isolated junipers near the bluffed pass dividing Piute from Lily Creek waters. A short distance beyond the saddle, an easy descent brings us to campsites at the crossing of Piute Creek. We quickly leave behind the little-used Studhorse Meadow Trail (Route BC-3) on the right, then the Piute Meadow lateral on the left, before rounding south into barren Groundhog Meadow.

We continue moderately up into a fine mixed coniferous forest, under the somber face of Peak 8124 to yet another col. Then, descending east, the path emerges from red fir at a rocky overlook from which upper Louse Canyon and the convergence of West Fork Cherry Creek and Buck Meadow Creek appear below. This vista point marks a return to drier, more rocky going, and our route switchbacks dustily down through huckleberry oak and phlox to a junction from which a trail going southwest to Rosasco Lake passes a number of campsites just downstream. This trail is described as Route PC-11. Early in the year, the ford of Cherry Creek immediately beyond this junction is a bit tricky, but it can be accomplished dry if you head upstream for a few yards to where boulders lead across the braided waters. Once more ascending, we traverse diorite slabs, following ducks across the monolithic rock, which shows glacial polish and striations. Considering that the highly polished surface was created by glaciers at least ten thousand years ago, it is in a remarkable state of preservation.

Gaining altitude via short, bouldery switchbacks on the north side of Buck Meadow Creek, the early-summer hiker will be presented with a multi-hued array of wildflowers—more than 20 species! Soon we come to the Gem Lake lateral, which traces ducks 0.4 mile up broken slabs to the east shore of Gem Lake, with some pretty camps. Cross the outlet stream of that lake and follow jointing fractures down to a boulder crossing of Buck Meadow Creek. The low roar of frothing water accompanies us along Buck Meadow Creek until we begin to climb away from its banks into deep hemlock forest. Features to our north include the dome south of Jewelry Lake, which would offer several pitches of severe climbing.

At a point where we level out under a granitic nose and begin to drop, the cross-country route to Coyote Lake (Route PC-12)

turns off southwest. A short distance beyond, we leap from rock to rock to cross Buck Meadow Creek, switchback quickly up and around a granite boss, cross the creek again via a large log-jam, and arrive at a junction with a lateral trail to Deer Lake, to be described momentarily. Only a few feet later we come into a large, damp, well-littered camping area at the west end of Wood Lake. Western tanagers, robins or varied thrushes might serenade us as we pause to lunch beside the shallow blue waters, gazing east to the horizon of Bigelow Peak. This 12-acre, 27-foot-deep, dumbbell-shaped lake offers very good angling for rainbow trout to 15″.

After lunch, consider a brief side-trip to Deer Lake: Retrace your steps a few yards west to the signed Deer Lake lateral, then walk east along the south bank of Buck Meadow Creek to a ford of that stream, which, in the first months of summer, is about 40 feet wide and 2 feet deep. Non-horsemen will no doubt choose to cross via

Deer Lake

the massive many-hundred-log-jam that dams Wood Lake. Skirting Wood Lake's north shore, our path passes its best campsite, on a forested promontory, and then another in a stand of lodgepoles, where we swerve north into a narrow gully. This rocky ascent soon levels off, and then our path drops to cross an intermittent creek. West of this stream, a few cobbly switchbacks take us moderately up a glacier-plucked step. Next on the itinerary is a shallow subalpine tarn. Passing through the water-logged grassland north of its shores, three tiny tarns are passed, one of which sits astride the trail, before we reach the second mapped lakelet. Moments later we intersect the Crabtree Trail (Route PC-4) in a forested heap of morainal debris, about ¼ mile east of Deer Lake.

Back at Wood Lake, we pass along the willow-obscured south shore, then turn south into a shallow gully from where the Karls Lake Trail heads southwest to solitude and good fishing, as described in Route PC-12. From this junction, we tread on spongy loam past fine campsites nestled in hemlocks along the wide "canal" joining the lobes of Wood Lake. Rounding the shallower east lobe, we come to a sign that points incongruously east, right across Wood Lake, indicating MAIN TRAIL! Early in the season it would seem a dubious enterprise indeed to follow this advice, though the route is soddenly passable later in the year. A better route, though longer, is to follow the trail south around the water to meet the main trail one third of the way east along the south shore of a yellow-pond-lilied tarn. This junction is marked well by ducks, so that those headed west may easily avoid a wade of Wood Lake.

Soon after this pond we come to the lodgepole-shaded head of an 8400-foot saddle, where we find the northbound Buck Lakes Trail (Route PC-4). Our route switchbacks east down among steep boulders and huckleberry oaks, on a pathway that was extensively reconstructed in 1988. We reenter forest at a sandy linkage with the North Fork Cherry Creek Trail (Route CL-5) beside musical North Fork Cherry Creek. Our route then makes two fords of the creek, which can

be icy cold and waist-deep at maximum runoff. We then wind past morainal tarns to the north shore of Cow Meadow Lake, which usually offers some of the best rainbow trout fishing in the central Emigrant Basin. Tight, rocky switchbacks, with occasional views of the lake, lead up into mountain-hemlock forest and to a gap, where we pass the Lertora Lake Trail, to be described below. Douglas Lake, a rectangular, granite-bound tarn, is skirted as we continue south toward Huckleberry Lake's southwest end. Douglas Lake provides good brook-trout angling, fine swimming, and the best campsites for miles around.

Wind gently down a joint-fractured valley, crossing the small stream therein many times, then turn east to switchback down to a mosquitoey lakelet, often glimpsing Bigelow and Haystack peaks, eastward in northern Yosemite. The final descent to Huckleberry Lake is negotiated by often-steep switchbacks in rocky, joint-controlled gullies. Surprising the hiker who expects another shallow, grassy mud puddle, Huckleberry Lake has clean blue waters enveloped in white rocks dotted with lodgepole groves, covering 200 acres to a depth of as much as 51 feet. Our trail winds south beside narrow arms of the lake, all the way to its tip, where this route ends. From here the Kibbie Ridge Trail continues both down-canyon and eastward to the Horse Meadow Trail, described as Route CL-1.

For hikers who would prefer to reach the east end of Huckleberry Lake, the Lertora Lake Trail is the logical choice. The faint trail begins at a signed junction atop a gap southeast of Cow Meadow Lake. Wind around a shallow mosquito pond, then turn east along a joint-controlled ravine to lovely Lertora Lake. Framed by small bluffs and pocket-groves of pines and hemlocks, and divided into small, intimate bays, Lertora Lake is a romantic spot, offering seclusion and many moods. The trail skirts only a tiny bit of its western shore before leading south along ledges to wind gently downhill. First, it passes two large ponds, and then it drops rockily to the head of a lakelet. Now, rather

Huckleberry Lake (southwest end of this big lake)

vaguely (look for ducks) clamber back up a short distance east, and gain the tarn's eastern side. Next on the agenda is a brief climb to the start of a long, narrow bench. The trail keeps more or less level on a northeastward traverse under a band of 100-foot-high cliffs—perfect for top-roped rock climbs. Anywhere along this stretch, walk south to see a wonderful panorama of Huckleberry Lake. The abrupt west face of Haystack Peak dominates the southern horizon; Sachse Monument and Bigelow Peak rise in the east.

Eventually, the well-ducked path begins to wind moderately downhill. After reaching a brushy gully south of tiny Frog Lake (not worth the uphill scramble), the descent becomes more earnest. Soon enough the descent ends near a murky lily pond, and then the path swings beside the northernmost bay of Huckleberry Lake. One short final climb over a low bench leads to flat ground and a large, cool grove of lodgepoles—site of a large complex of packer camps—at the unsigned junction with the Huckleberry Trail (Route KM-1) and the Kibbie Ridge Trail (Route CL-1).

PC-11

Hyatt Lake Trail and Big Lake Trail, Pingree and Yellowhammer lakes

Distances
1.6 miles to Rosasco Lake
4.5 miles to Hyatt Lake
3.7 miles to Pingree Lake
4.6 miles to Big Lake
5.2 miles to Yellowhammer Lake
6.4 miles to North Fork Cherry Creek Trail

Introduction

Fishermen, sunbathers, lovers of austere high country and, especially, connoisseurs of solitude will value the ice-scoured area reached by this exciting lake-hopping route. This is the least visited part of Emigrant Wilderness. Possibly, the gleaming white barrenness of the terrain, which appears much as it must have thousands of years ago when the last glaciers retreated, may seem lifeless to some wilderness visitors. To cognescenti, however, the polished landscape around Hyatt Lake and Big Lake offers a taste of alpine high country at warmer, friendlier elevations.

Trailhead

Same as the Route PC-10 trailhead.

Description

The signed junction of the Big Lake Trail and the Bell Meadow Trail (Route PC-10) is on the west bank of West Fork Cherry Creek in Louse Canyon, 8.2 miles east of the trailhead. The first 150 feet of this route, dropping gently to the right along Cherry Creek, was washed away by high water. Circle this washout to pick up good trail tread, then drop easily to a creekside sandbar overhung by tall lodgepoles and stately red firs. Numerous excellent campsites here line the chortling greenness of West Fork Cherry Creek. As we leave the camp complex, sauntering easily over marbled slabs of varicolored mafic and intrusive rocks, Cherry Creek slides beside us, winding through a corridor of lodgepoles.

Our track leads south to the high, cut banks of West Fork Cherry Creek. The 1–3-foot-deep, 20-foot-wide horse ford to red-fir-and-lodgepole groves on the far side is out of the question for pedestrians, but there is a wading ford due east at the top of a sliding cascade. From here, scrambling south over fallen timber and another small branch of Cherry Creek, we reach the point at the foot of Louse Canyon's east wall where the trail begins a steep ascent. Our way angles up the slope and through a granite notch 500 feet above Cherry Creek. A moment later we are on the west shore of small, wedge-shaped Rosasco Lake, named for an early cattleman. It sits snugly in a granite cup, rimmed by lodgepoles and labrador tea. Biennial air drops maintain a fair rainbow-trout fishery here.

From above Rosasco's southeast side, our eroded trail leads up to a divide, from where one can make out Haystack Peak in the east. Then, we drop first steeply and then moderately southeast on poorly ducked, rotting slabs of dark schistose rock. Levelling off on sand, we pass a signless junction with the Hyatt Lake Trail, described at the end of this route, and forty yards later, following blazes, cross a creek. Now our route becomes much harder to follow, but since the 250-foot ascent to Pingree Lake is over open slabs dotted with lodgepoles and some western white pines, we have no trouble heading for the small rivulet draining the saddle west of Pingree Lake, even if we lose the ducks. Following near the creek, we stay north of it and of the saddle's low point, crossing under soaring granite domes, and soon find the north shore of Pingree Lake. Belying its 54-foot depth, many sloping white islands, some graced by wind-stunted conifers, break the surface of Pingree Lake.

A large packer camp is passed as we traverse the north shore, and less "civilized" sites dot the forest when we turn south. At some point along this shore, the tread will disappear, leaving you to walk gently over mats of red heather and climb east to a granite ridge where awesome vistas of the desolate southern Emigrant Basin and northern Yosemite present themselves. Tower, Kibbie and Haystack peaks are all easily identified, and Mt. Clark, in the range of that name in the southeast, shows ample reason for its original appellation—The Obelisk. Mercur Peak, Gillette Mountain, and many of the other naked monolithic knobs so characteristic of this locality are seen in the south, across the immense, wind-torn expanse of Big Lake.

Our romp continues southeast, easily negotiating open slabs to reach a glaringly polished, dome-bounded granite trough, where we follow an orange-stained creek sliding merrily south to Big Lake. Before undertaking this 400-foot descent you might consider going up the canyon to Kole Lake, an isolated gem ideally suited for a base camp. Other routes to Kole Lake are outlined in Route PC-12. Aptly named Big Lake (90 acres; over 100 feet deep) supports some hard-to-catch rainbows. It has few good campsites, but the spectacular scenery invites a prolonged stay.

The next lake on our itinerary, Yellowhammer Lake, is a fine spot at which to base some explorations. We reach it by bearing southeast along a ducked path from a crossing of Big Lake's inlet stream. A pleasant stroll leads to a granite rib, which we ascend, to be presented with two choices. First, if you want to stay at narrow, rock-girdled Yellowhammer Lake, you can drop gently southeast to that lake's outlet. Second, you can follow ducks northeast along this ridge through a dome-bounded gap, and then descend into lodgepole forest along the outlet creek of Five-Acre and Leighton Lakes, where you will find Camp Yellowhammer. Once owned by Fred Leighton, constructor of the streamflow-maintenance dams found throughout Emigrant Wilderness, it consists of seven buildings and a corral, all made of logs handhewn from nearby trees. Yellowhammer Lake itself lies jammed between parallel granite bosses, which narrow its profile and limit camping to sites well away from the shore or, better, beside the small lake past its outlet. The 50-foot-deep waters must invigorate its inhabitants, rainbow trout.

To reach the North Fork Cherry Creek Trail from Yellowhammer Lake, head for the prominent ramp leading a bit north of east up to the ridge south of Peak 8206, which can be seen as the large dome with a technically difficult southwest face. Atop the narrow rib, we look east at North Fork Cherry Creek, flowing below in a textbook example of a joint-controlled streamcourse. In the northeast can be seen a tremendous friction face on the north canyon wall. Our route of descent is along a tight, huckleberry-oak-filled joint gully, to find the vague but well-

ducked trail along the cascades of North Fork Cherry Creek (Route CL-5).

Now the way to little-seen Hyatt Lake will be explained. This spectacular, unsigned lateral leaves south-southwest from the Big Lake Trail about 40 yards west of the creek ford in the glacially scoured valley separating Rosasco and Pingree lakes. From here a faint path proceeds down-canyon along an incipient creek. We keep close to the stream through meadow and forest, soon emerging onto water-oranged slabs on the lip of a barren cirque headwall. Stupendous vistas are had down this canyon to Kibbie Ridge and Cherry Creek Canyon, and we note the obvious cross-country route south past a grove of lodgepoles to Cherry Creek. From our 7780-foot overlook, the Hyatt Lake route follows ducks southwest, climbing slightly on the southern flanks of a slick dome. In a short time the ducks disappear, so we drop gently to the erratic- and conifer-littered saddle east of Hyatt Lake.

Hyatt Lake lies but a few joyous minutes west of the 7660-foot saddle. At the north end of this very deep (over 100 feet) expanse of shimmering water, is a clean quartz-sand swimming beach, a Sierran rarity. Very good campsites are found adjoining the picturesque sandbar. Those who desire absolute solitude for angling (sporadic for large rainbows), sunbathing, brisk dips, or merely lazy introspection will choose a lone site halfway around the southeast shore, the best camp on this little-visited jewel. If one desires to reach Cherry Creek Canyon, however, one must backtrack to the opposite shore, which consists of a monolithic granite sheet buffed to an eye-piercing luster by countless applications of fine glacial flour. Here there are no high bluffs to bar access to Cherry Creek.

The old route down to Hyatt Lake followed the outlet of Rosasco Lake southwest down a small canyon. It has its disadvantages: a narrow, talus-choked gorge at 7800 feet is rough, but not nearly as trying as this route's main difficulty—350 feet of poorly ducked thrashing in vengeful patches of huckleberry oak—definitely not for the faint-of-heart or, worse, the shorts-clad hiker!

PC-12

Karls Lake Trail: Cross Country to Leighton, Kole, Coyote, Red Can and Five-Acre lakes

Distances
0.6 mile to Karls Lake
1.3 miles to Coyote Lake
1.5 miles to Kole Lake
1.9 miles to Red Can Lake

Introduction
Six small lakes, each with its own distinct personality, and all harboring brook or rainbow trout, are found only a few minutes' walk from Wood Lake via easy combinations of trail and off-trail hiking.

Trailhead
Same as the Route PC-10 trailhead.

Description
The easiest route into the Karls Lake basin is via the Karls Lake Trail, which is found on the south shore of Wood Lake in a shallow ravine. This point is 11.5 miles east of the Bell Meadow trailhead. From the signed junction the path steeply ascends under a moderate pine cover to a narrow col. As we begin to descend, the broad depression that holds Karls and Leighton lakes comes into view, while Bartlett Peak, on the Yosemite boundary, rides the southern horizon. The basin that stretches before our feet is constructed of highly glaciated slabs overlain by a thin green shroud of lodgepole pines, and where the glaciers' weight was enough to excavate the granite sufficiently, there now rest sparkling blue lakes, flecked with islands of resistant rock or of heaped till. Ducks mark our way steeply down intervening slabs to the meadow-floored lodgepole groves that hide the north shore of Karls Lake. Our trail rounds the west shore of this shallow basin, visiting a few good campsites en route. Rainbow trout find a home in the warm water, which beckons the trail-grimy hiker to bathe near shores lined with red heather and labrador tea. At the western extreme of Karls Lake, three cross-country routes depart.

Coyote Lake is easily reached from this point by walking west past two mosquito-spawning mud puddles, then angling northwest over slabs under a haughty 100-foot granite nose. Underused Coyote Lake sits west of this outcrop, in a dense lodgepole forest. Its heather-rimmed waters, while a fine bivouac for transient mallard ducks, make a poor habitat for small brook trout.

Travelers with a sojourn to Leighton Lake or to Kole Lake in mind should, as on the route to Coyote Lake, proceed west past the second of two mud puddles, but should then turn south and climb gently. Dropping through a low gap, you arrive at Leighton Lake's north shore, surrounded by silver snags and fallen lodgepoles, victims of its dammed waters. These dead trees, combined with the murkiness of the shallow water, the barren granitic islands, the infinite, hostile mosquitoes, and the general lifeless ambiance of the environs, make this a place little-visited by hikers.

Heading for Kole Lake from Leighton Lake's west end, we easily negotiate, at a 250° bearing, a slope of exfoliating granite. Atop the western saddle, our field of view encompasses all the peaks of the eastern Emigrant Wilderness. Presently we arrive at Kole Lake, a natural water body with a poor rainbow-trout fishery greatly outnumbered by yellow-legged frogs or, in the shoreline grasses, by easily disturbed hordes of bronze dragonflies.

Hikers intent on Five-Acre or Red Can Lake should, from the west banks of Karls Lake, proceed south to its outlet, where Leighton Lake's snag-littered shores are but a minute away. Rounding this lake's east end, we reach a meadowed gully that climbs east to a gap. A profusion of wildflowers enhances our descent north-of-east to a corn-lily meadow at the west end of Red Can Lake. This lake is mostly in granite, with frequent bluffs dropping to the deep water. Fine camps are found in a north-shore cluster of lodgepoles and on the sandy east shore. From perches in hemlock trees, chickadees, goldfinches and warblers provide tuneless ditties by which to gauge the silence, while the water's ferocious rainbow trout, to 12″ in length, provide other pleasures.

To reach Five-Acre Lake from Leighton Lake, parallel the latter's outlet to a high cliff. Here, at the bench's lip, the mountain aficionado bags a view of northern Yosemite's finest—Tower, Haystack, Wheeler and Nance peaks, plus Colby Mountain, far to the south near Hetch Hetchy, and bits of Yellowhammer Lake. At our feet is the mosquitoey-meadowed, lodgepole-shrouded expanse of Five-Acre Lake. Our route down to it, obviously blocked by precipices in our vicinity, lies to the east, where a shallow chute can be followed south. Continuing all the way down the chute would mean a fierce battle with thick shrubbery—one which the shorts-clad hiker would never win. So leave this draw for broken slopes that allow easier passage down to Five-Acre Lake. Surprisingly deep for their small size, the cobalt-blue waters of Five-Acre Lake support fair numbers of rainbow trout. Continue down the outlet stream to Camp Yellowhammer and further adventures on the Big Lake Lateral Trail (Route PC-11).

Lertora Lake

Ch. 8: Herring Creek

HC-1

Cooper Meadow Trail:
Coyote Meadows to Whitesides Meadow

Distances
3.6 miles to Cooper Meadow
6.5 miles to Whitesides Meadow—Burst Rock Trail

Introduction
This heavily used path is a quick, relatively effort-free way into the western Emigrant Basin. It traverses a variety of large meadows and gives some fine vistas. Additionally, you'll pass some cabins built by pioneers over 100 years ago, and get some close-ups of the diverse volcanic terrain that makes up the Emigrant Basin's north rim.

Trailhead
Turn east from Sonora Pass Highway 108 just 3.4 miles east of Summit Ranger Station (at the Pinecrest Y) onto paved Herring Creek Road 4N12. It winds uphill, passing some good *de facto* campgrounds at Fiddler's Green in 3.1 miles. After 4.4 miles pavement ends and the route becomes a well-graded dirt road, passing more undeveloped campsites before a junction with the loop part of 4N12, 6.8 miles from the highway. Turn right (east) here, 0.1 mile to often-crowded Herring Creek Campground. Beyond, the rougher road switchbacks up to dirt Road 5N31, which branches south to Pinecrest Peak (Route HC-3) and the Waterhouse Lake trailhead (Route HC-2). To reach the Cooper Meadow trailhead, continue east on 4N12 1.7 miles to Road 4N12B, which branches south 1.0 mile to Coyote Meadows roadend.

Description
A short spur road leads to the signed trailhead information center. A few feet east is a verdant but trampled corn-lily-and-willow meadow, where any of a number of bifurcating trails soon coalesce into a trail-jeeptrack which climbs steeply southeast, returning to very dusty trail under red-fir cover. Atop Cooper Peak's southwest ridge we find the Emigrant Wilderness boundary and a stock-drift fence. A short way beyond, Sanguinetti Spring, with its diverse floral accompaniment of aster, rein orchid, mimulus, ligusticum, cow parsnip, lupine, mule ears and others, emerges from the hillside a few feet above our gently descending path.

Our wide track leads out of dark red-fir groves onto a volcanic slope mantled with lupine, scattered lodgepoles, and the bizarre-looking stalks of green gentian. Above, parapets of welded volcanic clastic rocks draw our eyes skyward. Shrill whistles, warning calls of the yellow-bellied marmot, punctuate the silence as we tromp northeast along the north side of Horse and Cow Meadow. Sweeping perspectives are had from here, from the spirey Three Chimneys to the east, south to precipitous Burst Rock. Much of Horse and Cow Meadow is really dusty sagebrush flats, but a few pockets of true meadow are found before we leave its east end to plunge steeply down toward Cooper Meadow.

The frequently bifurcating trail, showing ample evidences of its use as a stock driveway, forces the conscientious hiker to make his own switchbacks, so as to do the least damage to the terrain—and to his knees. Most of the descent is under lodgepoles, but the remainder of the hillside, on up to cubic Castle Rock, is draped solely in a velveteen of sagebrush and mule ears. About 400 vertical feet below Horse and Cow Meadow, we intersect a side trail to the Sanguinettis' range cabins which is the start of a cross-country hike down South Fork Stanislaus River (Route PC-2).

Here we angle south of east for only a short distance along a fence line that bounds a horse pasture to the signed Eagle Pass Trail (Route EM-1). To continue to Whitesides Meadow, we turn south, following the barbed wire across sedge-and-penstemon-covered Cooper Meadow, noting eminently photographable scenes of quietly grazing stallions, or, over one's shoulder, of the ruddy, sky-scraping form of Three Chimneys. Leaving the meadow, an ascent on cobbly trail in a veritable forest of undergrowth brings us to a saddle, from which we can gaze at the emerald expanse of Cooper Meadow as we pause for breath.

Next is Hay Meadow, reached by a gentle descent past a 10 × 20-foot log barn, built early in the second half of the last century by the Cooper for whom Cooper Meadow and peak are named. At one time, he pastured milking cows in these lush meadows, hauling the dairy products all the way out to the lucrative Sonora boomtown market! The wet meadow now supports only a battalion of blackbirds, emitting their harsh clicks as they forage for insects among the lupine and senecio.

Switchbacks lead rockily south from Hay Meadow, ascending a bouldery ravine to another, smaller meadow, this one surrounded by lupine, sagebrush and scarlet gilia growing on dark granitic rock. We skirt this meadow to climb a gully. At 8900 feet we emerge on a promontory just below the level of the overlying volcanic rocks, where, amid a handful of pines, one can see down the wide trough of South Fork Stanislaus River almost to Pinecrest Lake.

Here the route turns southeast to contour over shrublands of sagebrush and lupine, just below some weirdly shaped pinnacles and bluffs of autobrecciated volcanic rock. Beyond a saddle the route gently descends through a grove of conifers to the slopes that border Whitesides Meadow. After crossing the wide incision cut in the soft alluvium of Whitesides Meadow by the infant Stanislaus River, we amble northeast across this anemic pasture, its lumpy texture caused by the excavations of pocket gophers. At the east end of the meadow, we meet the signed Burst Rock Trail (Route PC-3).

Whitesides Meadow

HC-2

Waterhouse Lake Trail

Distance
1.2 miles to Waterhouse Lake

Introduction
Waterhouse Lake, easily reached in an hour's time, can be an overnight's destination by itself, or can be used to start the best day hike in the Pinecrest quadrangle—an exciting hike down the South Fork canyon to Pinecrest Lake.

Trailhead
Follow directions for Coyote Meadows Roadend (Route HC-1) but, after the right turn on the 4N12 loop road (6.8 miles from Highway 108), follow Road 4N12 for only 2.6 more miles, to Road 5N31. Turn south on Road 5N31 for 0.7 mile, to a signed junction at a saddle. The road to the Waterhouse Lake Trail is the middle of three leaving south from this gap; the other two are signed as dead end logging roads. Park near this junction; the road toward Waterhouse Lake is now blocked and signed for foot traffic only.

Description
Beginning at the Waterhouse Lake roadend, at 8200 feet among large red firs and some lodgepoles, our path, initially the closed dirt road, descends south. Now trail tread commences, and we descend gently-to-moderately south to a senecio-speckled meadow. Circling the meadow, we step across a branch of the Stanislaus River, then wind easily along another grassy swale, this one more lush. Turning from this meadow's edge, we pass under a dark canopy of red fir to the rocky rim of the South Fork's canyon, where one has comprehensive views of the upper reaches of that forest-bottomed trough. Here our route begins a scrambling descent south in a ducked gully. Ducks lead southwest out of the gully to broken slabs where the route is marked, at least for those returning from Waterhouse Lake, by stripes of luminescent yellow paint. Some of this slope is steep, but we soon level out north of Waterhouse Lake's outlet creek, which flows amid meadowy patches of lodgepole pines. Waterhouse Lake, 7425 feet, sits on a bench well removed from the Stanislaus River's path. Its sandy south and west sides are flanked by lodgepole forests in which good camps are situated. Much litter mars the bed of 17-acre Waterhouse Lake, but it won't detract from anglers' luck, for the lake supports good-sized rainbow trout.

HC-3

Pinecrest Peak Trail: Pinecrest Peak to Pinecrest Lake via Catfish Lakes

Distances
3.3 miles to Catfish Lake
4.5 miles to Pinecrest Lakeshore Trail
5.7 miles to Pinecrest Lake marina

Introduction
Sampling varied terrain and vegetation, the Pinecrest Peak Trail is a good day hike for those who haven't time for longer trips or who have energetic children in tow. Downhill all the way, with lunch-stop possibilities at the unusual Catfish Lakes or at Herring Creek, this path is a pleasant introduction to the lower elevation habitats of the western Emigrant Wilderness.

Trailhead
Follow directions for Coyote Meadows Roadend (Route HC-1) but, after the right turn onto the 4N12 loop road (6.8 miles from Highway 108), follow Road 4N12 for only 2.6 more miles, to Road 5N31. Turn south on this road, 2.7 miles to its end at 8025 feet atop the west shoulder of Pinecrest Peak. Park off the road (a shuttle is required).

Description

From our parking place near the site of the Pinecrest Lookout, now nothing but a few broken concrete footings, we stroll down to that spot to take in sweeping vistas of the upper Stanislaus River drainage. Dodge Ridge Ski Area and a bit of Pinecrest Lake, our day's destination, are visible in the south, while distant Mokelumne, Dicks and Round Top peaks are seen on the northern horizon, above the Dardanelles. The Stanislaus River's deep cleft disappears in the smog-haze to the west.

Our little-used trail begins here, on the very lip of Pinecrest Peak, whose domed northwest rib provides up to 600 feet of rock climbing from easy scrambles to multiple 5.10 leads. From the lookout, our sandy path, indistinct at first but marked by ducks, contours gently down, south, through sparse mixed conifers. Juncos and raucous gray, black and white Clark nutcrackers, named for William Clark of the Lewis and Clark expedition, are the most oft-glimpsed avian species. Our route makes a couple of easy switchbacks down into a timber pocket, then levels off over a sandy nose, where the way is ducked and blazed south just under its east side. We lose almost 350 feet of altitude, then cross to the steeper west face of the ridge, viewing Pinecrest Lake, and drop down a hillside clothed in red fir and Jeffrey pine. At 7100 feet, within yards of each other, we pass the first specimens of black oak, white fir, and sugar pine, as well as further proof of our entrance into the Transition zone—bright blue Steller jays. Later, linked switchbacks lead down a steep spur choked with head-high manzanita, huckleberry oak and chinquapin. A shaded saddle ends the descent at 6710 feet.

Past the saddle's low point, we skirt a shallow, grassy, but nonetheless perennial pond which would furnish adequate camping. A good overlook of Cleo's Bath in the South Fork canyon can be had from this gap. After contouring through second-growth white-fir forest around the north slope of Peak 6880+, we veer south, noting some spotted coralroot, a saprophytic orchid

Pinecrest Lake from the Pinecrest Peak Trail

which is rare in this area. In a dense grove of white fir, we ignore an old path heading straight, and instead take two switchbacks down to leveler terrain where there's evidence of old logging operations. The trail then goes west gently down to an unsigned junction with the Herring Creek spur, which leads to luxurious campsites beside Herring Creek, where small trout are easily caught. This junction, marked by an 18-foot-high erratic boulder, stands in a beautiful grove of mature conifers only yards from the rush-shrouded east shore of North Catfish Lake. North Catfish Lake is a delight for the novice angler. Its shallow, grassy expanse, though choked with duckweed and other aquatic vegetation, is teeming with brown bullhead catfish. Though only 5–7″ long, these fish, easily caught with a hook and 4 feet of line,

can provide hours of excitement, especially for children. Catfish Lake, over a morainal hump to the southwest, is the same.

Turning south at the junction, our route winds around a muddy pond. After a steep drop in a dark gully, the trail descends broken bluffs overgrown with huckleberry oak and black oaks. Levelling off, we turn southwest to traverse viewfully above Pinecrest Lake's north shore on a rock-and-sand trail which undulates in open terrain smelling strongly of mountain misery, a pungent member of the rose family. Cobbly switchbacks soon lead down near the lake level, behind summer homes in a quiet forest. Passing between two of these houses—please respect this private property—we emerge beside Pinecrest Lake at the signed Pinecrest Lakeshore Loop Trail (Route PC-1).

Ch. 9: Eagle Meadow

EM-1

Eagle Pass Trail: Eagle Meadow to Cooper Meadow

Distances
3.7 miles to Eagle Pass
4.7 miles to Cooper Meadow—Horse and
    Cow Meadow Trail

Introduction
    Cutting straight across remnants of Miocene volcanic mudflow deposits called the Relief Peak Formation, the Eagle Pass Trail treats hikers to geological enlightenment as well as spectacular subalpine scenery and expansive panoramas. It is a less used and prettier path into Cooper Meadow than the Horse and Cow Meadow Trail.

Trailhead
    Turn east from Highway 108 14.0 miles from Summit Ranger Station in Pinecrest, onto paved Eagle Meadow Road 5N01. This point is 7.5 miles west of The Dardanelles Resort. The first 0.3 mile of 5N01 is paved, but it turns to well-graded dirt where Road 6N24 continues straight ahead to Niagara Creek Campground (9 units, with stream water only). Follow 5N01 2.8 miles from Highway 108 to ford Niagara Creek, where more camping is available at often-crowded Niagara ORV Campground (12 sites). Then, 4.1 miles distant, reach signed Eagle Meadow and Martin's Cow Camp at a shallow gravel ford of Eagle Creek. Just south of the road is an unimproved campground in a stand of lodgepoles, with ample parking.

Description
    Our trailhead is found on the west side of Eagle Creek in Eagle Meadow, just across

that stream from the hand-hewn buildings of Martin's Cow Camp. The path begins as a deep-sand jeep road south through the willows and clusters of lodgepoles in Eagle Meadow, which is fenced and gated. A pleasant traverse of the meadow brings one to the southern drift fence and then to Eagle Creek, which burbles over rounded volcanic cobbles. A jeepers' camp is found beside this stream, which we hop across, leaving behind the tracks of all but the most dextrous vehicles. Here we earnestly begin a 1470-foot ascent to Eagle Pass, tracing a route up a hillside sea of tall herbaceous vegetation. Lupine, meadow rue, aster, penstemon, paintbrush, phacelia, farewell-to-spring, Queen Anne's-lace, corn lily, cow parsnip, scarlet gilia, mule ears, columbine, stickseed, and a host of other annuals thickly shroud the sparsely forested slopes. Across the creek in the west rises the precipitous east buttress of Eagle Peak, a 9385-foot tower of welded volcanic mudflows and alluvium.

    Our undulating but generally climbing path sticks to the eastern hillside, winding past occasional large Sierra junipers into lodgepole forests, sometimes meadowed, and groves of aspen. At 7900 feet, just after an open, steep stretch, the pines give way to red fir, through which we walk on deep duff past a good camp, to a ford of Eagle Creek. Climbing steeply through a sloping meadow on Eagle Creek's southeast bank, we pass a signed but nonexistent trail to Bloomer Lake, then level off through open mixed conifers growing on dusty gray soil. After dipping to cross a small side creek, we begin a very steep section under red fir, mountain hemlock and western white pine. One might startle a great horned owl in this quiet, bare-floored forest, or maybe sight a circling red-tailed hawk hunting the open areas.

The rough switchbacks abate at 8700 feet, soon after which we circle above another willowy expanse, this one growing on volcanic hardpan which, when wet from spring freshets or melting snowbanks, makes treacherous footing. A final steep pitch around the head of this meadow brings us to signed Eagle Pass, situated amid craggy volcanic boulders, and decorated with blossoms of red-tubular scarlet gilia and astoundingly bright yellow daisies. Vistas to the north are extensive. Looking past the ruddy

knob of Eagle Peak, almost the whole Carson-Iceberg Wilderness can be seen, and the high peaks of Desolation Wilderness, near Lake Tahoe, stand on the horizon.

Leaving this broad saddle, our route descends a cobbly slope clothed in sagebrush and mule ears down to a trickling rivulet in scattered pines. The rough trail continues south, soon presenting a view of Cooper Meadow below, and parallels and then crosses this stream, whose gorge is choked with an almost infinite variety of wildflowers in season. The rest of the hillside is a white velvet drapery of sagebrush, sprinkled with yellow mule ears and delicate clusters of mariposa lilies. Ending the 600-foot descent from Eagle Pass, we soon level out and find the signed Cooper Meadow Trail (Route HC-1) at the north side of verdant Cooper Meadow.

Castle Rock, Eagle Pass, Three Chimneys from the south

EM-2

Eagle Meadow Trail: Eagle Meadow to Dardanelle via Lower Eagle Creek

Distances

1.2 miles to Lower Eagle Meadow
4.2 miles to Bone Springs Trailhead

Introduction

The old Eagle Meadow Trail between Eagle Meadow and the small summer-home community at Dardanelle has fallen into relative disuse since the grading of Eagle Meadow Road has allowed passenger-car access to Eagle Meadow and beyond. This disuse, plus the ease of reaching each end of the path and the fact that the route lies outside of legislated wilderness, opens a wide range of recreational opportunities for the Eagle Meadow Trail. It is the only route in this book that is designated an Off-Highway Vehicle Route—though it is a very rare motorcyclist indeed who could muscle his dirt bike over the steepest, bouldery segments. As an OHV route, however, it is open to mountain bikers—possibly the finest use of the not-especially-scenic pathway. (See Chapter 18, "Mountain Biking".) For pedestrians the Eagle Meadow Trail offers solitude and the chance to enjoy unspoiled if unspectacular middle-mountain forest. Additionally, it has one of the longest seasons of any route in this guide, often being passable from mid-April to early December.

Trailhead

Since parts of the trail are quite steep, the downhill route, north from Eagle Meadow to Dardanelle, is the only one I recommend. Leave your shuttle auto at the trail's north end near Dardanelle. To get there, drive 21.5 miles east from the Pinecrest Y on Highway 108 to The Dardanelles Resort, which has a small store, a gas station, a lodge, a trailer park, and a post office, just across the highway from 28-unit Dardanelle Campground. Continue east on Highway 108 0.1 mile to cross Eagle Creek Bridge, then just 0.1 mile more to the first

right, an unsigned, narrow dirt road branching southeast from the highway shoulder into a stand of pines. Follow this through the Bone Springs Summer Home Tract, ignoring one right-branching road. At the second junction, find the signed Eagle Meadow Trail parking area. To reach the actual trailhead, walk south up a dirt road spur, signed DEAD END ROAD, to find the due-south-climbing trail just above a cluster of cabins.

To reach the beginning of the trail, now drive back west 7.5 miles on Highway 108 to Eagle Meadow Road 5N01. Take it, as described for the Route EM-1 trailhead, 6.9 miles to Eagle Meadow.

Description

The Eagle Meadow Trail starts at Martin's Cow Camp—named for a 1950's cattleman, the camp consists of a corral, a wonderfully constructed log barn and a small cabin on the dry bench just east of Eagle Creek. Walk left, north, between these buildings on a rapidly narrowing jeep road past a ladderlike black metal snow-survey marker—it is used to help predict yearly water runoff in the Stanislaus basin. A few yards later, the road becomes an obvious footpath, winding close beside Eagle Creek in an open grove of lodgepoles. With further descent, though, the path angles away from the stream and drops moderately into denser forest to find a 20-foot-wide rock-hop ford of quietly flowing Long Valley Creek. Now in a sunny stand of lodgepoles and aspens, we turn northwest and walk gently down along the creekside to a wider, cobbly crossing of Eagle Creek, just below its confluence with Long Valley Creek. Just a few minutes later we step into pleasant Lower Eagle Meadow, then wind through head-high willows to reford meandering Eagle Creek.

Now your path leaves the streamside for good. Wind sandily north to gain a broad granitic knob with a fine collection of mature Jeffrey pines. Trail tread from this point becomes substantially rougher and generally steeper. Descend in a joint-controlled ravine, with trailside mat manzanita and huckleberry oak. Rough switchbacks lead to a seasonal stream bed, easily stepped across. The remainder of our descent to Dardanelle is accomplished on the ensuing steep, boulder-strewn, morainal hillside. After we contour across it for just a bit, our trail plunges quite directly down it, over boulders and logs, shaded by open groves of white fir

and Jeffrey pine. A few anemic switchbacks fail to moderate the steep descent, and, almost before we know it, we abruptly level out, 1200 feet lower, in cool forest on the outflow plain where Eagle Creek debouches into Middle Fork Stanislaus River canyon. Here we turn a bit more east, glimpse cabins of the Bone Springs Tract, and meet the trailhead on a dirt spur road, just uphill from a group of summer homes. Now walk right, northeast, down a few hundred yards to the signed Eagle Meadow Trail parking area and your waiting car.

EM-3

Long Valley Creek: Cross Country to Lower Relief Valley

Distances
0.8 mile to pass north of East Flange Rock
1.8 miles to Upper Relief Valley Trail

Introduction
This cross-country route up Long Valley to Lower Relief Valley is a good short-cut for those who want to get into the Relief Valley region in a hurry. The 1000-foot climb over the north shoulder of East Flange Rock is fully 600 feet less than the longer climb out of Kennedy Meadows, and the vistas are spectacular.

Trailhead
Follow Road 5N01 as described for the Route EM-1 trailhead, but continue past it 1.3 miles to a ford of Long Valley Creek. At an undeveloped campsite at this ford, turn right (southeast) on Road 5N01A, following it to near the limits of your vehicle's capability, probably near 7900 feet.

Description
From our parked car, we follow the very rough dirt road as it parallels Long Valley Creek southeast over volcanic terrain hallmarked by cobbles, sagebrush and mule ears. To the south, an unusual perspective of the Three Chimneys presents itself. Those who have a powerful, high-clearance vehicle will save a walk on this road, which ends at 8160 feet, at a crossing of Long Valley Creek near

a poor campsite. Just before this ford the road passes through a willow thicket, and from it another, poorer track heads east, climbing to 8240 feet and another camp, before it terminates. From this highest road-end, we begin an ascent southeast to the ridge separating the Eagle and Summit Creek waters. Cottonwoods and aspens grow in the narrow, loosely cobbled ravine that we start in, supplemented by mule ears, lupine, lovage, pennyroyal and scarlet gilia. Clambering up the dusty slopes, which force many rest stops from which we can see a "window" in the face of the most northern of the Three Chimneys, we cross gullies, large and small, headed for the 8900-foot col just north of Peak 9200+. Much of the hillside is covered with mat manzanita or dwarf lupine, but near the top most of the vegetation disappears on friable slopes which range in composition from fine-grained, platy gray rock (a welded tuff), to many-hued andesitic cobbles. All these rocks are grouped into the Relief Peak Formation, the oldest of many layers of volcanic debris that once spewed over the northern Sierra. At the ridgetop, we catch our breath and enjoy the views east and south: Lower Relief Valley is the patch of green at our feet, while the eastern horizon is dominated by the long sweep of Relief Peak.

Tower Peak stands in the distant east. To the southeast lies aptly named Granite Dome, while at the right edge of our vision the sheer precipice of East Flange Rock drops for 600 vertical feet.

To reach Lower Relief Valley, we have only to scramble down the hard-pan slopes to our east. Leveling out at the dung-littered grassland there, we cut south behind a sprawling dome to hit the Relief Valley Trail (Route KM-6) near an incongruously signed junction with the nonexistent Silver Mine Creek "Trail" (Route EM-4).

Granite Dome from Lower Relief Valley

EM-4

Silver Mine Creek Roadend: Cross Country to Lower Relief Valley

Distances
1.1 miles to Silver Mine Creek Ford
2.9 miles to Relief Valley Overlook
3.8 miles to Upper Relief Valley Trail

Introduction
The fastest route of all into the Relief Valley area, this hike along the Silver Mine Creek Road involves only one mile of cross-country walking—all downhill.

Trailhead
As described in the Route EM-1 trailhead, follow Road 5N01, but continue past Eagle Meadow and the Haypress Meadows Road (private) to an unsigned junction with Road 5N01D (8.4 miles). Road 5N01 here turns southeast down the slope to some private summer homes, while we take 5N01D, which continues south-southeast. Beware that after this junction, the road deteriorates rapidly and, after fording Silver Mine Creek, is passable only to 4-wheel-drive vehicles. It is recommended that one park at the 5N01/5N01D junction.

Description
From the 5N01/5N01D road junction, we climb gently to moderately along little-used and dusty Road 5N01D. About a mile along, we dip to ford Silver Mine Creek—which really once was the site of a silver mine—at 7440 feet. Now, as we swing southwest, switchbacking up quite steeply, we see, under a dense canopy of white pine, red fir and hemlock, evidences of exploration for the latest earth-treasure: uranium. Diggings and claim-marking posts scattered through-

out this forest—and all the country
hereabouts between Highway 108 and Emigrant Wilderness—are for autunite, a yellow-
green uranium-bearing mineral found in
pegmatite dikes. At 8700 feet our road
gentles to swing east around a nose, then
leaves shady fir groves behind for more open
sagebrush. Presently we drop down to a
roadside campsite near a small spring that
emanates from a pocket meadow that is
wedged between the volcanic hillside to our
west and 8760-foot granitic knob to its east.
Our road turns east to ascend this knob for its
superb views of the eastern landscape. Relief
Peak, a huge red ridge to the east, dominates
the scene, while Leavitt and Night Cap
peaks, farther north, backdrop Relief Reservoir, which is impounded between chaparral-
cloaked hillsides. Turning our gaze south, we
see massive Granite Dome and East Flange
Rock, a route-marker for early pioneers.
Leaving this sunny spot, a final jeep track
drops southeast on the ridge's nose, then becomes a steep use-path that fades out as we
clamber down. Here we cut either east or
south, depending on which direction we wish
to take upon leaving the valley, to strike the
Relief Valley Trail (Route KM-6).

**East Flange Rock
seen from lower Relief Valley**

Ch. 10: Kennedy Meadows

KM-1

Huckleberry Trail: Kennedy Meadows to Relief Reservoir, Lunch Meadow, Emigrant Lake and Huckleberry Lake via Mosquito Pass

Distances

2.4 miles to Relief Station—Kennedy Canyon Trail
5.1 miles to Upper Relief Valley Trail
8.5 miles to Sheep Camp
11.8 miles to Emigrant Lake Trail
14.1 miles to Maxwell Lake Trail
14.9 miles to Horse Meadow
17.9 miles to Huckleberry Lake

Introduction

The Huckleberry Trail is the time-honored main thoroughfare into the central Emigrant Wilderness, and the route that most equestrian parties use to reach the backcountry. From Kennedy Meadows pack station to Relief Reservoir, the path follows a wide, historic donkey engine skid-path which was built among the turn of the century during the construction of that reservoir. Beyond the reservoir, the trail stays near Summit Creek, and is marked by reminders of the hardy pioneers who travelled this route in the 1850's. Beyond Mosquito Pass, the trail reaches Emigrant Lake and then Huckleberry Lake—the two largest in the entire Wilderness.

Trailhead

Drive 25.7 miles past Pinecrest on Highway 108 to Kennedy Meadows Road. Public trailhead parking is found on Kennedy Meadows Road a short distance before its end (which has private parking only) at Kennedy Meadows Resort. This rustic, hospitable enclave, privately owned since the Kennedy brothers of Knights Ferry patented it in 1886, boasts rental cabins, a restaurant, a bar, a store and gift shop, a gas station and a fine pack station which offers day rides, fishing guides and full services for extended backcountry horse packing or base camps.

Description

The signed Huckleberry Trail begins beyond the pack station's corrals, where a cool green sweep of Middle Fork Stanislaus River bends near a large gate across a jeep road. This is our route. Follow it moderately uphill in mixed-conifer forest for a few hundred yards to a small saddle, where the signed Night Cap Trail (Route KM-10) branches up to the left, east. Keeping to the sandy road, we descend slightly to the sunny northern fringe of pretty Kennedy Meadow. The Middle Fork Stanislaus River chortles past gravel bars and beaver-gnawed cottonwoods here, and affords some angling for rainbow trout. Granite bluffs up-canyon make this area quite photogenic—indeed, a mock-log cabin once stood here, a prop for the Hollywood film "Mail Order Bride". Continue south around the meadow, then up into open Jeffrey-pine shade where we enter Emigrant Wilderness. Presently, the Stanislaus' burbling becomes a roar, and we find an 80-foot-long steel-and-wood bridge across its small gorge. Just beyond it, two trails, the first signed, constitute an alternate route to Relief Station that was in use for some years after a bridge washout in the heavy winter of 1969.

We keep to the widest trail—previously a steam-donkey skid-path—close along the cascading river's south bank. Soon, where our way has been massively dynamited out of the small cliffs above, we see enormous iron eyelets and spikes set into the granite, cemented in place by molten sulfur. These were used to attach cables, so that donkey engines could drag themselves uphill to the Relief damsite. A few minutes later we come to a sweeping 150′ iron bridge spanning a spectacular gorge just above the confluence of Kennedy Creek's waterfalls and green-pooling Summit Creek. Across the bridge, tiny switchbacks lead moderately up over sunny granite benches, and we find a rusting steam-donkey. Now broken in two, the cylindrical boiler used to sit atop the two reciprocating pistons, clutch, brake and cable-spool assemblies. These, in turn, sat on wooden skids. Powerful cold steam engines such as these were widely used in the early days of Sierran construction and lumbering. Attached by cables to a succession of trees or rocks, they could pull themselves up to worksites, where they were then firmly anchored and used to haul logs or construction materials. At Relief Dam, donkey engines powered an overhead-bucket line that carried rock for the dam.

After taking a few minutes to ponder this example of Yankee ingenuity, resume your own "steam donkey" mode and pull yourself onward. After passing an unsigned trail to a horse ford on the old alternate trail, come to PG&E's 3-story green woodframe Relief Station. It serves seasonally as a maintenance facility for the reservoir.

At Relief Station we find the left-branching Kennedy Lake Trail (Route KM-9). Just uphill from the building a few yards are two junctions with an older route back down to Kennedy Meadows. For variety,

why not follow it on the return trip: A few rocky switchbacks lead down to a large white-water cauldron on Summit Creek. A narrow, swaying, 45-foot-long log bridge here carries us nervously to the west bank, where we pant up sandy switchbacks to a gap between two domes. Now the way descends northwest in the huckleberry-oak-choked cleft. We momentarily touch a small creek, then swing north via rocky switchbacks to drop beneath a high cliff. Later we actually ascend for just a moment to strike the main Huckleberry Trail, next to the first bridge across the Stanislaus River.

Bound for Mosquito Pass, our trail climbs moderately south from Relief Station, soon gaining a granite nose where we find a donkey engine and an old trail west to a powder house and two rusted winches at an overlook of Relief Dam. Here, too, the unmarked Grouse Creek Trail (Route KM-8) meets our route. Now we get our first up-can-yon views, to Granite Dome and East Flange Rock. Heading in that direction, the path ascends a rocky hillside then traverses above the reservoir to a cool aspen grove at a cobble-and-log ford of Grouse Creek. A few big campsites are found here—usually quite crowded on weekends.

Next on the agenda is an up-and-down leg to reach a small, permanent creeklet at the signed Relief Valley Trail (Route KM-6). Tank up on water here. Above, tight, rocky, volcanic switchbacks lead 400 feet up, onto a dry hillside cloaked in huckleberry oak-manzanita chaparral. Eventually you drop slightly past large junipers to small, spring-fed Saucer Meadow, overgrown with corn-lilies and willows. Still climbing, pass under the sheer gray cliffs of a volcanic outlier of Relief Peak and come to a large camp complex in a shady red-fir grove, marking the start of Route KM-7, up to Lewis Lakes. For the next mile, we keep within earshot of Summit Creek in dense forest punctuated by zones of avalanche blowdown from the multihued battlements of Relief Peak, above. Later, the path drifts away from creekside, to begin dynamited switchbacks through huge talus blocks. Easier climbing now leads to a forested gap through which we drop to a sandy flat signed, SHEEP CAMP. A large camp complex here also marks the start of a scramble to <u>Blackhawk Lake</u> (Route KM-7).

Changing character, the Huckleberry Trail now undulates east on a gentle ascent. Alternately, we pass open volcanic meadows sprinkled with sagebrush, snowbush, paintbrush, pussy paws, buckwheat and green gentian, and lodgepole stands, each with a good campsite. Above 8880 feet, we swing out onto the lower end of Lunch Meadow, which has the same dry character as those meadowy pockets downstream. One mile after entering Lunch Meadow, we reach a signed junction with the east-ascending Brown Bear Pass Trail (Route KM-2). Here the Huckleberry Trail veers from the Emigrant Pass wagon route, (which crossed Brown Bear Pass), and, hopping 10 feet of cobbles, turns south across Summit Creek.

The next leg of our journey, over Mosquito Pass to Emigrant Lake, is on new trail constructed in summer 1986. Its route is intended to keep traffic off of fragile subalpine meadows around Mosquito Pass. Our brief climb via rocky, dusty switchbacks soon leaves hemlock and pine cover behind, as we traverse upward through pocket meadows, then skirt a small stream and a swampy pond. The nicely engineered trail then veers southeast, steeply up tiers of sloping granite slabs. Presently, the grade levels off atop 9410-foot Mosquito Pass—a rolling grassland dotted with knee-high lupine, senecio, pussy paws and paintbrush. Beyond, we descend gently into open pine-and-hemlock groves to cross Mosquito Lake's outlet creek.

From here, a short detour up to 14-acre Mosquito Lake is well worth the effort. Leave the Huckleberry Trail and climb steeply, paralleling Mosquito Lake's small outlet creek. A few minutes' exertion brings you to a lush, knee-high field of lupine, willow and sedges. This in turn yields to open fell fields surrounding delightful Mosquito

Beside the trail near Lunch Meadow

Lake. Its shallow, warm, west end has a clean, sandy beach, offering an invigorating swim. At 24 feet deep, it supports a fair colony of rainbow trout, up to 14 inches. Camping is found in clustered pines near the west shore. A small dome above the camps would offer some clean climbing routes. As an alternative to retracing your steps, you could easily continue north of the lake, then east over a 9800-foot granitoid saddle, and down easy slabs to intersect the Brown Bear Pass Trail (Route KM-2) at the east foot of Brown Bear Pass.

After returning to the Huckleberry Trail, further descent leads across the main stream via an 8-foot horse ford. Now in heavier lodgepole forest, descend moderately, soon finding the meadowed valley floor at the head of Emigrant Lake. Here, too, is the Buck Lakes Trail (Route PC-4) which can be followed a few yards west to fine campsites near Emigrant Lake. Bound for Maxwell and

Huckleberry lakes, our path continues a few yards south to a 12–15-foot-wide sandy horse ford of meandering North Fork Cherry Creek. To avoid removing boots, hikers should instead walk east 0.1 mile up a streamside use-trail; cross via rocks near a small cascade. Once on the south bank, well-graded trail quickly leaves the meadow for an easy, switchbacking climb eastward. In a very few minutes, we descend slightly in a joint-controlled slot to find the northwest shore of two tiny Blackbird Lakes and the signless, left-branching Middle Emigrant Lake Trail (Route PC-4).

As the third part of an overhaul of the Huckleberry Trail, the segment between Emigrant Lake and Huckleberry Lake was reconstructed in summer '88, at a cost of $158,000. From the Middle Emigrant Lake Trail junction, walk easily south on refurbished tread, passing picturesque Blackbird Lakes—really just shallow tarns—in dry

At Maxwell Lake

meadow of short-hair sedge, rice grass and Brewers ryegrass. Patches of dwarf bilberry here turn brilliant red in the autumn. We soon pass an obscure junction with a faint use-trail to W Lake, (see Route KM-5), then cross a low divide, with a glimpse of (from this side) unprepossessing Sachse Monument. Now we descend in a sweeping zigzag over broken slabs with open shade. Near the bottom of the hill, we hop across a seasonal creek and drop just a moment more to the signed Maxwell Lake Trail, beside a large, pretty tarn. This side trail leads right, southwest, to a packer camp, then peters out as it leads along a narrow canal connecting the tarn with Maxwell Lake. However, even horses can make their way to this larger, 46-acre lake. It has numerous bays and islands and offers secluded camping and a large population of eastern brook trout. One may easily continue down to another fine lake below, or make the easy, recommended walk up slabs and broken rock to the viewful summit of Sachse Monument. Charlie Sachse was a local cattleman who pioneered many of the Emigrant Basin's trails.

Back on the Huckleberry Trail, climb briefly on a tortuous course, controlled by dominant master joints in the granite, up to the north shoulder of Sachse Monument. Beyond, drop quickly on rocky, badly eroded tread. Soon, the broad, green sweep of Horse Meadow is apparent below. After a bit the trail moderates, traversing southeast past two horse-traffic shortcuts down to Horse Meadow. We don't have to contribute to further hillside erosion, however—our signed intersection with Horse Meadow Road (Route SP-2) is just a minute farther, atop a low rise at the south end of Horse Meadow. Here we join the road and follow it, rockily down at a moderate-to-steep incline, close alongside cascading Cherry Creek. A huge yellow engine-now-gone-to-rust is passed, reminding us of the eventual fate of this primitive mining road. A minute later, the descent abates at a signed branching of the Twin Lakes Trail (Route KM-4). A short distance later the road makes a broad, shallow ford of Cherry Creek, and almost immediately

comes to a road junction. From here the left branch climbs just a bit, then descends in forest, eventually ending at the fascinating Cherry Creek Mine. Bound instead for Huckleberry Lake, our way takes the right road branch, which heads downhill for just a few yards before becoming trail. It winds down in slightly damp, meadowy lodgepole forest under the spectacular visage of Sachse Monument. This dark granite cliff is criss-crossed by white dikes, black water streaks and orange rust stains, and has some impressive climbing routes. In a short while, the forest cover opens and we find the previously mentioned abandoned mining road only 30 feet south of our trail. Stash your backpacks here, and follow the road up the fragrantly sagebrush-dotted southern hillside to the south to the Cherry Creek Mine—an abandoned tungsten claim. Ruins of the ore-crushing mill—built in 1967—and a side-dumping ore cart are still identifiable. The mouth of the main tunnel is accessible atop a heap of rubble—look around it for brown and green crystals of tungsten minerals.

Returning to the Huckleberry Trail from the Cherry Creek Mine, walk gently down canyon, always within earshot of Cherry Creek, to enter cool forest, primarily lodgepole, but with some red fir, hemlock and western white pine. All the while, we get tantalizing glimpses of many excellent climbs that are possible on bluffs on the skirt of Sachse Monument. We pass through a stock-drift fence, and later—now almost on level, wide bottom land—we wade to the north bank of Cherry Creek via two 10–12-foot-wide, shallow fords. A planned trail re-routing will keep our trail on the south bank, avoiding these crossings. Pass through small meadows to hop across Maxwell Lake's outlet stream, then come into a large complex of horse-packer campsites near the northeast end of Huckleberry Lake. Here the Huckleberry Trial ends at a junction with the south-branching Kibbie Ridge Trail (Route CL-1) which passes south of 2-mile-long Huckleberry Lake, and the Bell Meadow Trail (Route PC-10) which skirts north of Huckleberry Lake, bound for Lertora Lake.

KM-2

Brown Bear Pass Trail: Bond Pass via Emigrant Meadow Lake and Summit Meadow

Distances

1.3 miles to Brown Bear Pass
2.9 miles to Emigrant Meadow Lake
4.4 miles to Horse Meadow Road
5.8 miles to Summit Meadow
6.6 miles to Bond Pass
7.3 miles to Pacific Crest Trail in Jack Main
     Canyon

Introduction

This fine stretch of near-timberline trail is the key link between Emigrant Wilderness and the Pacific Crest Trail in Yosemite's North Country.

Trailhead

Same as the Route KM-1 trailhead.

Description

Ascend the Huckleberry Trail (Route KM-1) 11.8 miles from Kennedy Meadows to Lunch Meadow, where that trail turns south across Summit Creek at a signed junction with the Brown Bear Pass Trail. Now

continue up-canyon, keeping to its north, volcanic side, climbing at a gentle-to-moderate pitch. Soon we leave behind all timber but a smattering of scattered lodgepole and whitebark pines, and tread pockets of short-hair sedge meadow. Brown Bear Pass is the obvious low point ahead on the division between brown volcanic rocks north of Summit Creek and cream-colored quartz monzonite, to its south. A final, very steep but well-engineered grind leads to the top—9765 feet—and a startling emerald vista over Emigrant Meadow's rolling alpine grassland. At our feet, Emigrant Meadow Lake looks as inviting as it must have to California-bound pioneers who toiled past here, with their wagons and oxen, in the 1840's. Beyond, dark Grizzly Peak and the bright spires of Tower Peak stand above the scene. Drink your fill of the view, then reshoulder your pack and descend east over slopes of tan and purple andesite to the grassy flats below. At

Looking east from Brown Bear Pass

the bottom, step across a small branch of Cherry Creek. From here one could scramble southwest, up a series of white granite slabs to a saddle. As described in Route KM-1, lovely, subalpine Mosquito Lake is just a few minutes beyond it. Even more remote and less-fished Lost Lake lies upstream to the north from the foot of Brown Bear Pass. It is a trivial matter to get there—a gentle 1½-mile ascent through delightful meadows brings one to its grassy shore at a spectacular overlook at the head of Kennedy Canyon. Although treeless and often windy, and set in an austere bowl rimmed by red peaks, Lost Lake is worth the trip, partly because it has a good population of eastern brook trout.

After you've tried your luck at Mosquito Lake or Lost Lake, return to the Brown Bear Pass Trail and walk southeast across often-muddy Emigrant Meadow. Swing close to some tarns at the tip of Emigrant Meadow Lake, then make a long leap of its inlet stream, which drains High Emigrant Lake. A short distance beyond, pass a few poor, exposed campsites (much better ones are to the north, against the hillside) and find a post marking the south-branching Middle Emigrant Lake Trail, Route PC-4. You can take it about ⅓ mile south to fair camps near Emigrant Meadow Lake's south shore. Emigrant Meadow Lake is a good choice for backcountry fly fishermen, since it has a large population of 10–12″ rainbow trout and no surrounding trees.

Bound for Bond Pass, our pathway ascends east from the obscure Middle Emigrant Lake Trail, winding through a meadow-ring of low willow thickets to ascend a morainal hillside. At least two varieties each of lupine and paintbrush, as well as ranger-buttons, senecio and some less common western blue flax lend color to the moderate undertaking. Beyond the ridgetop we angle down across a small granite-locked basin holding small, shallow West Grizzly Peak Lake, which has rainbow trout. We come closer to the north shore of similarly meadow-fringed East Grizzly Peak Lake, which is larger (12 acres) and similarly stocked with rainbows. Step across a

swampy creeklet east of this pleasant tarn and find the obvious but usually unsigned Grizzly Meadow Cutoff Trail, down into East Fork Cherry Creek Canyon. Moments later we reach wide dirt Horse Meadow Road, Route SP-2.

Here, beside the western skirt of layer-cake Grizzly Peak, the Yosemite-bound traveler is presented with two options, each route eventually crossing into Yosemite Park via Bond Pass. The Bond Pass High Trail, certainly the more scenic route, will be described below. Most hikers, however, will choose the lower Summit Meadow route, initially following Horse Meadow Road, Route SP-2. On it, we descend steadily southeast, first gaining and then losing panoramas over lakes of the East Fork Cherry Creek basin. Beyond a small tributary of that drainage, the road turns abruptly southwest, directly downhill. Here we leave Horse Meadow Road and drop southeast out of a screen of conifers to enter large, hummocky Summit Meadow. At mid-meadow, near a black metal ladderlike aerial snow-survey marker, the Snow Lake Road (Route KM-3) branches obviously south across the lazy stream.

Here our final 300-foot climb to Bond Pass (named for a Yosemite Park boundary commissioner) begins. The narrowing, cobbly roadway parallels the creeklet up a willowy, bouldery hillside, switchbacks twice, and then arches across the cirque headwall onto rolling, dry, rocky fells. 9730-foot Bond Pass is attained, with the usual fanfare of trail signs and restriction signs that attends entry into Yosemite National Park. Views from the pass are actually meager. I recommend a side trip from Bond Pass for peak-baggers, geologists, and panorama-lovers: the summit of Quartzite Peak, which caps the ridge south of Bond Pass. A continuation of the Bond Pass mining road winds south up this ridge to reach a number of eagerly dug but universally disappointing prospect pits made by tungsten miners in the 1940s and '50s. They now pockmark an invigorating windswept alpine hillside like the workings of giant ground squirrels. After a climb of some

Closed mining road near Bond Pass

400 feet, the jeep track splits, the right branch climbing onto the mountain's north slope to a large digging and a good overlook of Snow Lake. The left, south branch ascends almost to the viewful apex of 10,420-foot Quartzite Peak, which was named by miners for the white-creamy quartzite (a metamorphic rock, made of heat-congealed beach sand) that caps its summit. Panoramas are extensive.

A brief descent into Yosemite from atop Bond Pass finds the terminus of the Bond Pass High Trail, now to be described, starting from the Emigrant Pass environs. The poorly signed but well-trod foot path angles gently up and away from the descending

Horse Meadow Road. A high-desert assemblage of sagebrush and rabbitbrush clothes this sandy hillside, which is dotted with red and purple boulders of volcanic breccia that have tumbled from the ramparts of Grizzly Peak above. Trail tread alternates between light, fine-grained volcanic earth and deep granitic sand, formed during an ancient age of wet rain forests that prevailed at the same time that this ancient gigantic upland was being covered by volcanic eruptions. Beyond, the trail steepens momentarily to gain a small ridge where long, down-canyon looks at Maxwell Lake and Huckleberry Lake can be had. Now on more-friable metasediments, the path makes a descending traverse toward the Yosemite boundary. Here we gear down for rough switchbacks to drop not, as one might expect, to the summit of Bond Pass, which we can see below, but a bit to the pass' east, where, at an unmarked junction, we merge with the much more heavily used Bond Pass-Summit Meadow Trail.

From the convergence of the two Bond Pass routes, our trail swings east in open lodgepole forest. A very short walk leads down to a well-signed, triangular junction with the southbound Pacific Crest Trail (Route YP-2) bound for Grace Meadow. The PCT also continues northeast from here, as Route SP-1, toward Sonora Pass. Ten minutes' level walk along this meadowy path will bring one to beautiful Dorothy Lake, home to some of the nicest camps and largest rainbow trout for miles around.

KM-3

Summit Meadow to Snow Lake, Bigelow Lake, Black Bear Lake and Upper Twin Lake

Distances
0.6 mile to Snow Lake
2.5 miles to Bigelow Lake
3.9 miles to Black Bear Lake
5.4 miles to Upper Twin Lake

Introduction

Running parallel to the Yosemite Park boundary, this short trail is jam-packed with lakes, scenery and fascinating mining ruins. Once, this part of Emigrant Wilderness was excluded from federal wilderness protection, due to the presence of tungsten mines. Now more-or-less abandoned, these diggings serve to highlight the tremendous geologic diversity of the Bigelow Peak region.

Trailhead

Same as the Route KM-1 or SP-2 trailhead.

Description

Either of two northeastern arterials into the Emigrant Basin—the Huckleberry-Brown Bear Pass Trail (Routes KM-1 and KM-2), or the Horse Meadow Road (Route SP-2) can be used to reach Summit Meadow, occupying a small cirque at the head of East Fork Cherry Creek Canyon.

Virtually in the middle of Summit Meadow, the signed Snow Lake-Twin Lakes Trail branches south from the dirt road bound for Bond Pass (Route KM-2). Itself a jeep road, bound for the Montezuma Mine above the east end of Snow Lake, our route is easily seen as it quickly fords the lazy stream draining Summit Meadow, then bends westward to gently climb the low hill separating Summit Meadow from Snow Lake. Just beyond the top of the rise, another road, now fallen into disuse, branches left, southeast, quickly reaching the ruins of the Montezuma Tungsten Mine. Both adits (horizontal tunnels) have been dynamited closed, and nothing remains of the nearby cabins except their stone foundations. In the heyday of these claims in the 1950's, the tunnels totalled 215 feet in length, but only a few tons of tungsten ore were recovered.

Backtracking to the main road, an easy descent leads to a dry, rocky meadow on the north shore of lovely Snow Lake. Two vandalized cabins here were bunkhouse and storage shed for workers at the Montezuma Mine. Here our jeep road ends, and a good foot trail leads west along Snow Lake's breezy north shore. Numerous large campsites are passed, each in a small stand of pine and hemlock. Vertical white metamorphic bands on the cliffs of aptly named Quartzite Peak, and the sharp spire of a dark, unnamed peaklet to the west, make a stunning backdrop for the 40-acre lake, which also offers the invitation of fair angling for large rainbow trout. Near the west shore, the trail drops to rock-hop across the two outlet streams under sections of 10-foot-high stream-flow-maintenance dams. Turning south along the west side of Snow Lake, the path now becomes hard to follow—it frequently bifurcates to pass through and around low thickets of willows, then begins to climb, first gently and then very steeply, up the hillside southwest of Snow Lake. If you lose the path, head for the dark, rocky gap between Quartzite Peak and the aforementioned peaklet. Our poor trail gains this gap via a final narrow, bouldery gully, rewarded by a delightful overshoulder panorama of Snow Lake, Summit Meadow, Grizzly Peak and Big Sam.

From atop the pass, our indistinct but well-ducked trail makes tiny zigzags up to the east before dropping south into a rugged cirque, which is lined by black metamorphic mudstones near its head. Soon the route finds a comfortable, traversing descent. Rocks hereabouts run a gamut of metamorphic and granitic types, including glaring white quartzites and lizard-skin-rough tan marble. Passing under the cliffy shoulder of Quartzite Peak, the trail switches back up to the south, soon gaining a dry flat on the north shore of large, windswept Bigelow Lake. Our trail's intersection with the much more obvious lakeshore trail is inobvious—northbound hikers should watch out for the north-branching ducked trail just a few yards before a large campsite, after gaining Bigelow Lake's north shore. Bigelow Lake has only a poor fishery of small rainbows. Some controversy surrounds the origin of the lake's name: Packers claim it commemorates "Big Low", a corpulent Sonora prostitute who skinny-dipped here with cowboys. Scholars have opined that the nearby peak was named to honor Major John Bigelow, Jr., the caval-

ryman who was Yosemite Park superintendent in 1904. It is reasonably certain, in
either event, that he was unacquainted with
the young lady from Sonora!

Resuming our walk to Black Bear Lake,
we now follow the lakeshore path west,
dipping under a series of small rock-and-
concrete stream-flow-maintenance dams that
block Bigelow Lake's multiple outlets. West
of the lake, the trail heads west, down a joint-
controlled meadowy ravine. It is only a few
minutes' work to descend, first gently and
then steeply on cobbly tread, to a pocket
meadow of willows and vernacular sedge on
the north side of Black Bear Lake. Here a
use-trail branches south to a campsite com-
manding a good overlook of the eastern
shore. Just a moment beyond, the signed
Black Bear Lake Cutoff Trail (described at
the end of this route), continues straight
ahead, while our route, aiming for Upper
Twin Lake, branches indistinctly left, south.
After climbing a few feet, the path drops
moderately in dry, open forest to a fringe of
red heather along Black Bear Lake's northwest edge. A black-and-white outlier of
Bigelow Peak that towers above the southeast shore will beckon photographers to
spend some time at this pretty, unpopulated
tarn, while a plentiful supply of hungry rainbow trout will lure anglers. A small campsite
is located on Bigelow Lake's far western bay,
just before the continuing trail surmounts a
small rise.

Now the path drops steeply, only to get
lost in a boggy hanging meadow. To stay on-
track, continue directly downhill. Later, an
easy, traversing descent ensues, under heavy
hemlock, lodgepole and western white pine
timber. We trace the course of a broad hillside terrace, intermittently meadowed by a
knee-high assemblage of lupine, senecio,
meadow rue and aster. Eventually, the
descent abates to yield a mild southward
climb, quickly reaching a low ridgetop and
the well-marked Yosemite Park boundary.
Only a minute down the other side, we find a
well-signed 4-way trail intersection on the
north shore of exquisite upper Twin Lake. A
carpet of sedge and bilberry reaches to the
shoreline, while the sparkling blue waters reflect the gentle broken cirque of granitic
Michie and Kendrick peaks. A well used trail
runs near the northern shore to the meadow
at its upper end. Numerous fine camps, large
and small, are found along it, in mountain-
hemlock forest. The two west-branching
trails from upper Twin Lake lead to lower
Twin Lake and back down to the Huckleberry Trail. They are described as the Twin
Lakes Trail, Route KM-4.

A faster way to access Black Bear Lake
from the Huckleberry Trail in East Fork
Cherry Creek is to use the following steep
cutoff from Horse Meadow (see Route SP-
2): From the USFS snow-survey cabins on
the east side of Horse Meadow, follow a fair
trail south, right along the meadow's margin,
passing an aerial snow-survey stake and a
telemetered weather station. In about 0.1
mile a sign points uphill, aptly warning of a
steep, rough trail. Turn east, very steeply up
into a cool forest. The duff tread is heavily
eroded by horse traffic, and is marked by
only token switchbacks. The ascent quickly
brings one to a small saddle beside a granitic
knoll, an excellent overlook of East Fork
Cherry Creek Canyon, the dark-veined south
face of Sachse Monument, and Maxwell
Lake. Now the climb moderates, and we
leave the forest for a traversing ascent southeast across an open hillside composed of
variegated metamorphic and intrusive rocks.
Short, rocky switchbacks lead up, over a low
shoulder, then we step across the creek from
Bigelow Lake, its banks lined with fragrant
onions and corn-lilies. Beyond, we once
again find steep duff tread and shady forest.
Almost 400 feet higher, find the signed junction with the faint Snow Lake–Twin Lakes
Trail, just north of Black Bear Lake.

KM-4

Twin Lakes Trail: Then Cross Country to Peninsula Lake, Schofield Peak, Bear Lake and Otter Lakes

Distances

1.4 miles to Upper Twin Lake
2.3 miles to Lower Twin Lake (East End)
6.0 miles to Peninsula Lake
9.0 miles to Otter Lake
10.3 miles to Pacific Crest Trail in Jack Main Canyon

Introduction

Only a cartographer who had never visited them could possibly have named "Twin Lakes". Both are interesting, but completely different—the upper, eastern lake is a true gem, surrounded by dense, cool forest, meadowy margins, and with dancing water reflecting the surrounding cirque of Michie and Kendrick peaks. The much less visited lower, western lake is larger, open and rocky, with fewer camping possibilities on its blocky shoreline. However, as unlike as they are, both are good and little frequented destinations. From lower Twin Lake, an exciting cross-country adventure can lead to almost never-seen Peninsula Lake and Bear Lake, and on to lovely Otter Lake, which holds golden trout.

Trailhead

Same as the Route KM-1 and SP-2 trailheads.

Description

Use the Huckleberry Trail, Route KM-1, or Horse Meadow Road (Route SP-2) to find the well-signed Twin Lakes Trail junction, lying on Horse Meadow Road at the foot of a long hill south of Horse Meadow. The route immediately makes a rocky ford of broad East Fork Cherry Creek (may be difficult in early season). Now, without ado, steep trail attacks the southern hillside, usually under cool cover of pine, hemlock and some fir. About one third of the way up, the path makes an ascending traverse southwest to a broad ravine, and then follows it up, over granites, gabbros, other ultramafics, metamor-

phic rocks and even some seams of marble, to level off eventually at the signed ridgetop boundary with Yosemite National Park. The path turns levelly east here for a few minutes to a signed intersection with the Black Bear Lake Trail (Route KM-3) near the outlet of lovely upper Twin Lake. A nice trail proceeds around its densely forested north shore, reaching numerous camps before fading out in a meadow in the upper cirque. Both Twin Lakes have lightly fished colonies of rainbow trout.

A poor, little-used trail may be followed down to lower Twin Lake. It starts at the 4-way intersection at upper Twin Lake, then winds south to its outlet. Now the way becomes less distinct. At a large campsite, trail tread actually disappears, but by sighting ducks and blazes, the path can be followed west. A bit later, it begins dropping steeply downhill, and almost all semblance of tread disappears. Although ducks and an occasional blaze can be followed, too many downed trees cross the route to make following it worth much trouble—just continue down-canyon, preferably on the more open north side. Soon enough, you'll reach wet meadows of tall sedges at the head of lower Twin Lake. The vicinity hereabouts is not conducive to camping, but fair camps can be made farther along the north shore or, better, near the outlet. Which shore is better to walk around is debatable. The north shore offers gentler walking, but is longer and has innumerable fallen logs. The south shore, on the other hand, is steep but open, with low bluffs and much talus. Take your pick. In any event, you're likely to be alone—I saw only a few firerings along the entire shore—all unused for years. After you reach lower Twin Lake's outlet, the way to Fawn Lake gets easier for a while: drop moderately down open slabs, keeping generally east of sliding Kendrick Creek. Drop around either shoulder of a prominent bluff into a large, level basin. Later, the stream meanders out into an open meadow, which we cross, then clamber down over broken mafic intrusive rocks to a tangled lodgepole grove where the creek draining Peninsula and Bear lakes joins the flow of Kendrick Creek. Here, the cross-country route from Huckleberry Lake joins ours—just upstream from narrow, unremarkable Fawn Lake. (It does have rainbow trout.)

If we wish to push on to Peninsula and Otter lakes, we now turn upstream, southeast, through dense forest litter and tall grasses. The better route keeps north of Peninsula Lake creek, but is nonetheless rather strenuous. Soon, we have scrambled to a position under a tall, dark, brooding buttress on Haystack Peak's northwest shoulder. Just a bit farther up, the brown, broken summit cliff, which would be an easy rock-climb, and the vertical lower apron of Haystack Peak come to loom overhead. This view signals that our climb is almost over. Soon we find the outlet of aptly named Peninsula Lake—this large (34 acre), shallow lake is almost bisected by a long, low ridge of light-colored granite. The western shore has more trees and better camping. I did not see any fish rising during my stay here, although Peninsula Lake has been planted with rainbow trout to 15 inches in the past. Small, pretty Bear Lake, also stocked with rainbows, and an unnamed, intervening lake (which is even nicer), can be reached by a short, easy climb southwest.

The steep-walled cirque containing Upper Peninsula Lake is reached by a brief ascent east, up nice slabs. This alpine lake is rock- and meadow-bound, with only poor camping in prostrate hemlocks around its outlet. I doubt that it has fish, although it, too, was once planted with rainbows. But the reflected profile of Haystack Peak in its waters is striking.

To reach Jack Main Canyon or Otter Lake from Upper Peninsula Lake, hike east up benches and meadowy steps to the north side of the broad saddle between Haystack and Schofield peaks. The summit of either peak is a "must"—views are excellent. The descent east into Otter Lakes' basin is straightforward and relatively easy. Otter Lake is visible from the ridge, with Chittenden Peak and Tower Peak in the distant haze. A few low step-offs are the only minor obstacles to descent, down sandy slopes and steep meadows of knee-high vernacular sedge. Presently, one reaches the meadow north of "big" Otter Lake, and turns south to its meadowy north shore. This very shallow, lagooned lake has been planted with golden trout, but they are probably outnumbered here by mountain yellow-legged frogs. Otter Lake has the distinction of draining both east and south, into the Falls and Frog creek drainages, respectively. Little Otter Lake is just a bit south of us, and it has good camping and rainbow trout.

To end our cross-country jaunt at the Pacific Crest Trail in Jack Main Canyon, turn east, rounding well north of Otter Lake's bayed margin, and then descend in mixed forest near the south bank of its small outlet creek. Without much difficulty you will eventually hit the PCT (Route YP-2) quite close to its junction with the Tilden Lake Trail (Route YP-9) on the forested floor of Jack Main Canyon. "Jack Main" is a corruption of "Jack Means," who, like Thomas Richardson, for whom the nearby summit was named, was an early sheepherder and explorer of northern Yosemite.

KM-5

Cross-Country Route to W Lake, Shallow Lake and Fraser Lakes from Blackbird Lake

Distances
1.3 miles to Shallow Lake
1.8 miles to Fraser Lakes
2.3 miles to Emigrant Lake outlet

Introduction
All of these little lakes are off the beaten track, but easy to reach and worth the trip, for their solitude and angling for eastern brook trout.

Trailhead
Same as the Route KM-1 trailhead.

Description
Take the Huckleberry Trail 12.4 miles from Kennedy Meadow to Blackbird Lakes. Proceed south from those shallow tarns 0.6 mile, gently up a bilberry-and-sedge meadow, passing the southern ridge of a large dome that forms the hillside west of Blackbird Lakes. Here our route commences as an indistinct, unsigned use-trail climbing due west away from the Huckleberry Trail. In a moment, the track ducks into a stand of mountain hemlocks. Less than 5 minutes later we stand beside 1-acre W Lake, commemorating a Fish and Game surveyor named Wilson. Its morainally dammed, lupine-clothed meadow banks have a good camp, where one can try his luck for eastern brook trout. W Lake will always be a haven of solitude, close as it is to the Huckleberry Trail.

If Shallow Lake is our destination, our route now continues southwest, through a low gap, on discontinuous trail tread through bouldery meadows. The way descends along a seasonal stream past another small lake, then bends west in a drier, more open valley, via a ducked route south of the stream. Soon we see many lagoons of well-named Shallow Lake, below. In many years, Shallow Lake is

Fraser Lakes, near Emigrant Lake

considerably larger than the 38-acre size shown on the topo—it may occupy almost the entire basin. It is home to an underfished population of large eastern brook trout. Its nicest camp is in a clump of trees at its far south end. Shallow Lake also has many islands to camp on, if one is willing to wade or has a raft.

A highly recommended trip to Fraser Lakes leads north from Shallow Lake, up a broad ravine, over slabs and steps. Almost atop the hill, turn west over a gap to larger, eastern Fraser Lake. The four clustered Fraser Lakes are, to me, the friendliest, most secluded subalpine jewels in the Emigrant Basin. Each is rimmed by white granite slabs

and fringes of meadow and heather. A shining dome between the two main tarns gives excellent views across the sweep of Emigrant Lake.

To continue your loop to the outlet of Emigrant Lake, cross the isthmus between the largest lakes, swing around the meadowed north shore of the western lake, and climb west up over a shallow gap. Now descend a broad ravine, alternating talus with knee-high sedge meadows. Near the bottom, keep right, and walk across a short concrete-and-rock stream-flow dam at Emigrant Lake's outlet. Meet the poorly maintained, slightly vague North Fork Cherry Creek Trail (Route CL-5) on the far bank.

KM-6

Relief Valley Trail: Summit Creek to Whitesides Meadow and Salt Lick Meadow via Relief Lakes

Distances
4.1 miles to Upper Relief Lake
6.0 miles to Burst Rock Trail at Salt Lick Meadow

Introduction
This historic trail follows a wagon road travelled across the Sierra by early settlers. Today, as then, it affords the easiest link between the Kennedy Meadows region and the Burst Rock Trail in the central Emigrant Wilderness.

Trailhead
Same as the Route KM-1 trailhead.

Description
The Huckleberry Trail KM-1 climbs 5.1 miles up Summit Creek from Kennedy Meadow to 7600 feet, where, in a shady forest of red fir and lodgepole, the signed Relief Valley Trail leaves the Huckleberry Trail just beyond a trickling creek that emerges to cross our path from a thicket of alder, meadow rue, paintbrush and columbine. Our route quickly switchbacks up and over a domed nose, then parallels the dome's south face on a gentle northwest descent to a wading ford of Summit Creek. On the far bank, amid shading

lodgepoles, are two campsites just north of the trail. Abruptly, we climb out of the trees on sandy, rocky trail lined with Indian hemp and huckleberry oak to traverse steeply above the roiling gorge of Summit Creek. Buttress-rooted Sierra junipers give little shade on this slope, but we soon enough level out beside the now-less-raucous stream under aspens and lodgepoles. Trudge away from Summit Creek, working south, then west, on deep sandy trail.

Meeting the old trail alignment, we swing southwest around a decomposing outcrop of light intrusive rock to Lower Relief Valley. Here the stupendous volcanic prominence of East Flange Rock comes into view, dominating the western skyline as it did for pioneer parties in gold-rush days. After traversing along the overgrown meadow's north fringe, we turn across it, noting a sign indicating a nonexistent trail to the Silver Mine Creek Road (our cross-country route EM-4), as well as colorful sunflowers, buckwheat and pussy paws. Only a few trees protect us as we leave a campsite beside Relief Creek for a steep, dusty ascent on poorly maintained trail, bearing southwest under East Flange Rock's brooding face.

The angle presently abates to make a switchback down to a fir-canopied hop of Relief Creek, but not before we pause to examine a sand plate and wheel rim from one of the Duckwall Party's prairie schooners, which was abandoned here in late 1853. These artifacts are nailed to a granite boulder beside the trail. We skirt a large camping area across Relief Creek, then climb steeply to another simple ford. A final section of steep volcanic tread leads through lush vegetation, scattered hemlocks and lodgepoles, and possibly a lingering snowbank to finish the ascent in a sandy flat that has seen heavy camping use. Here, those whose angling urge dictates a visit to North (lower) Relief Lake should strike east to Relief Creek, where fishing is fair for brook trout to 12″, then drop gently along its grassy banks, crossing to the lake when opposite it. North Relief Lake, where anglers will fare much the same as in Relief Creek, is a much more hospitable place to be based than its southern counterpart, owing to its more rocky surroundings, which inhibit wind and mosquitos.

From the entrance to Upper Relief Valley, the path stays along the west side of a lush meadow. Shallow South Relief Lake, lying in a meadowed depression, is easily reached from any point on this pleasant walk. A short distance later we meet the well-marked linkage with the Whitesides Meadow Cutoff Trail. This 1.2 mile lateral, a time-saver for those bound for western Emigrant Basin, climbs gently up, southwest, through meadowed lodgepoles to gain viewful sage-brush- and mule-ears-clad volcanic slopes. A contouring traverse soon ends at the well-signed Deer Lake Trail (Route PC-3) on a low ridge just east of Whitesides Meadow.

Bound for Salt Lick Meadow, we proceed south across the meadow to cross Relief Creek one last time. After winding around tiny tarns strewn amid stunted lodgepoles and crystalline boulders which mark the Stanislaus-Tuolumne divide, we track south, descending gently into deeper forest floored with a meadowy consortium of red heather, twinberry and bilberry. The signed Deer Lake Trail (Route PC-3) is reached shortly after the path switchbacks twice and levels out.

KM-7

Granite Dome's Golden Trout Lakes: Blackhawk Lake, Iceland Lake, Ridge Lake, Sardella Lake and Lewis Lakes—Cross-country Route

Distances
1.7 miles to Sardella Lake
1.9 miles to Iceland Lake
1.7 miles to Ridge Lake
1.9 miles to Upper Lewis Lake

Introduction

If it's the exquisitely beautiful, delicious golden trout you're after, this is the trip for you. No other spot in Emigrant Wilderness or northern Yosemite has so much good fishing water packed into such a small space as here. And the setting is awesome—a pair of high, rocky cirques tucked right under the dizzying summit of Granite Dome.

Trailhead
Same as the Route KM-1 trailhead.

Description

The Lewis Lakes can be reached from a number of directions. Most walkers and almost all equestrians will start up from the Huckleberry Trail, and this way will be outlined first. Other approaches are via Iceland Lake creek, or from Sheep Camp, and both routes will also be described. Alternatively, one can drop into the basins from atop Granite Dome, to the south, by following cross-country routes from Pinto or Wilson Mcadow Lake, as described in Route PC-9.

The easiest and fastest approach to the high lakes under Granite Dome leaves the Huckleberry Trail (Route KM-1) south of Saucer Meadow. Here, at 8300 feet, low granite slabs dominate the southwest side of Summit Creek and, for the first time, the high dark cliffs above Lewis Lakes heave fully into view. This point is a few yards downhill from where the Huckleberry Trail first enters open, mature red-fir forest. Here, ford Summit Creek (may be difficult in early season) to its southwest bank at its confluence with Lewis Lakes creek. Now follow the latter steam for 100 yards, then clamber up a hillside to the southwest. This gains a sloping bench, from which we turn west up an obvious, forested draw, climbing moderately to granite slabs and a snowfield atop a gap south of Peak 9332. Beyond, contour southwest around the canyon's head, then up slabs to a boulder-dotted open ridge shoulder near the north end of Ridge Lake. Impressively sited under the dark dihedrals of Granite Dome's 10322-foot summit, rockbound Ridge Lake has golden trout and poor camps near its outlet.

Better than stopping at Ridge Lake, drop northwest past a pair of tarns to lovely, entirely rockbound Iceland Lake. It is my favorite, since it too has golden trout and it occupies a spectacular perch overlooking Relief Valley and East Flange Rock. Iceland Lake can be reached more directly from the Relief Valley Trail (Route KM-6): From the east edge of Lower Relief Valley, look south to see Iceland Lake's stream cascading down over slabs and talus, almost directly below the summit of Granite Dome. Crash through tall willows to reach Relief Creek where it meets the descending stream. (The ford will usually require a long, knee-deep wade.) Now work steeply up the glistening slabs along Iceland Lake's creek.

To reach Sardella and upper Lewis lakes, horse parties should ride up the shallow, meadowed canyon of Sardella Lake's outlet, without first riding to Ridge Lake. On foot, most parties will traverse the moraine north of Ridge Lake, then wander over slabs to the north end of upper Lewis Lake. Here,

glistening white slabs slope gently into the tarn's sky-blue waters, and light plays across the water and the pockets of meadow fringe as a frequent breeze blows. Camping is poor, but fishing for brookies is not. My preferred route to Black Hawk Lake sweeps along upper Lewis Lake's border, then undulates over slabs on the canyon rim to reach that tarn, passing a similar tarn halfway along the viewful traverse.

Very close to upper Lewis Lake, Sardella Lake sits in a round, tidy bowl. Meadow-fringed, it has no trees or campsites, but is stocked with golden trout. It was named for the patriarch of a prominent local family.

To descend to middle and lower Lewis lakes and back to the Huckleberry Trail, walk north from the north end of upper Lewis Lake, contouring a short distance into the cirque above Sardella Lake, then climb quickly to a gap just south of Peak 9772. Now drop easily over fairly steep slabs, directly downhill. Spectacular middle Lewis Lake soon comes into view. As upper Lewis Lake is a study in dancing light, middle Lewis Lake is a study in darkness—an incredible 500-foot cliff of brooding black rises vertically from its west shore, above its dark waters. Silver snags frame the vista—as stark as an Ansel Adams print. Below middle Lewis Lake, we can either descend along its outlet stream or continue down slabs to the north, traversing at times to avoid small cliffs. Reach a ribbon of lodgepole pines along a now-gentle stream in the canyon bottom, just below lower Lewis Lake. Totally unlike its higher sisters, this smaller tarn is typical of the Emigrant's lakes, with a willow-and-meadow fringe and stands of pines. Like its sisters, it supports brook trout.

To return to the Huckleberry Trail, now follow Lewis Lakes' creek down, north, back to your original crossing of Summit Creek.

Hikers (but not horsemen) can approach Black Hawk Lake directly from Sheep Camp, on the Huckleberry Trail (Route KM-1). From Sheep Camp, descend west along the south bank of Summit Creek, to where the waters turn abruptly north. Black Hawk Lake

Middle Lewis Lake

sits above the black-streaked bluffs to the southwest. Its outflow steam tumbles down the hillside into a grove of lodgepole pines. Turn up along its east bank and clamber over slides, steps and pockets of wet meadow to the canyon lip, some 900 feet above. Here, abruptly, the lung-searing ascent abates at a pair of rock-bound tarns under the broad summit of Black Hawk Mountain. Here, turn northwest and drop just a few feet to equally diminutive Black Hawk Lake. Almost completely rockbound, it offers no good camping, and the small fishery of golden trout is subject to frequent freezing winter kill.

KM-8

Grouse Creek Trail to Grouse Lake

Distance
2.9 miles to Grouse Lake

Introduction
This rough, little-used path is known mostly to deer hunters. It visits a pleasant hanging valley under Relief Peak.

Trailhead
Same as the Route KM-1 trailhead.

Description
Take the Huckleberry Trail 2.8 miles to the first overlook of Relief Reservoir. Here a 10-foot-long iron steam donkey lies just west of the trail, on an open granite rib, beside two large junipers, just a few feet before a spur trail to Relief Reservoir branches west. The Grouse Creek Trail lies up to your east: scramble 50 feet southeast up a granite slab, past a 5-foot juniper stump, to find the trail branching on a 136° bearing from the dynamited road bed. The first few yards of trail presage what is to come: rocky, dusty, eroded, overgrown, and steep-to-very-steep.

The trail is not recommended for horses, beginners or hot days—there is a 900-foot climb without shade. Soon, you get vistas over Relief Reservoir to East Flange Rock, the Three Chimneys and Red Peak. Eventually, the rough switchbacks lead up to a stock-drift fence and some welcome shade. Here the climb moderates but does not entirely abate. Continuing south under the open shade of mixed conifers, we come to a sloping meadow where we can look south up Grouse Creek to white snow slopes contrasting starkly with the dark red of Relief

Peak. The trail now takes a gently ascending gradient, alternately through pines and meadows above the east side of the little stream. We keep well away from the creekside, and pass a few good campsites. Above 8580 feet, we emerge in a dry sagebrush meadow, littered by an obvious avalanche track. From here on, the trail is less obvious, due to disuse. If you have been able to trace the path this far, it ends at tiny, almost-silted-in Grouse Lake. The pond has no fish, and camping is much better in the meadows back down-canyon.

KM-9

Kennedy Creek Trail: Kennedy Lake and Soda Springs

Distances
5.6 miles to Soda Springs
5.5 miles to Kennedy Lake
8.9 miles to Horse Meadow Road at Kennedy Canyon head

Introduction
Three-thousand-foot-deep Kennedy Creek canyon is the deepest in the area of this guide, outside of Hetch Hetchy. But snow melts quickly from its floor, making an early-season fishing trip to Kennedy Lake a good choice.

Trailhead
Same as the Route KM-1 trailhead.

Description
Reach Pacific Gas and Electric Company's Relief Station maintenance building, in the sunny draw below Relief Reservoir, by walking 2.4 miles up the Huckleberry Trail (Route KM-1) along Summit Creek. The Kennedy Creek Trail, often unsigned, begins near the northeast corner of the three-story institutional-green structure. Starting up a cobbly, mixed-moraine hillside draped with manzanita, huckleberry oak and snowberry, the path makes a few steep switchbacks, then levels out behind a small dome. Catch your breath here while enjoying pine-framed views of Granite Dome and East Flange Rock. Now eastbound, the way contours

easily on sandy tread above the roar of Kennedy Creek. Later, drop across Kennedy Creek's roiling pools via a sturdy 30-foot-long wood-and-steel bridge. Now on a broad north-bank bench, we begin a long, easy ascent under an open canopy of Jeffrey pines and junipers. In about one mile, we pass, unsigned, the obvious rut of the Night Cap Trail (Route KM-10). Ambling on, we glimpse the volcanic prow of Kennedy Peak through gaps in the conifers. These gaps become more numerous, widen into pockets, and become broad expanses of sagebrush-dotted meadows as we near the mouth of Soda Canyon. Here we will likely see summer-grazing horses and cattle. A bit upstream from Soda Canyon's confluence we step across a small creek draining the massive slopes of Leavitt Peak. Here in a cluster of lodgepole pines, just yards before the two cabins of Kennedy's Cow Camp, is the unsigned Soda Canyon Trail.

A wild, alpine cirque, ringed by red and black volcanic cliffs and spires of Kennedy and Relief peaks, Soda Canyon is also home to an unusual carbonated spring. This is easily reached by the short side trail starting from Kennedy's Cow Camp. It first leads south to a 40-foot log-hop crossing of Kennedy Creek (possibly a wade in early summer), then ascends southwest in dark forest over the medial moraine forming a low ridge beside the mouth of Soda Canyon. This gives way to a much easier contouring ascent once we turn the corner into the spectacularly craggy canyon. At first, we walk well above Soda Canyon's creek, alternating muddy hillside meadows with stands of sagebrush-floored lodgepoles. In less than a mile, however, we are beside the willow-banked creek and the path becomes less obvious. In just a few yards we find Soda Spring, bubbling quietly from the volcanic hillside, a few feet from the stream. No camping is available hereabouts.

Return to the Kennedy Creek Trail and continue up-canyon toward Kennedy Lake. First, the good track skirts east around a fenced, soggy meadow. Here we have good views east to the canyon's headwall, overhung by Kennedy Peak. Presently we near Kennedy Creek, where we could walk across

logs to its south bank use-trail and a number of large camps—the best ones near Kennedy Lake. Now we come to the wide-open meadowed shores of 28-acre Kennedy Lake. Except for near some thickets of willow, it offers excellent flycasting for large (to 24″) brown and rainbow trout.

To reach Horse Meadow Road (Route SP-2) or the Pacific Crest Trail (Route SP-1) at the saddle at the head of Kennedy Canyon continue around the boggy north margin of Kennedy Lake. While the slopes above are barren gravel, the lakeside is speckled with the yellow of senecio, the pink of wild onion and spreading phlox, the blue of iris, and the pale green of chest-high green gentian. We quickly climb onto drier gravel terrain and hop across a permanent stream coming from a hanging valley. Now we undertake a steep—sometime extremely steep—rocky ascent, paralleling Kennedy Creek's headwaters. Either of two paths can be used—the

Kennedy Lake and Big Sam

one closer to the creekside may have a slightly easier grade. Both routes offer the rewards of fine over-shoulder vistas down-canyon across Kennedy Lake to the Dardanelles, and up to the smooth face of Kennedy Peak. Above 8700 feet, the two paths join and the incline decreases somewhat. An open grove of western white pines and lodgepoles now offers a chance for shade, and Kennedy Creek is close by. At 9000 feet we pass a dry meadow, with evidence of avalanches from the north face of Big Sam. Then, we pant up another steep valley-step to a small, hanging valley. Here the trail peters out. Thankfully, we are only 5 minutes from Horse Meadow Road (Route SP-2) up on the Sierra crest to the northeast. Alternatively, continue east along the creekside to good camps just below Horse Meadow Road.

KM-10

Night Cap Trail:
Kennedy Meadows to Kennedy Creek Canyon

Distances
3.4 miles to Kennedy Creek Canyon
7.3 miles to Kennedy Lake

Introduction
This is a rough but highly scenic alternative to the heavily used Huckleberry Trail for reaching lower Kennedy Creek canyon. It is recommended especially for off-season use, since its south-facing exposure renders it free of snow earlier in summer. By midsummer, however, the route may be waterless and uncomfortably warm.

Trailhead
Same as the Route KM-1 trailhead.

Description
Named for the small volcanic peak on the divide between Deadman and Kennedy creeks which is so prominent from Highway 108 around Kennedy Meadows, the Night Cap Trail begins atop a small saddle that forms the north end of Kennedy Meadows proper. This point is just a 5-minute uphill walk along the Huckleberry Trail (Route KM-1) from Kennedy Meadows store and stables. Atop the saddle, a sign points out the east-branching path, which immediately sets the tone for much of its length: a steep, cobbly ascent via tiny, heavily horse-eroded switchbacks, under a series of small granitic cliffs. After gaining about 150 feet, the incline moderates and we turn north through a little gap, actually descending for a moment eastward above the gorge of Deadman Creek. Then we resume the ascent, turning south through huckleberry-oak brush.

We presently find a tiny bench and an equally diminutive pond, which the path skirts on the east. Above, a handful of very tight switchbacks leads to a nice viewpoint. Directly below, Kennedy Meadow is home to the meandering Middle Fork Stanislaus River. Farther south, Granite Dome rises on the horizon, usually ringed by snowfields below its summit cliffs.

After getting your bearings, continue up the trail, which initially traverses to the right, around the south side of a small ridge to gain a gully that leads up to another, shaded saddle. Now the trail undertakes a traverse south across the hillside, but, gradually, the traverse yields to ascent, which later turns extremely steep, up a ravine that is an early-season creekbed. After gaining almost 700 feet, the route finally moderates and we amble over to a delightful vista: Now we have gained sufficient altitude to gaze south over rock-dammed 7215-foot-high Relief Reservoir. Beyond, the black scarp of East Flange Rock stands as it did 100 years ago, a beacon marking the wagon route for Forty-Niners' emigrant trains.

After a well-deserved rest, continue southeast on the sometimes-vague path as it climbs, now at an easy angle, into a nice stand of red fir. Presently, the tread underfoot changes from granitic to tan and black volcanics, and we can glance upslope to the red volcanic parapet of our trail's namesake, Night Cap Peak. A short distance later, our climb finally ends atop an 8100-foot saddle, behind a low knoll. Now begins a steep descent, occasionally punctuated by eroded switchbacks and fallen trees. The way keeps generally to the west side of a small ravine as it drops 500 feet into the dry, open Jeffrey-pine forest on the floor of Kennedy Creek canyon. Here, at a vague, unsigned junction, the Night Cap Trail merges with the prominent Kennedy Creek Trail (Route KM-9). Many campsites are nearby, both up and down canyon.

The morning mist dissipates

Ch. 11: Sonora Pass

SP-1

Pacific Crest Trail: Sonora Pass to Dorothy Lake

Distances

4.9 miles to gap above Latopie Lake
8.1 miles to Horse Meadow Road near Leavitt Lake Pass
9.2 miles to head of Kennedy Canyon
13.8 miles to West Fork West Walker River at Emigrant Pass Trail
16.9 miles to Cascade Creek Trail
17.9 miles to Harriet Lake
19.4 miles to Dorothy Lake Pass
20.9 miles to Bond Pass Trail at Head Jack Main Canyon

Introduction

The first 8 miles south of Sonora Pass of the famous border-to-border Pacific Crest Trail are possibly the finest of the entire 2650-mile route. True to its name, the Crest Trail here follows the naked edge between earth and sky, yielding the most easily obtained alpine panoramas of the entire northern Yosemite Sierra. The first part of this route makes a fine day hike, especially if combined with an ascent of 11570-foot Leavitt Peak, or done as a loop trip, combined with the start of the Horse Meadow Road from Leavitt Lake. To continue south into the verdant Yosemite North Boundary Country at Dorothy Lake makes one of the finest 3- or 4-day backpack trips in the northern Sierra.

Trailhead

Highway 108 at the summit of Sonora Pass, 35 miles east of Pinecrest and 9.2 miles east of Kennedy Meadows. Parking is available ⅛ mile west of the pass, at the USFS PCT trailhead parking area.

Description

The southbound PCT begins right atop 9628' Sonora Pass. It climbs easily northwest from a large sign that commemorates this historic thoroughfare across the Sierra Nevada. Our path turns southwest to parallel the Sierra divide, ascending through open stands of whitebark pines. We soon cross to the east side of the divide, descend slightly along dry hillsides sporting mule ears, lupine and green gentian, and hop across a small creek, our last on-route water until Kennedy Canyon, a long 10.4 miles distant—be sure to fill your canteens! Now the ascent begins in earnest. The PCT initially arcs east up to an alpine, volcanic nose, giving fine views east over Sardine Meadow to Pickle Meadows, the West Walker River basin, and the distant Sweetwater Range. Beyond, swing south into a broad cirque under peak 10960+, and climb moderately on good trail over volcanic gravels and boulders of andesite autobreccia, below a large permanent snowfield. Note that this damp, barren hillside is the northernmost known home of the Mount Lyell salamander, a rare, exclusively alpine amphibian with an adhesive-tipped tail.

The path curves northwest to regain the Sierra divide, then parallels it steeply up to a tiny switchback at a flat spot on the ridge. Here, although vistas to east and west are themselves impressive, the greatest interest lies at our feet—thousands of agates are scattered over the thin, ruddy earth, derived from volcanic tuff. Ranging in color from creamy white to pale blue, pink and yellow, and in size from BB's to large grapes, these oval agates are believed to have formed when trapped bubbles of mineral-rich water slowly evaporated within the surrounding, cooling volcanic rock. Escape of the water left behind concentric layers of gypsum and silica crystals to fill each bubble. These layers can easily be seen by cracking open one of the agates, and many agates can be found, still held in the vesicles of the rock that spawned them.

Leaving this thought-provoking spot, the way ascends, now steeply across a very steep slope where until mid-season, a snowfield straddles the path. A slip then could well be lethal, and inexperienced hikers should avoid walking on this snow. Hopefully, the USFS will relocate this dangerous bit of trail farther to the west. We soon top out at a 10870-foot saddle, and now most of the serious climbing of the entire hike is behind us. Here the trail enters Emigrant Wilderness and commences a delightful, nearly level stroll southward, just west of the Sierran spine. Ahead, Leavitt Peak looms above a large rock-glacier at the head of lovely, meadowed Blue Canyon. Our immediate environs consist of incredibly dense thickets of 3–4 foot-high whitebark pines, their tops pruned to a lawn-like texture by icy winter winds. The tops of these thickets, called "krummholz" ("crooked wood"), show the usual depth of winter snows on this hillside.

Pressing on, we soon contour into one pass and then another, just south of Peak 11245, where the trail makes one switchback to cross east of the Sierra crest and descends slightly into the head of McKay Creek canyon. Under the dark, vertical ramparts of Peak 11265, Little Ice Age glaciers here left behind a pair of fresh terminal moraines, enclosing an early-season pond. The PCT traverses these morainal rings, then clambers steeply south to a narrow 10780-foot notch. A breathtaking panorama presents itself in the south: at our feet, Latopie, Koenig and Leavitt lakes sparkle in the sun. On the horizon, much of northeast Yosemite Park is in view, from the battlements of Tower Peak

and the Sawtooth Ridge to far-off Mts. Conness, Lyell and Ritter and Banner Peak.

Now our trail swings southwest under a steep, avalanche-prone wall. Soon an obvious cross-country route down to wind-swept Latopie Lake is passed, but, unfortunately, the trail is routed 400 feet above the lake. The path eventually climbs a bit to gain Leavitt Peak's east shoulder. This stretch crosses another lingering snowfield that should be avoided by novices. The 10880-foot east shoulder of Leavitt Peak is the highest attained by any trail north of southern Yosemite. This is a good starting point for a ½ mile climb (steep walking) to the viewful summit of Leavitt Peak. The PCT now drops into a broad, virtually lifeless bowl, and leads yet again to a crossing of the Sierra crest at a saddle southeast of Leavitt Peak. Here the crest bends southeast, and we turn to follow it, undulating far above Kennedy Creek Canyon and meadow-fringed Kennedy Lake. Occasional stands of whitebark pines are encountered, but mostly we traverse open volcanic slopes with a sparse alpine flora of low currant shrubs, bright yellow hulsea, orange wallflowers, rose pussypaws and delicate ivesia. Three times, our windswept route gives views down onto Leavitt Lake, through gaps in its cliffy headwall. Eventually, we strike dirt Horse Meadow Road (Route SP-2) just shy of the brink of Kennedy Canyon.

Here, congruent momentarily with the rough, gravelly road, the PCT drops quickly south to again find the Sierra crest at a gap. Just a few yards later, the PCT branches left, south, away from road, steeply down the bare cobbly hillside above the head of Kennedy Canyon. Eventually, it rejoins the mining road at a switchback below which we follow the road for only a few minutes to find a signed junction with the PCT, just north of a broad saddle at the head of Kennedy Canyon. Looking east down-canyon, we see large areas of toppled trees—residue of a very severe avalanche. Initially, our descent is moderate and open, passing stands of whitebark pines, but soon enough comes under more dense lodgepole-pine cover, then hops a permanently flowing branch of

Avalanche result in Kennedy Canyon

Kennedy Canyon creek. A half-mile later the PCT comes close to the main stream, in dry lodgepole stands, where it used to cross to the south bank, but is diverted onto a refurbished old Kennedy Canyon Trail, to remain along the north bank. This change was instituted in 1986, after a tremendous avalanche covered the new PCT route with thousands of upended lodgepole pines. Our detour proceeds down-canyon, often vaguely, keeping quite close to the stream bank. Presently it passes the easternmost border of avalanche-downed timber and enters a boggy area fed by numerous ice-cold springs. At this point, the new PCT route lies only a few yards uphill, across the usually shallow creek. I recommend hopping across here and resuming a walk on excellent tread, leading gently down-canyon. (If desired, one may remain on the old trail, north of the stream— early-season PCTers will find it more snow free).

The PCT itself poses no further route-finding difficulties. The path heads down, on easy duff tread, in dappled open forest, soon with a sprinkling of Jeffrey and western white pines. Eventually, it turns the corner at Kennedy Canyon's mouth and proceeds south on undulating footing, between a large volcanic cliff, above, and the meadow-dotted West Fork West Walker River bottomlands, below. A bit later, we dip to cross a small creek under a two-tiered waterfall, then continue on to ford wider, seasonal Dry Creek. Beyond, we tread the level forest fringes of one of Walker Meadows, then traverse onto granitic terrain for the first time on this hike. This leads east to find a 30-foot-long wood-and-steel bridge over the West Fork West Walker River. A large campsite lies just before the bridge. Just across the bridge, a four-way junction with the Long Lakes Trail (Route WB-5) and the Walker Meadows Trail (Route WB-3) is encountered, just east of Upper Long Lake. Here the PCT turns gently southwest up-canyon in open lodgepole forest. Soon we come upon a well-signed junction with the Emigrant Pass Trail (Route WB-3) branching southwest, up along the Walker River.

The PCT climbs left, south, from this junction, ascending gradually for about ½ mile on a frustrating, expensive alignment that keeps us very close to the prettier, better-constructed Emigrant Pass Trail just below. Eventually, our trail bends eastward up to a low divide. Beyond, a contouring descent leads across a fascinating hillside of gray, banded marble—a relict of the Paleozoic seas that once covered California. One-hundred-eighty-degree vistas here encompass the Sweetwater Mountains, the Little Walker River divide and the Sierra crest above Piute Meadows. Pushing on, pass the right-ascending Cinko Lake Cutoff (Route WB-4), cross a deep, narrow stream via a rickety log bridge, and ascend moderately in shady mountain-hemlock forest to a saddle with two small tarns. Here the PCT swings south into the Cascade Creek watershed, passing a signed junction with the north-descending Cascade Creek Trail WB-4. Fairly level walking presently finds a log crossing of Cascade Creek, just short of a large, hospitable camp in a dark lodgepole grove. Lake Harriet is next on our menu, reached by an easy grade that sticks close beside its raucous outlet stream. We step across to the west bank just below the outlet, then wind halfway along Lake Harriet's rocky western shore. The best camps are on the far side; fishing pressure is high, but the lake has a good population of rainbow and brook trout. If we choose not to stop here, we can push on, up a short series of tight switchbacks to a low divide that separates the two halves of Cascade Creek's cirque. Now, lovely Bonnie Lake is below (drop cross-country to the best camps on its west shore); smaller Stella Lake is ten minutes away, across the wide-open basin.

Just a minute beyond Stella Lake, we ascend just a bit more to 9590-foot Dorothy Lake Pass and a plethora of signs heralding our entrance into Yosemite National Park. Here we doff our packs and pause at the overlook of large, frequently wind-swept Dorothy Lake and its backdrop, a large rock-

glacier descending from the gray ramparts of Forsyth Peak. When you are ready to camp, drop easily to Dorothy Lake's head, then wind near its meadowy north shore, passing a number of good campsites. Fishing at Dorothy Lake is usually good, for rainbow trout to 24 inches. Below Dorothy Lake, the path winds through a pretty rice-grass meadow to a signed intersection with the west-branching Bond Pass Trail (Route KM-2) and the PCT's continuation south into Jack Main Canyon (Route YP-2).

SP-2

Horse Meadow Road: Leavitt Lake to Horse Meadow via High Emigrant Lake and Emigrant Pass

Distances
1.7 miles to Leavitt Lake Pass
3.8 miles to head of Kennedy Canyon
6.3 miles to Big Sam
9.0 miles to High Emigrant Lake
9.8 miles to Emigrant Pass
11.8 miles to Summit Meadow
16.0 miles to Horse Meadow at Huckleberry Trail

Introduction
If you want to get to the heart of the Emigrant Basin the fast way, this is it. An amazing mining road was gouged along the Sierra crest to reach tungsten claims near Snow Lake and Horse Meadow. Today, closed to vehicular traffic, the route now yields a bonanza of two-mile-high panoramas. Descending from the peak called Big Sam, the Emigrant's loftiest viewpoint accessible by trail, this route then swings near some justifiably famous flycasting waters before ending at a strategic hub of trails for exploration of the Emigrant's wilderness of lakes.

Trailhead
Drive over Sonora Pass 3.8 miles (38.8 mile from Pinecrest) to signed Leavitt Lake Road, which leaves Highway 108 at a switchback. This steep, rough, deeply rutted

dirt road is not recommended for low-clearance passenger cars. Driving up, pass through debris of two major avalanches dating from spring '86, and make two stream fords. In 2.9 miles, find a parking area at Leavitt Lake's outlet. Myriad branching roads lead to nearby RV campsites in small clusters of whitebark pines.

Description
Leavitt Lake sits in a spectacular, massive cirque of maroon volcanic rocks—derived from lava flows and ash of the Tertiary Relief Peak Formation. Its wind-swept waters, a good producer of golden trout, are fringed with a scant, cobbly meadow and clusters of whitebark pines. Hiram L. Leavitt, for whom many local features are named, built a lodging at the eastern foot of Sonora Pass, soon after a road was constructed, in 1863. He later served as a Mono County judge.

Our hike to Emigrant Pass follows a nearly abandoned jeep road which is closed to all vehicular travel. This amazing road was constructed in 1943, to reach the rich Cherry Creek Tungsten Mine below Twin Lakes. Then, during WWII, tungsten was a valuable strategic mineral, used in hardening steel for the American war effort. Hence, a 18.1 mile,

Leavitt Lake from Pass 10640

precarious track was bulldozed to the mine site. However, very little ore was trucked out, and after the war, the expense and danger of obtaining ore via this avalanche-scoured route exceeded the ore's value, and mining ceased. The road's continued existence, however, prevented the adjacent corridor from being included in Emigrant Wilderness until 1984. In 1984 and '85, the USFS helicoptered out much of the old mining equipment.

Ponder this conflict in land-use values while you fill your canteen for the waterless ascent ahead. Then, shoulder your pack. Your first objective is a gap on the Sierra Crest, called, "Leavitt Lake Pass" by many, on the southern rim of Leavitt Lake's cirque. The route along the sandy jeep road wastes no mileage to attain the pass—easily seen from Leavitt Lake. After crossing Leavitt Creek via logs at the lake's outlet, the track begins climbing east, winding up past whitebark pines and spur roads. Presently, we turn south and climb steeply, soon panting past a locked gate. Above, we level out for a moment atop a spur ridge, where the Ski Lake Trail, an old road, branches northeast. Ski Lake is surprisingly little-visited, and is a good choice for a short fishing trip or a day-hike. To reach it, turn northeast across a

wide-open hillside fell-field dotted with yellow ivesia and follow the road as it leads gently down across a trickling, permanent creek, then climbs just a bit to a nice overlook of little Ski Lake, nestled in its tan volcanic cirque. Here the track turns down, soon winding to a fair but windy camp in a small stand of whitebark pines on Ski Lake's otherwise barren west shore. Golden trout are reputed to inhabit the waters.

Returning to the Horse Meadow Road, now we can pick our poison—the jeep road swings southeast to climb steeply as a broad switchback, while a shorter but murderously steep trail climbs straight south to rejoin the road's dogleg. Once they rejoin, one has only to gasp and stagger up two more steep switchbacks to attain the 10640-foot gap just east of the Sierra crest. All but the most jaded or hypoxic hikers will admit that the view is worth the effort—views southeast encompass the entire North Boundary Country of Yosemite National Park from Forsyth and Tower peaks to Hawksbeak and Matterhorn peaks, Mts. Conness, Dana, Lyell and Maclure. To our east lies the West Fork West Walker River basin. North, we see Sonora Pass, Carson-Iceberg Wilderness and distant Round Top.

From this exhilarating but usually windy

gap, we descend southwest along the Sierra crest. Our route quickly finds the northbound PCT (Route SP-1) at the end of a switchback. Below, we descend to a saddle, where the PCT branches left, south, from our obvious road, which we follow as it makes an aggressive switchbacking descent of the almost barren rhyolitic hillside at the head of Kennedy Canyon. Four switchbacks and 500 feet lower, the PCT rejoins our road, and we continue down to a broad saddle where the marked PCT again leaves us, dropping northeast into Kennedy Canyon (Route SP-1). Just beyond are some fair camps under scattered clumps of whitebark pine, understoried by fragrant purple pennyroyal. Water is available from the head of Kennedy Creek, to our west. Here too, is the terminus of Route KM-9 from Kennedy Lake, which we glimpse far below.

Next on our agenda is an ascent of Big Sam (10824')—even more work than our first climb from Leavitt Lake! Initially, the road ascends moderately westward, under a battlement of volcanic cliffs. Rounding a corner, the road is often buried under a long, treacherously steep snowfield that usually persists into late August. Use caution here—many inexperienced hikers (and bulldozer drivers) have taken long slides! Once across

this obstacle, the way climbs into a side canyon, where a monkeyflower-decked creek always flows into late season. Above this welcome rest spot, the final ascent to Big Sam ensues—first a leg east, then an ascending traverse west across the upper cirque, on rocky, muddy tread, to a finale of five switchbacks.

Then—voila—you are standing on the highest summit attainable by trail in Emigrant Wilderness or northern Yosemite. Vistas from Big Sam are even more extensive than from Leavitt Lake Pass: In addition to sweeping vistas of northern and central Yosemite, south to the Hetch Hetchy rim, an encompassing panorama of all the major peaks and lakes of the eastern Emigrant Basin is presented at our feet. Descending south from the top, a moderate set of rocky switchbacks leads past tufts of hardy alpine gold and yellow buckwheat, eventually reaching easier going in a subalpine meadow at the peak's base. A riot of wildflowers celebrates our arrival there: Alpine paintbrush (both white and green), Brewers lupine, yellow senecio, magenta Lemmons paintbrush, violet Rydbergs pentstemon and white mariposa lilies. Next, the gravelly track passes east of shallow Red Bug Lake (1.2 acres—no fish) to broad, emerald meadows

Tower Peak (right) from Pass 10640

High Emigrant Lake

framing High Emigrant Lake. Larger (14 acres), and deeper (22 feet), this lakelet affords superb flycasting for rainbow trout. Our way crosses a stream-flow dam at the outlet, then undertakes an easy ascent south, overlooking the larger expanse of Emigrant Meadow Lake, with glimpses down-canyon of Middle Emigrant Lake. Some clustered whitebark pines below the road offer the closest good camping for High Emigrant Lake. One hairpin turn leads easily up to historic Emigrant Pass, 9740 feet, the objective of Gold Rush wagon trains. Gently, the road descends from this pass to the actual low point on the Cherry Creek-Walker River divide. Here, the headwaters of West Fork West Walker River have cut a 12-foot-deep trough in the granite sand, and next to it, the unmarked Emigrant Pass Trail (Route WB-3) begins. Our way, still on road, turns south, levelly through an alpine meadow to a junction with the right-branching Brown Bear Pass Trail (Route KM-2) marked by a usually vandalized sign.

At this point, walkers bound for Horse Meadow may choose to take a cutoff down to the headwaters of Cherry Creek. Note, however, that this is a steep, hot, sandy, dusty trail, heavily eroded by pack stock—it is recommended for *down* hill traffic only. Begin by walking about 0.1 mile northwest along the Brown Bear Pass Trail, to atop a sandy rise, where we get our first glimpse of East Grizzly Peak Lake. Here, unsigned, our obvious path branches, south, going up a bit, then gently down past a small pond at the headwaters of East Fork Cherry Creek. We descend an open, willowy hillside meadow, and then reaching the canyon lip, we begin a willy-nilly downhill plunge on deeply eroded tread. A few token switchbacks do nothing to slow our precipitous descent. Almost before we know it, we reach the canyon floor and strike dirt Horse Meadow Road, in a stand of lodgepoles. This junction is unsigned but obvious.

If, however, we choose to continue on Horse Meadow Road itself, we leave behind the Brown Bear Pass Trail and wind lazily south past dry meadow and sagebrush. Long views are had here, down East Fork Cherry Creek Canyon to Sachse Monument and Wheeler Peak. An intricate array of red and brown volcanic tuffs and ash flows looms above, on Grizzly Peak, making it resemble a medieval fortress. In just a minute or two, you pass the often-unsigned, left-branching Bond Pass High Trail (KM-2). After you round a low ridge, the road descends rockily to re-enter coniferous forest. We step across a branch of Cherry Creek, then a few minutes later, turn southwest, straight downhill. Here we pass, in rapid succession, a short, steeply descending trail, then a branching jeep road, described in Route KM-2, bound southeast across Summit Meadow toward Bond Pass. Horse Meadow Road continues right, west. For a while, it is near the tumbling stream that drains Summit Meadow, but later it turns north, arcing around the head of Cherry Creek Canyon to its north side. Here, just yards beyond a seasonal creek that flows from Grizzly Meadow, the unsigned Grizzly Meadow cutoff trail described above merges with our road.

Continuing down-canyon, the dusty road drops on a moderate incline in open lodgepole forest. Eventually, the decline becomes more gentle, and we pass through a stock-drift fence. Later we pass under a large white dome—it and a nearby cliff could offer steep and sound rock climbs up to two pitches long. As our march progresses, the canyon bends more southward and we burst onto the lush upper end of Horse Meadow. At about this point, we pass a horse trail branching northeast to a large packer camp. A bit later, pass two log cabins just back in the forest fringe east of the meadow. These are snow-survey cabins administered by the USFS. Farther along, we pass a side trail (unsigned) that winds across the deep meadow turf, makes a shallow, 50'-wide ford of East Fork Cherry Creek, and reaches the two exquisitely hand-crafted buildings and adjacent snow-survey plot. Near the meadow's south end we pass through another stock-drift fence, then climb just a bit to end our route at the signed Huckleberry Trail (Route KM-1) branching right, west, up to Maxwell Lake.

(The final mile of our mining road, down to the Cherry Creek Mine, is described as part of the Huckleberry Trail, Route KM-1.)

SP-3

Koenig and Latopie Lakes

Distances
1.0 mile to Koenig Lake
2.3 miles to Latopie Lake
2.6 miles to Pacific Crest Trail

Introduction

Fishermen or hikers in search of golden trout or solitude may choose this short hike, to little-visited Koenig and Latopie lakes. Koenig Lake is a particularly good destination for overnight family backpacks—even toddlers could be ushered over the short, mostly gentle trail to reach it. Latopie Lake, although requiring steep cross-country hiking and some route-finding ability, is only an hour beyond Koenig Lake, and an exilarating destination. Linking this hike with the Pacific Crest Trail (Route SP-1) to loop southeast along the Sierra Crest back to Leavitt Lake, makes a long alpine day hike.

Trailhead

Same as the Route SP-2 trailhead.

Description

High, windswept Leavitt Lake, back-dropped by an impressive wall of brooding volcanic cliffs, is itself a justifiably popular destination for car-campers, day hikers and fishermen. Cozy stands of lodgepole and whitebark pines to the north and east afford numerous camps. Fishing in Leavitt Lake is good for rainbow and golden trout to 20 inches.

Begin the hike to Koenig Lake by walking west along a jeep road on the windblown, willow-lined north shore of Leavitt Lake. After 200 steps, turn right, uphill, on the gravelly slope, going directly away from the lakeshore. This dry hillside is in season vibrantly colored with valerian paintbrush, buckwheat, mule ears, lupine and starwort. Find the trail after ¼ mile on a tree-dotted ridge. Now ascend gently west and then north over platy gray andesite to a conspicuous ridgetop. From here, the trail drops abruptly left, west, down through a grove of pines to lush, damp meadows surrounding a large pond just east of Koenig Lake. Our path again disappears as we approach the shoreline, but it is a simple matter to wend through chest-high willows, corn lily, lupine and senecio to the isthmus separating the two lakes. Here, pleasant camps have been established in clusters of pines. Even better camps may be made in a stand of larger trees some yards to the northeast. Fishing is fair for golden trout to 10 inches.

To reach Latopie Lake, ignore the clearly visible trail that rises northward on the lake's west side, and follow the lake's outlet stream for a few hundred feet until it is possible to hop to its west bank. Just a few yards above its bank is a closed jeep road which deadends beside Koenig Lake's west shore. Follow this road left, southwest, for just a few yards to another, less used, very steep jeep track that branches right, north. Alternatively, you could follow the fisherman's trail around the southwest side of the lake to find a jeep road continuing around northward, and the jeep road branching left, steeply uphill, mentioned above. Huff and puff up this very steep track for about ⅛ mile, to its deadend, where Mother Nature and steep cobbly slopes finally won out against Yankee four-wheel-drive technology and mindless persistence. Continue uphill along a faint trail which parallels the gorge of Latopie Lake creek. Quite abruptly, level out beside a pocket meadow and skirt it to the left, still heading uphill, past a tiny pond to a step-across ford of the Latopie Lake creek. Now, with half of the ascent behind us, we climb south-southwest to an easy ridge that lets us avoid a waterfall and a clump of whitebark pines in the west. We rejoin the stream just above the fall, and from there a few minutes' easy walking leads to a pocket meadow on the north shore of Latopie Lake. A large snowfield often persists along the west shore, but a stand of low whitebark pines on the east side shelters a few cozy campsites with superb views. Fishing in Latopie Lake is fair for small golden trout.

The Pacific Crest Trail (Route SP-1) makes a fine alternative route for our return trip to Leavitt Lake. It can be reached in two ways from Latopie Lake: The most straightforward route is to simply head uphill from the outlet; the PCT will be encountered in about ⅓ mile. But for hikers who will be southbound on the PCT, the most interesting way is to climb southwest along the south edge of the large snowfield above the lake, then contour into the large, barren cirque southeast of Leavitt Peak. In midsummer this gentle basin, its rock formed from ancient clouds of volcanic ash, is awash in beautiful yellow "alpine gold" hulsea—a member of the sunflower family. The PCT is met at the saddle above the basin's head. Now follow route SP-1 southeast along the Sierra Crest to Horse Meadow road (Route SP-2). Follow the road north, steeply down to your car at Leavitt Lake.

SP-4

Sardine Falls

Distance
1.2 miles to Sardine Falls

Introduction
Sardine Falls catches many a motorist's eye while they drive east down the upper reaches of Sonora Pass Highway 108. In early summer, its thunder is also carried to the highway, while later, it offers only a thin, dancing veil of water. Both shapes are enjoyable and, only 1.1 miles from the pavement, Sardine Falls is a good objective even for daytrippers with young children.

Trailhead
Drive east over Sonora Pass, 2.5 mile from its summit (37.7 miles from the Pinecrest Y) to Sardine Meadow. Park here beside the highway, about ⅓ miles west of Highway 108's bridge over Sardine Creek. Sardine Falls can be seen in the southwest.

Description
The trail begins in small, sagebrushy Sardine Meadow as an old, closed jeep road. The trailhead is often signed, but vandals periodically destroy the marker. Start south across the meadow (ROAD CLOSED sign), quickly nearing wide, chortling Sardine Creek, home to sardine-sized brook trout. Cows graze here, so, although it's fine for the fish, you should purify the water before drinking. For just a bit, the old jeep road swings back, upstream, around a boggy patch which in late May has a gorgeous display of Western blue flag iris. Beyond it, the road makes a broad take-off-your-shoes ford of Sardine Creek, then heads southwest, easily up on sandy tread to the north of McKay Creek. Soon, the jeep road ends and a fair trail rises north for a few yards, then climbs through a patch of willows and a bit of dry hillside before swinging back near McKay Creek. Now we can see Sardine Falls, but a small patch of avalanche debris must be negotiated before we arrive at a pleasant campsite in a grove of lodgepoles at its foot. Sardine Falls is about 50 feet high, dropping

over a resistant ledge of volcanic breccia. Columbine, valerian and monkshood nod in the misty shadows at its base.

Sardine Falls in late summer

SP-5

Blue Canyon and Deadman Lake

Distances

1.7 miles to Blue Canyon Lake
2.3 miles to Deadman Lake
3.3 miles to Pacific Crest Trail

Introduction

This is a wonderful short day hike into an alpine cirque with living glaciers. As a bonus, you will likely have it to yourself. It makes a very easy overnighter, and is especially attractive if combined as a loop-trip with part of the Pacific Crest Trail just south of Sonora Pass.

Trailhead

Blue Canyon is reached by driving up Highway 108 7.2 miles beyond the Kennedy Meadow turnoff (32.9 miles from the Pinecrest Y) to the third hairpin turn above Chipmunk Flat. Park on the shoulder of this turn and walk 200 yards up the road. You will see Blue Canyon Creek entering Deadman Creek via a waterfall.

Description

Starting high, at 8820 feet, we lose our breath merely scrambling down to the banks of Deadman Creek. Here we are standing on an obvious junction between orange-pink 80-million-year-old granodiorite and crumbly brown cobbles and mud of the younger, volcanic Relief Peak Formation. Some 20 million years ago, these volcanic flows and mudslides covered over a pre-existing rolling granitic upland, but that old granitic surface is being reexposed now, as Deadman Creek erodes the weaker volcanic sediments away. Rock-hop 10–12 feet across Deadman Creek to its south bank, then scramble through waist-high willows and steeply up a rubbly slope to a small stand of lodgepole pines on the bench just west of Blue Canyon creek. Here, our pathway is much better defined. It leads southeast, past a sign indicating the Emigrant Wilderness boundary. Quickly, reach a step-across ford of the main stream in a willowy pocket of meadow. Now the path leads moderately uphill on open slopes, dotted with widely scattered seasonal wildflowers and stunted lodgepole and whitebark pines. Resembling the stern of a sinking ship, an unnamed 10320-foot peaklet, directly up-canyon, serves as our volcanic beacon. A pitch of steeper climbing, with a few switchbacks, leads to a crossing of the easternmost fork of Blue Canyon creek. Beyond, we curve across a barren slope under the aforementioned peaklet, now seen to be splashed with vibrantly colored lichens, then dip to cross back to the west side of the main stream to a small gorge. Just a moment later we recross the trickling stream and amble up over platy gray rhyolite flakes, which create an unnerving sound underfoot, much akin to a bull in a china shop!

The ascent soon ends at the pretty alpine meadow surrounding the outlet of 3½-acre Blue Canyon Lake. The lake itself is bounded by a narrow strip of meadow turf which blends into the scree slopes above. A fair campsite lies in a low thicket of whitebark pines just north of the outlet. The fishability of Blue Canyon Lake is questionable—until the Seventies, California Department of Fish & Game occasionally planted the 30-foot deep, moraine-dammed tarn with golden trout, but these were subjected to frequent, freezing winter kill. Recently, anglers of my acquaintance have returned empty-handed.

To reach Deadman Lake and the Pacific Crest Trail, an easy cross-county walk leads east from Blue Canyon Lake. Clamber uphill over broken rock and meadowy benches. Once you gain the ridge, the upper cirque, dominated by Leavitt Peak, heaves into view. Now pick an easy route south up to the desolately barren moraine which forms the cup for Deadman Lake. Too stark to be pretty, Deadman Lake is nonetheless a startling blue—owing to the finely ground glacial silt it contains, drained from the nearly buried glacieret in the cirque above it. You might think that you would die if you tried to camp here—it is certainly too rocky and inhospitable to be recommended—but Deadman Lake's name actually derives from an event on the creek above Chipmunk Flat. There, in the winter of 1860–61, young Tim Hazeltime died while attempting to reach Sonora from the Bodie mines.

Instead of retracing your steps, continue east to join the PCT by walking atop the moraine bounding Deadman Lake. Later, descend to Blue Canyon Creek's east branch, just downstream from another glacial tarn. Above it, a jumbled rock glacier—a moving ice glacier covered with debris—occupies the floor under Leavitt Peak's red cliffs. Before crossing the stream, note the prominent saddle on the eastern ridge—the Pacific Crest Trail will be found there. Now, find any of a number of easy routes up the sandy hillside to the saddle. This 500-foot ascent will show you fine specimens of yellow alpine hulsea (a sunflower) and the "krummholz" ice-pruning effect on low thickets of whitebark pine. On gaining the obvious Pacific Crest Trail, turn north to reach Highway 108 at Sonora Pass, described in reverse as part of Route SP-1.

Looking up Blue Canyon

Ch. 12: Walker Basin

WB-1

West Walker River Trail: Leavitt Meadow to Upper Piute Meadows and Tilden Lake via Tower Lake

Distances
- 3.5 miles to Roosevelt Lake
- 6.7 miles to Hidden Lake Trail
- 7.2 miles to Fremont Lake Trail
- 8.3 miles to Long Canyon
- 10.9 miles to Cascade Creek Trail
- 12.0 miles to Kirkwood Pass Trail (Upper Piute Meadow)
- 15.7 miles to Tower Lake
- 17.6 miles to Mary Lake
- 21.6 miles to Tilden Lake outlet at Tilden Lake Trail

Introduction
This relatively low-level route into the heart of the North Boundary Country is also the main thoroughfare for the entire upper Walker Basin—under study for addition to the Hoover Wilderness. The first few miles of the trail approximate the historic Emigrant Pass Wagon Trail, while the last part of the route cuts easily cross-country over a spectacular alpine pass to reach Tilden Lake, possibly the epitome of the verdant, pastoral North Boundary Country.

Trailhead
Drive east over Sonora Pass on Highway 108 to Leavitt Meadow Campground, 42.9 miles beyond the Pinecrest Y. This point is 7.1 miles west of the Highway 395 junction. Park in the campground, or at a hiker's parking area just 0.1 mile west.

Description
The West Walker River Trail leaves Leavitt Meadow Campground and drops east a few yards to bridge the wide West Walker River under a typical east-slope volcanic-soil forest association: robust, widely spaced Jeffrey pines, squat junipers, streamside Fremont's cottonwoods, and a sagebrush understory. East of the river, our well-trod path climbs briefly east, then traverses briefly south to a west-dropping use-trail. From this junction we climb east momentarily to a low ridge and, 0.3 mile from our trailhead, reach an important signed junction. From it an older trail (Route WB-2) to Roosevelt Lake via Secret Lake continues east before climbing south.

We take the newer trail, which swings south and quickly drops to a sunny, sagebrush-dotted bench on the east side of giant Leavitt Meadow. It stays along this side for 1.4 miles, keeping well above wide meanders of the West Walker River. Across it, one may hear the shouts of Marine mountain troops practicing rock-climbing techniques on a cliff, near Leavitt Meadow Store. Later, pass the horse trail from Leavitt Pack Station (not a recommended route, since it involves a deep, dangerous river-wade). Upon leaving Leavitt Meadow, you begin to climb, and in several minutes reach a junction with another

Leavitt Meadow trail on the right, then in several minutes top out at a diminutive pond. Immediately beyond it we encounter a long, slender pond, with a trail junction nearby. Route WB-2, which passes Secret Lake, descends southwest to this junction. Ahead we traverse about 130 yards to a junction with the last Leavitt Meadow trail—the route one would take if he were to follow the meadow's westside road.

We continue south, going through a gulch between granite bluffs. This easy walk leads quickly to the north shore of Roosevelt Lake, which, with its southern twin, Lane Lake, is usually overcrowded but makes a good lunch stop. Both of these small shallow lakes harbor small brook trout and crayfish, and some lunker rainbow trout, to 24 inches, as well as a teeming variety of insect and attendant bird life. Lane and Roosevelt lakes are separated by a broad isthmus of wind-transported sand, possibly of glacial origin, and it is possible that wind, as well as mineral-rich lake-bottom springs, bring the nutrients to support this unusual abundance of life. Here, even some beaver-felled lakeside logs are covered with plants—a verdure more commonly seen in the wet Cascades.

The West Walker trail passes some adequate camps on the isthmus between Roosevelt and Lane lakes, then climbs gently above the latter, returning soon to camps at its southern outlet. Here a recently constructed trail branches from the old, mapped route, which can still be followed southwest down to the West Walker to large, secluded campsites. The new trail climbs, via switchbacks, southeast up volcanic tuffs to a rising mile-long traverse through open aspen groves and sage flats on a bench east of the West Walker River. Later, we rejoin the old riverbank route and drop to a lodgepole-and-aspen grove that borders the West Walker's trench. Here, under a 400-foot bluff of solidified volcanic mud flow, we could share shaded campsites with tinkling-belled cattle that summer throughout the upper Walker basin in accordance with the Forest Service's Mutiple-Use policy.

We quickly leave this cooler haven to swing southeast across a side stream, then steeply attack an eroded trail that climbs over a chaparraled spur. Once across this obstacle, which gives our first up-canyon views of Forsyth Peak, we descend to the signed Red Top Lake Trail.

Although they lie only 10–20 minutes from the main West Walker River Trail, Red Top and Hidden Lakes are surprisingly little visited. They make a good destination for a spring warm-up day trip, or the first night out on longer excursions. To reach them, cross the West Walker River via a fallen tree, then climb steeply up a sandy hillside to the west. This 100-foot climb leads to a gap with a narrow view down a brushy ravine to a drowned forest of sickly lodgepole pines that rim Red Top Lake. Our path fades as it drops to near the east shore, then rounds south to some poor campsites in dense forest. To reach even smaller, shallower and less-appealing Hidden Lake, continue around the west shore, then up along a faint use-trail to a saddle with some large Jeffrey pines. Hidden Lake's dry camp is just a short walk farther west.

Returning to the main West Walker River Trail, resume a pleasant streamside stroll south past good camps. After ¼ mile, the West Walker River's course becomes a 15-foot deep gorge through jointed granodiorite, and we follow it closely on some dynamited tread. Just beyond this gorge, the old trail fords the river, but most hikers will prefer to stay on the new trail on the east bank for another ½ mile, until a signed junction points back—north—across the river via an easy, sandy ford.

On the far bank we find campsites, the westbank West Walker River Trail (Route WB-5) and the signed Fremont Lake Trail (Route WB-3) which climbs steeply northwest ¾ mile in deep sand to Fremont Lake, the best bet for our first night's camp. Fremont Lake lay directly on the route of the pioneers' Sonora Trail route to the gold fields. In fact, emigrants once had to lower the outlet level of this good-sized lake so that their wagons could pass around its lodge-

The West Walker River

pole-and-juniper-lined western shore! Heavily used camps greet us at Fremont Lake's south end. Fishing for large brookies and rainbows is fair.

The next morning, return to the West Walker River, regain the east-bank trail, southbound, and climb moderately up a wooded gully and over a col to Long Canyon, where Route WB-6 leads southeast 4 miles up to Beartrap Lake. Leap Long Canyon's creek, then continue southward through a forested groove to a stock fence and a small pond which herald Lower Piute Meadow. Keeping well back in the dry eastern fringe of lodgepole forest, our way turns south along

that sandy grassland, then undulates over small ridges to the signed Long Lakes Trail (Route WB-5) which branches west across a small, moist meadow. After a few more minutes of easy walking, we pass the Cascade Creek Trail (Route WB-4) and continue up-canyon in pleasant lodgepole forest.

After a mile of usually easy climbing, we level off at a well-signed junction at the north end of Upper Piute Meadow. Here the good Kirkwood Pass Trail (Route WB-7) continues ahead, along the meadow-side.

Our route, the well-signed Tower Lake Trail, branches right, south, momentarily reaching a broad, deep horse-ford of West

Walker River. A log crossing is just downstream. Now on the west bank, walk past USFS' "Piute Cabin"—a patrol cabin built during the Great Depression, and a beautiful example of log architecture. Continue past a corral and through a stock gate, then out into stunningly beautiful Upper Piute Meadow. Graceful, sweeping Hawksbeak Peak dominates the southern horizon. Underfoot, shooting-stars, dandelions and buttercups color the springy turf.

Walk south around the meadow's perimeter, following on-again, off-again tread. About halfway along its length, blazes mark a resumption of good trail, angling slightly uphill into dry lodgepole forest. This leads quickly to a small, wetter meadow, then to a nice packer camp on the verge of lovely Rainbow Meadow.

Now our path turns uphill, into Tower Canyon. Initially, the way is moderate, under heavy forest cover. Above, steep, short, rocky switchbacks lead onto sunny slopes between two metasedimentary *roches moutonees* that guard the canyon mouth. Beyond, the trail levels out and finds a log crossing of Tower Canyon creek in a charming forest of mixed conifers. A nice camp here is the last good one before exposed, rocky sites in the environs of Tower Lake. Now, with the impressive "Watchtower" spire as our beacon, trace the steep trail up to a vest-pocket willowy meadow at the canyon's head. Here the route leaps back to the west side of the main stream and proceeds more-or-less directly uphill to the west, close by the falling, tumbling outlet stream of Tower Lake. The rocky way is punctuated by only a few half-hearted switchbacks—its steepness gives us plenty of excuses to pause and gaze at the graceful Watchtower's cliffs or beyond it to equally imposing Hawksbeak Peak. Eventually, we arrive at the rocky outlet of 9570' Tower Lake, which is often ice-bound until mid-season. The lake's rocky shore yields acceptable camping only in a stand of whitebark pines beside the outlet—better sites may be found in small stands of trees beside a satellite tarn above the north shore. Tower Lake supports a small population of beautiful golden trout.

Our route from here is cross country. From the lake's south shore we climb south nearly 600 feet up to a conspicuous saddle.

Upper Piute Meadow, Hawksbeak Peak, Ehrnbeck Peak

From the 10,150-foot saddle between Saurian Crest and Tower Peak we can gaze southwest down the canyon of Tilden Creek, over barren, windswept Mary Lake to long, forest-girded Tilden Lake and its southern guardian dome, Chittenden Peak. Leaving this austere gap, we scramble easily down to the clustered whitebark pines that afford the best camps above the inlet of Mary Lake, which is stocked with beautiful golden trout. Follow Mary Lake's rocky northwest shore to reach the outlet, then descend moderately through frost-shattered hummocks and a velvety alpine fell-field of Brewer's reed-grass, rice-grass, and red heather to about 9420 feet, about ¼ mile below the outlet, where a poor, ducked trail begins to define itself. This use-trail leads southwest, always quite near the west bank of raucous, dancing Tilden Creek, down through a step-ladder of delightful meadows and subalpine conifers. Once, at 9120 feet, Tilden Creek makes a small waterfall, and wildflowers explode onto the moist slopes, overlooked on the east by mitre-capped Craig and Snow peaks. A long hour below Mary Lake, we traverse the final lumpy meadow to the head of lovely Tilden Lake.

The trail follows the west shore of 2-mile-long Tilden Lake, which is conspicuously better clothed in lodgepole pines than the east side, which is slabby and lacking soil. Almost halfway down this narrow gem, we find a sandbar which offers the best swimming beach for miles around. Farther on, our lakeside path bends southwest and enters open subalpine meadows near the base of black-streaked Chittenden Peak. This summit, named for an early Yosemite boundary commissioner, is easily climbed and provides the best overlook of Jack Main Canyon. Rounding south of Chittenden Peak, we find some good camps under a lodgepole canopy, then reach the end of Tilden Lake's long outlet lagoon. Here we boulder-hop south to find well-used Tilden Lake Trail (Route YP-9). Even if you don't plan to camp at Tilden Lake, you may want to walk ¾ mile east on this trail for storybook views up-canyon, where Tilden Lake mirrors the cockscombed Saurian Crest. Excellent camps are also found here, near emerald shoreline meadows. Bears and inquisitive deer are seasonally a nuisance, so plan your camp accordingly.

Mary Lake

WB-2

Leavitt Meadow High Trail, To Millie Lake, Secret Lake, and Poore Lake

Distances

1.0 miles to Millie Lake
2.6 miles to Secret Lake
3.8 miles to Poore Lake
3.6 miles to Roosevelt Lake

Introduction

A more scenic alternative to the new Leavitt Meadow Trail, this short path allows visits to three distinctly different lakes. It is short enough and varied enough to serve as a good first-time backpack with children, in combination with the new Leavitt Meadow Trail, for a loop trip to Roosevelt and Lane Lakes. It's sunny, so it's snow-free early. Use it as an inspirational early-season warm-up hike.

Trailhead

Same as the Route WB-1 trailhead.

Description

The West Walker River Trail leaves Leavitt Meadow Campground and drops east a few yards to bridge the wide West Walker River under a typical east-slope volcanic-soil forest association: robust, widely spaced Jeffrey pines, squat junipers, streamside Fremont's cottonwoods, and a sagebrush understory. East of the river, our well-trod path ascends moderately south, then east, and soon, 0.3 mile from the trailhead, we depart from the West Walker River Trail (Route WB-1). Beyond the junction a short ascent reaches a meadow fragrant with blue iris, where a north-branching trail strikes off for Millie Lake and a poor use-trail leads southwest down to the West Walker River Trail.

To reach small, grassy Millie Lake (a fair early-season picnic destination), follow the unsigned trail, a faint rut in the knee-high iris. Climb briefly north out onto a hillside of mountain mahogany, from where Millie Lake comes into view below, in a sagebrush-lined bowl, with Pickel Meadow beyond. Our trail drops moderately on the gravelly-dusty brown volcanic hillside, then peters out in grasses just south of the shallow lake. Look for an unusual plant—water smartweed, with pink flowers—in the shallows.

Returning to the Secret Lake-Roosevelt Lake Trail, we begin a hot, exposed, sometimes steep climb south along the axis of a ridge where the rock is friable, tan-gray welded tuff. This climb affords excellent panoramas north over huge Pickel Meadow and the Marine Corps' Mountain Warfare Training Center to the chalk-white Sweetwater Mountains. Beside the trail we enjoy sunny-yellow mule ears, shrubby rabbitbrush and treelike mountain mahogany, easily recognized by its long, silken seed plumes.

Eventually our route climbs above the 7600-foot level and begins to undulate gently on the dry ridgetop. Here, vistas open up to the south, up the broad, forested trough of the West Walker River to ragged Tower and Forsyth peaks. Below, the river cuts lazy loops through patchy, willow-dotted Leavitt Meadow, where pack horses graze near the ruts of pioneer 49er wagon trains, still visible in the meadow turf. After a mile of ridge walking, the trail descends to an overlook for glimpsing sagebrush-rimmed Poore Lake in the east, then quickly arrives beside the shaded north-shore camping area at Secret Lake. Tall rushes, willows and wild roses rim the rock shoreline of this small, heavily used lake, and tall Jeffrey pines and junipers frame vistas southeast across it to Peak 10006, on a pastel-banded volcanic ridge. Only the most rabid anglers will want to pursue Secret Lake's harried population of small brook trout, but everyone should try his luck with a length of string and a bit of salami for the small crayfish that abound in the algae-bottomed shoreline waters.

Two trails continue south from Secret Lake; the better one branches west from the northwest shore and leads up and over a shoulder, then down to the signed Poore Lake Trail, branching east. The second path scrambles along Secret Lake's west side to another group of camps before ascending briefly south for just a moment in a sandy ravine to strike the Poore Lake Trail beside a tiny mosquito pond.

Via either route, the Poore Lake Trail can be followed for a few dusty minutes steeply down to the southern tip of mile-long Poore Lake. If you choose to stay here, you'll likely have the spot to yourselves—the desertlike shoreline and scattered juniper and Jeffrey pine trees do not create the most idyllic campsites.

From the Poore Lake-Secret Lake trail junction, it is just a minute's walk down to where our route joins the signed Walker River Trail (Route WB-1). To reach Roosevelt Lake, we keep south, going through a gulch between granite bluffs. This easy walk leads quickly to the north shore of Roosevelt Lake, which, with its southern twin, Lane Lake, is usually overcrowded but makes a good lunch stop. Both of these small, shallow lakes harbor brook trout, huge rainbows, and crayfish, as well as a teeming variety of insect and attendant bird life. Lane and Roosevelt lakes are separated by a broad isthmus of wind-transported sand, possibly of glacial origin, and it is possible that wind, as well as mineral-rich lake-bottom springs, bring nutrients to support this unusual abundance of life.

WB-3

Emigrant Pass Trail: Fremont Lake, Long Lakes, Chain of Lakes, Walker Meadows

Distances

2.1 miles to Fremont Lake
3.4 miles to Chain of Lakes
6.0 miles to south Long Lake at West Fork West Walker River

Introduction

Fremont Lake is probably the number-one destination for visitors to the Walker Basin. Historically, it was an important resting point on the Emigrant Pass Wagon Trail, which this route generally follows, up to that historic crossing of the Sierra Crest. Imagine, as you walk, the incredible difficulties that must have been encountered 150 years ago, negotiating this trail via oxen-drawn wooden wagons!

Trailhead

Same as the Route WB-1 trailhead.

Description

Follow Route WB-1, the West Walker River Trail, 7.2 miles up to the first of two signed junctions with the Fremont Lake Trail. Here we branch right, west, from the main trail just above a narrow, joint-controlled river slot between broken, sunny cliffs. To cross the West Walker River here, one can choose, depending upon your mode of transportation, between a 40-foot-wide, sometimes waist-deep horse-ford and a multi-log bridge. Once on the west bank, turn south past a few pleasant camps, quickly reaching the signed Fremont Lake Trail, just before the inobviously-branching west-side West Walker River Trail (Route WB-5) and a wide river ford which connects back to the main Piute Meadow Trail. We branch right again and immediately climb west very steeply up a hot, sandy trail, showing heavy erosion by stock. Picturesque junipers and fragrant sagebrush line the route. Soon enough, the path levels mercifully to find a signed junction with the Fremont Lake Spur Trail, at a narrow gap. The signed Chain of Lakes Trail can here be followed around the south side of a viewful, rocky divide to reconnect with the Fremont Lake Spur. If you want to camp at Fremont Lake, drop down the spur to find adequate camps on the rocky southeast shore, or continue along the trail to a dank lodgepole grove on the south end, with larger campsites. Rimmed by broken granite and a fringe of gray, drowned pines, Fremont Lake is far from the most beautiful lake in the Walker Basin, but it is the largest and it does afford fair angling for rainbow and brook trout to twelve inches.

To regain the Chain of Lakes Trail without retracing your steps, continue due south from Fremont Lake via a hideously steep, but thankfully short, track up a gully to the rim of the lake basin. This route was almost certainly the one used by 49ers to winch their wagons up from Fremont Lake—imagine the logistics involved! Once atop the ridge follow the wagon route southwest up to a low divide. Beyond it, drop easily to the northernmost of the Chain of Lakes—shallow and grassy—and a signed junction with a little-used lateral west to Walker Meadows. That path closely follows the probable emigrant wagon route to reach the Walker Meadows Trail, described below.

The Chain of Lakes Trail here turns south, follows a log across the lakes' small stream, and winds above and beside the three largest lakelets in quick succession. A few fair camps are found, the best alongside the largest, most southern lake. Fairly level going in open forest next finds a linear, unnamed lakelet, which we swing east around to reach Lower Long Lake. This pleasant, multi-bayed expanse does not have the developed campsites—or the traffic—of Upper Long Lake, which is found just a few minutes farther on. Our path leads to its swampy west end, crosses the rarely-flowing outlet, and hops up the far bank to strike the signed Long Lake Cutoff Trail (Route WB-5). Here we jog east for just a minute to an important 4-way trail junction with the Long Lake Cutoff and the Pacific Crest Trail, which, southward, climbs up the West Fork West Walker River, and northward crosses a steel bridge to a large campsite on the Walker's west side.

The fourth trail, the old PCT-Kennedy Canyon route via Walker Meadows, is a good late-season choice for a detour to more-secluded camping. It curves north around a swampy lakelet, passing a riverside packer camp, then rockily parallels the river for a few minutes. Abruptly, the trail veers west through a thicket of willows and monkshood to a shallow wade, usually about 20 feet wide, of West Fork West Walker River. Across it, we quickly enter one of the largest of the Walker Meadows, where the trail is usually almost impassably marshy (not to mention, mosquitoey) in all but late summer. North of the meadow, the trail returns to open forest and drops across the sandy wash of seasonally flowing Dry Creek. Beyond it, trail peters out in another meadow. Trail tread resumes very close to the river some 250 gravelly yards later. Just north of tread's resumption the Fremont Lake/Chain of Lakes lateral trail branches right, southeast, to ford the river. Our path continues north to leave the meadow and, a bit later, we pass through a barbed-wire drift-fence gate, then traverse a north-trending linear meadow. Beyond it, we ignore a short, right-branching spur trail, instead continuing north to a hop-across ford of Kennedy Canyon Creek, here marked by an aging PCT post (in the early 70's, this was the temporary PCT route). Proceeding north, the path becomes increasingly vague, and passes the almost impossible-to-find intersection with the decrepit old Kennedy Canyon Trail. A few minutes later the path fades out in a cow pasture.

Retracing our steps to Upper Long Lake and the PCT, we continue on toward historic Emigrant Pass by turning southwest, up along the West Walker River, momentarily congruent with the Pacific Crest Trail. Our route diverges in less than ¼ mile from a well-signed junction—the PCT climbs left, while we stay low, on the right-hand branch. Probably, wagon trains that traversed this route used the easier northwest bank. Our trail winds along the southeast river-side, alternating between open granitic benches and pockets of meadowy, damp forest. Eventually, we cross the river by a 20-foot-wide bouldery ford to its western bank. Now with a smattering of mountain hemlocks and western white pines added to the open lodgepole canopy, the trail arcs under the steep, broken face of granitoid Peak 10010. Once in the sunnier environs south of that peak, we find the signed Cinko Lake Trail (Route WB-4) branching south. A bit later, the path veers away from the stream to clamber up a steep hillside on cobbly, poorly switchbacked tread. Soon enough, however, the way becomes a level traverse on a volcanic hillside bench. Ruddy outcrops of volcanic breccia loom above; alongside the path, sagebrush, aster, snowberry and green gentian lend color.

Farther on, the trail takes on a more subalpine flavor as it climbs up onto open benches dotted with clusters of whitebark pines. The twin castellated summits of Grizzly Peak now heave into view—the expanses of white, resembling snowfields, that are draped on Grizzly Peak's lower northern slopes are actually light-colored outcrops of fine volcanic ash, probably deposited as mud flows from an ancient volcano. Further ascent leads to the northeast edge of a large meadow, just below Emigrant Pass' low saddle. Here, trail tread ends in the thickly matted meadow grasses. No problem—proceed across the meadow, keeping to the north of West Fork West Walker River's shallow head waters. At the far southwest

end of the meadow, the river emerges from a red gorge of highly altered sands. Just south of that gorge, a steep trail proceeds directly up the hillside. Follow it up a short distance to a sandy saddle with a poor camp in a cluster of whitebark pines. A minute beyond, our route ends, unsigned, at a horseshoe bend in the Leavitt Lake-Horse Meadow Road (Route SP-2) just a bit south of historic Emigrant Pass.

Grizzly Peak and Grizzly Lake are both very worthwhile side trips from the Emigrant Pass environs. To get to Grizzly Lake, climb east through hillside meadows from the meadow below Emigrant Pass, then traverse a very sandy bench to the cirque where Grizzly Lake lies, nestled between two granitic bluffs. Grizzly Lake is too shallow to support fish, but it makes a delightful, isolated basecamp. Grizzly Peak is an easy, if somewhat loose, scramble from Grizzly Lake. Climb up to its eastern ridge, over a hillside of deeply weathered granitic sands. The lower part of the mountain is firmly packed light-gray volcanic ash. Its summit cap is a collection of gargoyle-like pinnacles composed of red-brown welded cobbles.

WB-4

Cascade Creek Trail and Cinko Lake Cutoff

Distances
1.8 miles to Pacific Crest Trail
3.8 miles to Cinko Lake
4.5 miles to Emigrant Pass Trail

Introduction
    The short lateral up Cascade Creek from the West Walker Trail is the main route into Yosemite from Leavitt Meadow. It also connects to an old section of Pacific Crest Trail that reaches Cinko Lake. Well off the beaten track, sparkling Cinko Lake is the premier base for explorations of the Emigrant Pass country.

Trailhead
    Same as Route WB-1 trailhead.

Description
    Follow the West Walker River Trail (WB-1) 10.9 miles to a well-signed junction in a damp, dark riverside stand of lodgepole pines above Lower Piute Meadow. Here our way angles right, southwest, to quickly find the West Walker River's banks. Cross via any of a number of fallen trees. Look for the Cascade Creek Trail angling up and left, on the uphill side of a sloping, boggy meadow. Soon, the trail is switchbacking aggressively under a shady mix of Hudsonian-zone conifers. About one third of the way up, take a break to view pretty Cascade Falls—a short, signed spur leads to its brink. Beyond, the

way becomes gentler for a bit, then makes a final very steep 400-foot climb to gain the Walker Canyon rim. After traversing south for a bit, we eventually find the signed Pacific Crest Trail (Route SP-1) bound south for Dorothy Lake Pass.

We follow the PCT north for the next leg of our journey, proceeding levelly to a gap where the duff-treaded path winds north of two tiny tarns. Beyond, an easy descent leads to a rickety log-bridge over an unnamed stream. On it west bank we find the Cinko Lake Trail, diverging left, southwest, up from the Pacific Crest Trail (Route SP-1).

Now on rockier terrain, including meta-sedimentary rocks, we amble over a number of rocky ridgelets, presently encountering

quaintly signed BILL'S LAKE—a small tarn that is *someone's* favorite spot! Now head more westward, coming back beside the stream momentarily before making a final short ascent to lovely Cinko Lake. As you traverse along the eastern shore, look for a number of fine campsites, nestled in hem-lock-shaded crannies between the lake's small bays. A large packer camp is found just before we drop from the lake's outlet. An easy descent swings near a swampy pond, beyond which we step across the West Fork West Walker River—here only a small stream. Just a minute up the north bank, in a dry volcanic flat dotted with sagebrush, find the Emigrant Pass Trail (Route WB-3).

WB-5
West-Side Walker River Trail and Long Lake Cutoff

Distances
3.4 miles to Long Lake cutoff
5.3 miles to south Long Lake

Introduction
The quiet path along the west side of the West Walker River can be a pleasant alterna-tive to the much more frequented, horse-dusty main trail on the east side. Hikers should be cautioned, however, that the path is unmaintained and is, in early summer, muddier going, with many more mosquitos than on the main trail. The short, pleasant Long Lake cutoff is the "fast track" between the West Fork and main West Walker basins.

Trailhead
Same as the Route WB-1 trailhead.

Description
The start of this route is hard to find. It begins just 100 feet south of the signed Fremont Lake Trail (Route WB-3) on the west side of the West Walker River, some 7.2 miles from Leavitt Meadow Campground. Walk back into the lodgepole grove from the horse ford, and look west through a thicket of fallen trees for blazes that show the route. After just a minute, the trail becomes quite

obvious, close beside the river's edge. Quickly, the way steepens a bit to match the now-cascading stream, then climbs well above the water where it transforms into an impressive cataract. Abruptly, we re-enter forest, and begin a mile-long traverse in dark, damp lodgepole forest. Keep a sharp eye out for blazes. Beyond a log-crossing of a creek that drains the region east of Cinko Lake, the terrain becomes drier, and we once again near some cool, green bends of the West Walker River. Minutes later, we step out onto Lower Piute Meadow, with its profusion of wildflowers and, alas, summer-ranging cattle. Our often-faint trail keeps mostly back from the meadow's edge, meeting the apex of each lazy meander of the Walker River—each deep pool an invitation to fish or swim. Beyond Lower Piute Meadows, the sandy path ascends easily in dry forest. Presently, we strike an unsigned but obvious junction with the Long Lakes Cutoff Trail, which climbs back to the northwest. If we wanted, instead, to regain the main West Walker Trail to Upper Piute Meadows, we would keep left, southeast, to find a broad, waist-deep (in

The West Walker River

early season) horse ford of West Walker River. A signed junction with the main West Walker Trail (Route WB-1) lies on the east bank.

If, however, Long Lakes are one's goal, choose the Long Lakes Cutoff, which climbs right, making some moderate switchbacks up the canyon wall. Eventually, gain a tiny gap, beyond which the path winds levelly past a trio of yellow lily-dotted ponds. The way now bends west, crosses a fair-sized stream, then ascends easily to the soggy southeast end of cigar-shaped Upper Long Lake. We undu-

late around its pleasant southern shore, passing a few large campsites and the signed Chain of Lakes Trail (Route WB-3). A minute past the lake's northwest end, we find a 4-way trail junction beside a swampy pond. From here the PCT (Route SP-1) heads upstream along the raucous West Fork West Walker River, and also west, across that stream via a steel bridge. The little-used Walker Meadows Trail (Route WB-3) branches north, down along the West Fork to some nearby horse-packer camps.

WB-6

Long Canyon Trail to Beartrap Lake

Distances
4.4 miles to Beartrap Lake
6.7 miles to Kirkwood Pass

Introduction

One of the best-kept secrets of the West Walker Country, tiny, alpine-meadowed, fragile Beartrap Lake is protected by a long, steep, hard-to-follow trail, now made all the more difficult by recent avalanches which have ravaged upper Long Canyon. It is a destination only for expert outdoorsmen.

Trailhead

Same as the Route WB-1 trailhead.

Description

The Long Canyon Trail leaves the main West Walker Trail (Route WB-1) from a well-signed junction just north of the latter trail's ford of Long Canyon creek, some 8.3 miles above Leavitt Meadow. Not inclined to waste time, the route undertakes the first leg of its 2000-foot ascent via an unabashedly steep, rocky grade—a style of travel which will soon become familiar. Some small switchbacks do little to ease the chore. The hot, sunny hillside, with poor shade provided by fibrous-barked junipers, pungent Jeffrey pines and trailside coffeeberry shrubs, also affords little comfort. Later, the way becomes steeper still, but thankfully is more shaded by lodgepoles. (Adding insult to injury, the climb is waterless—the cascades of Long Canyon creek are inaccessible to us, deep in the rocky gorge below.) Eventually almost 800 feet above our start, the gradient abates, and we come close enough to burbling Long Canyon creek to find a much-deserved drink. The next 2 miles are much easier: make a steady ascent, never more than a few yards from the meadow-fringed streamside. Later, the path becomes indistinct as we walk into a larger meadow, the upper end strewn with broken and uprooted trees, swept down in a 1986 avalanche. Here, trail tread crosses the narrow creek to its southwest bank. For almost the next mile, the trail (as of 1988) is very difficult to follow. A huge avalanche swept across and down-canyon above 9200', cutting a gigantic swath through a grove of pines and hemlocks. Immense trees were tossed like jackstraws across the old trail. To replace the lost trail, blazed trees now mark a passable but indistinct and virtually treadless route steeply up along the cool, deeply shaded west canyon wall. Once above about 9600', the old trail is again passable, winding through progressively thinning stands of hemlock and lodgepole and whitebark pines to the boggy, pond-dotted meadows below the outlet of Beartrap Lake. Shallow and subalpine, Beartrap Lake is almost entirely fringed by a springy turf of sedges, which are rapidly encroaching upon the lake's waters.

To reach Kirkwood Pass or Buckeye Canyon from Beartrap Lake, simply walk southeast up over rolling willow-dotted meadows to the broad saddle (10100') between Long Canyon and Buckeye creeks. To gain the head of Buckeye Canyon, one may now simply amble down the meadowy, trailless but obvious route into the canyon. About halfway down, enter dense timber. Finally, find the Buckeye Canyon Trail near the north bank of Buckeye Creek.

A more direct route to Kirkwood Pass, which does not entail such elevation gain and loss as dropping into Buckeye Canyon, involves making a traversing ascent south from the saddle above Beartrap Lake. Amble up across open fell fields, passing a tarn to gain a low ridge. This leads to granite ramps which give access to a talus-heaped terminal moraine under the northeast cliffs of Peak 10790. Continue levelly south now, around the brow of the ridge. Here Kirkwood Pass and Hawksbeak Peak heave into view. Follow easy ramps down to the pass' low point and a gorgeous lakelet, a dramatic foreground for Tower Peak. The Kirkwood Pass Trail (Route WB-7) is found in the next major notch south of this tarn.

WB-7

Kirkwood Pass Trail; Kirkwood Lake

Distances
1.6 miles to Rainbow Meadow
4.3 miles to Kirkwood Pass
5.6 miles to Kirkwood Lake

Introduction
This scenic trail reaches a delightful windswept vista atop 9960-foot Kirkwood Pass, but its greatest value comes from the other routes that branch from it—up Rainbow Canyon to wilderness Northern Yosemite, to Kirkwood or Beartrap Lake, or down Buckeye Canyon and then over Buckeye Pass to meet the Robinson Creek Trail (Route YP-1) in Upper Kerrick Meadow.

Trailhead
Same as the Route WB-1 trailhead.

Introduction
From the signed trail junction with West Walker River Trail WB-1, just inside a stock-drift fence at the north end of Upper Piute Meadows, the Kirkwood Pass Trail proceeds levelly southeast. In just a moment, a fringe of small lodgepole pines parts, giving a thrilling vista south to the rocky spires of Hawksbeak Peak and Ehrnbeck Peak, standing above immense, lush Upper Piute Meadows—the emerald in the crown of the West Walker basin. Our path skirts the pasture's eastern verge on level tread which passes numerous meanders in the deep river bed. Near the meadows' south end, the trail ascends slightly through muddy hillside meadow littered with coniferous debris from a 1986 avalanche. Rerouted trail takes us up over a small knob, then down to cross pretty, but similarly avalanche-swept, Rainbow Meadow. Here, the airy spires and buttresses of 11755-foot Tower Peak, monarch of the North Boundary Country, can be seen, framed by two *roches moutonees* that guard the entrance to Tower Canyon. Across Rainbow Meadow, pass a pair of nice camps which mark cross-country routes WB-8 and WB-9 into Rainbow Canyon. Now turn mod-erately uphill—the climb to Kirkwood Pass has begun. Often indistinct or muddy, and occasionally steep, our route stays within earshot of tumbling Kirkwood Creek, usually under open shade of lodgepoles, western white pines and hemlocks. As we pass below the waterfall that drains Kirkwood Lake, a switchback heralds a steeper final ascent. This ends just beyond another switchback, some 600 feet higher, atop Kirkwood Pass— 9960'—a barren, windswept, granitic notch. Extremely scenic (but still windy) camping may be had, at least until late season, at the small lakelet in the divide's actual low point, just a few minutes' walk to the north.

Kirkwood Pass is the jumping-off point for three other fine cross-country destinations. The traverse north to Beartrap Lake and Long Canyon is described in reverse as part of Route WB-6. South from Kirkwood Pass, a 400-foot ascent past rocky steps, hanging meadows and clusters of whitebark pines leads to a series of deep, joint-controlled notches weathered from the orange granitic bedrock. These in turn lead up to an unusual sandy saddle at the head of Thompson Canyon. Follow it south, through delightful subalpine fells, to join the Thompson Canyon cross-country route, WB-9. From atop the saddle, one could alternatively ascend just a bit southwest over a rounded, sand-and-krumholz-topped ridge to find alpine Kirkwood Lake. Sitting in a rocky morainal bowl under the spectacular north face of aptly named Hawksbeak Peak, Kirkwood Lake affords remote, windy camping in small groves of whitebark pines beside its outlet. Hawksbeak Peak itself is easily reached, via a sandy use-trail on its north-east ridge, to gain a short final scramble up the summit rocks.

WB-8

Stubblefield Canyon (Cross Country)

Distances

2.8 miles to Upper Rainbow Canyon
4.1 miles to lakelet under Ehrnbeck Peak
11.9 miles to Pacific Crest Trail at confluence of Thompson Canyon

Introduction

Mile upon mile of unspoiled subalpine meadows and absolute solitude are the rewards for any hiker who ventures into Stubblefield Canyon. Wide-open countryside and easy navigation make this route a good choice for experienced hikers who are new to cross-country travel, just as it afforded an easy avenue for 19th century sheepherders.

Trailhead

Same as the Route WB-1 trailhead.

Description

The route begins at Rainbow Meadow on the Kirkwood Pass Trail (Route WB-7). At a pair of packer's campsites above the meadow's southeast side, contour south, away from the trail to a careful rock-hop crossing of seasonally rowdy Kirkwood Creek. Now under the watchful gaze of a prominent *roche moutonee*, ascend easily south along the east bank of a larger stream that drains the valley—known as Rainbow Canyon to local horsepackers—between Hawksbeak and Tower peaks. Dense stands of lodgepole and western white pines shade the way, which presently steepens to gain a morainal bench at about 8900 feet. A half-mile later, following an on-again, off-again

Tower Peak and upper Stubblefield Canyon (aerial view)

use-trail, we emerge in the first of a lovely string of tree-fringed meadows through which Rainbow Canyon's creek cuts deep, lazy meanders. Flanking this pastoral scenery, Hawksbeak Peak throws up its stunning western wall—a climber's dream—three airy orange cliffs cleaved by innumerable vertical cracks. On our right, Tower Peak's summit battlements are almost incandescent in an evening's alpenglow. And a fine spot to spend an evening this is—as attested to by at least two fine horsemen's camps beside the meadow edge. The next morning, continue easily up the main valley, possibly hopping the stream once or twice to ease your travel. A delightfully easy climb over hillside meadows, around blocks of morainal granite, and through patches of knee-high willows gradually curves southeast, under Hawksbeak Peak's breathtaking precipice. Just above 9600 feet, and directly under the cliffs, we find a beautiful triad of glacial tarns, nestled on a meadowy bench. Trees scattered hereabouts would afford spectacular campsites for backcountry rock climbers.

These lakelets mark a critical branching point for travelers bound for Stubblefield Canyon. While one easy way to Thompson Canyon (see Route WB-9) continues southeast up to a windy pass at the head of Rainbow Canyon, the way to Stubblefield Canyon from here climbs southwest, away from the stream, up the north slopes of Ehrnbeck Peak. Initially, clamber up a hillside of broken rock, with scattered patches of thigh-tall vernacular sedge, rosy spiraea, willows and a few whitebark pines. Soon, the cliffy summit of Ehrnbeck Peak heaves into view, and we angle up, below and around it to the southwest, over slopes of glacial moraine and through bands of ice-trimmed whitebark-pine thickets. Over-shoulder views of Hawksbeak Peak give it a passable resemblance to Mt. Whitney. Above 10200 feet, probably crossing a snow patch or two, we contour almost levelly southwest to a 10340-foot pass at the head of Stubblefield Canyon. Ehrnbeck Peak (11240') can be easily reached from this saddle, via a sandy walk up to the northern summit, then a brief scramble

(class 3) south to the top. Views encompass almost all of Yosemite Park and Emigrant Wilderness.

Back at the pass, reshoulder your pack and drop easily south along a sandy slope to a small, beautiful lake cupped in a narrow cirque. A few clumps of low whitebark pines here offer a windy, cold camp, but the sunrise view of Tower Peak would be well worth an icy night.

Now begins a long, thoroughly delightful trailless romp down the length of Stubblefield Canyon. Probably named for an early illegal sheepman who herded his flocks in this area around the turn of the century, Stubblefield Canyon is flanked by bare granite peaks that memorialize the men whose duty it was to keep the shepherd *out* of Yosemite Park—Ehrnbeck, Wells, Craig, Price, Forsyth and Keyes peaks, as well as Macomb Ridge, are all named for U.S. Army cavalrymen who patrolled the north country. Nearby Jack Main, Thompson and Kerrick canyons are, appropriately, named for other meadow-poaching shepherds.

Either side of Stubblefield Canyon will do for your descent, though the west side is more free of avalanche debris. Below 9600 feet, the valley dog-legs southwest, and its entire length comes into view. The way is obvious and virtually treeless for the next 5 miles. Chortling Stubblefield Canyon creek makes a musical accompaniment to a visual feast of red Brewer's reed-grass, Lemmon's paintbrush, heather and willow. Below 8100 feet, we begin to find patches of lodgepole pines—welcome shade, after so much sunny walking. From here on, the easiest route will lead most walkers away from the immediate streamside, along paralleling, joint-controlled benches northwest of the stream. Below 8000 feet, the way opens up again but now over slabs of bare, hot granite. (Avoid the many gullies choked with huckleberry oak.) Presently, the additive roar of Thompson Canyon creek heralds its confluence with Stubblefield Canyon's stream. Now we re-enter dense forest and quickly strike the Pacific Crest Trail (Route YP-2) just downstream from the creek confluence.

WB-9

Thompson Canyon (Cross Country)

Distances

2.8 miles to Upper Rainbow Canyon
4.0 miles to Upper Thompson Canyon
12.3 miles to Pacific Crest Trail at confluence of Stubblefield Canyon

Introduction

Were it closer to a road-end, Thompson Canyon would surely have a popular trail running its length. In times past, Thompson Canyon probably saw more traffic than it does today, when marauding herds of sheep were driven here to dine illegally on its lovely meadow grasses, and U.S. Cavalry patrols swept through to apprehend them. Now Thompson Canyon provides an easy subalpine cross-country hike that may be used to link the West Walker country, Buckeye Creek or the Peeler Lake region with the Pacific Crest Trail. As a bonus, you can be fairly certain of being alone the entire while.

Trailhead

Same as the Route WB-1 trailhead.

Description

There are at least 3 fairly easy ways of reaching the head of Thompson Canyon. The first, via Rainbow Canyon, will be described momentarily—it allows access from the Hoover Wilderness Addition. The actual head of Thompson Canyon may be reached from near Kirkwood Lake, just off the Kirkwood Pass trail, as described in Route WB-7. This allows slightly easier but less direct access from the West Walker River or Buckeye Creek. Finally, hikers coming from the east, via Peeler Lake (Route YP-1), can proceed west across the head of Kerrick Meadow and moderately up an open-forested slope to a broad 10080′+ saddle overlooking Thompson Canyon. This is certainly the fastest way to reach Thompson Canyon, in terms of hours.

Because it is the prettiest, I recommend using the following cross-country route via Rainbow Canyon. Follow Rainbow Canyon,

Stubblefield (left) and Thompson canyons (aerial view)

as described in cross-country route WB-8, up to a trio of tarns at 9600 feet, under the southwest face of Hawksbeak Peak. Continue easily up-canyon through bouldery subalpine meadows, finally gaining a sandy gap overlooking the windswept head of Thompson Canyon. Descend east past a sand-rimmed tarn, then turn south along Thompson Canyon's incipient creek. Occasional clusters of lodgepole or whitebark pines dot a broad expanse of meadowy, bouldery benches, which we follow south, then southwest down a very gentle grade. Below 9600 feet, a thick forest of lodgepole pines bounds the north side of the canyon.

At 9300 feet, we find the upper end of a 2-mile-long, unnamed meadow. Although the meadow is very picturesque, and a fine foreground for the sharp, classically triangular north face of Acker Peak, veritable clouds of mosquitos that breed in ponds dotting the meadow here may drive an early-summer hiker to literally jog along the meadow's length! While passing by, note the very good examples of "meanders" here in the meadow—any obstruction, in the form of boulders or resistant ledges of meadow turf, has caused the stream to veer from a direct course, resulting in multiple oxbow loops. Near the meadow's southwest end, one may choose an easy alternate route by climbing for a few minutes southwest in forest to a low gap, then down a joint-controlled, meadow-floored ravine to a series of small tarns. These each have nice, intimate camping, but no fish, to my knowledge. The main route on the floor of Thompson Canyon can be rejoined by following their outlet stream down a linear gully cut along a joint in bare granite.

If you choose to stay in Thompson Canyon, your route below the large meadow has only the difficulty of deciding which bank has the best way—both are easy. Most of the next 4 miles are now densely forested, but not so much as to obscure sweeping cliffs on the south face of Dome 9775. Thompson Canyon creek is hereabouts very large in early season, alternating long stretches of relatively quiet water with short, noisy cascades. Below the confluence of an unnamed creek draining 2 strings of lakelets (the alternate route, above), the valley floor seems to narrow appreciably, forcing us up onto open granitic slabs. We alternate between these and some brush and pockets of lodgepoles, often keeping well above the stream bed. As you near the confluence of Stubblefield Canyon, look carefully for an easy ford in your intended direction. It is usually easiest to cross either stream somewhat upstream of the forested flats around their confluence, where they pool up to 6 feet deep during spring-time runoff. I was once swept a considerable distance downstream while trying to cross in 5-foot-deep water at the traditional ford of the Pacific Crest Trail in Stubblefield Canyon, despite an 80-pound pack! On either bank, the obvious Pacific Crest Trail (Route YP-2) will be joined near large campsites.

WB-10

Lakes of the Upper Cascade Creek Basin: Cora, Stella, Ruth and Helen (Cross Country)

Distances
0.7 mile to Ruth Lake
1.4 miles to Lake Helen
1.9 miles to Cora Lake
2.4 miles to Pacific Crest Trail at Harriet Lake

Introduction
The cirque basin lying at the foot of Forsyth Peak holds six distinct and delightful subalpine lakes, strung together like a sparkling necklace. Although each lake is only a few minutes from the Pacific Crest Trail, hikers will usually find secluded camping at the upper lakes, and good fishing in season. Their proximity to one another allows easy exploration on a layover day.

Trailhead
Same as the Route WB-1 or Route SP-1 trailheads.

Description
A counterclockwise traverse allows the most downhill travel while scouting the Cascade Creek basin. Start at Stella Lake. Drop your pack in any of the numerous parallel gullies that were chiseled by glaciers in the banded metasedimentary rocks hereabouts, and scramble south, "across the grain" of both the rocks and their gullies, to the large rocky southern arm of Stella Lake. Strike south across talus, then up dry-meadowy benches along Lake Ruth's outlet stream to Lake Ruth. Here, windswept clumps of whitebark pine and mountain hemlock offer fair camping. Angling for brookies and rainbows, to 12", is good, as it is in each lake of the basin.

Lake Helen, named for the daughter of Colonel Forsyth and wife of Lieutenant Keyes (names given to peaks above Grace Meadow), is reached by walking most of the way south along Lake Ruth's east shore, then cutting east over a low divide. Descend momentarily to meadowy Lake Helen. This is certainly the central gem of Cascade Creek's paternoster necklace. It is also a wonderful spot to practice your fly-casting. A few squat trees below the outlet afford protection for suboptimal but beautiful camps.

Two fairly easy cross-country routes, both passable to skiers, reach Tower Canyon from Lake Helen. The more difficult and spectacular way climbs southeast rockily up to a 10320+-foot saddle, just north of a prominent brown peak. Tower Lake is now easily reached, after drinking in awesome vistas of overshadowing Tower Peak and the Watchtower. The easier way heads east from Lake Helen's outlet into an adjacent basin, then up to a less prominent saddle at 10080+ feet. From it, descend southeast to a bench with 2 tarns and wind-trimmed whitebark pines. Contour southeast along the bench to reach Tower Lake (see Route WB-1).

Return to the Pacific Crest Trail by descending Cascade Creek from Lake Helen to small, more-forested Cora Lake. You can camp on a bench to its east. Finally, drop over a steeper hillside to the large lodgepole forest pocket rimming Lake Harriet. The trail crosses just below its outlet; the most secluded camps are near its southeast corner.

Ch. 13: Yosemite Park

YP-1 Maps 2, 1, 4

Robinson Creek Trail: Kerrick Canyon via Barney and Peeler Lakes

Distances
4.6 miles to Barney Lake
8.2 miles to Peeler Lake
9.3 miles to Upper Kerrick Meadow
16.5 miles to Pacific Crest Trail near Seavey Pass

Introduction

The Robinson Creek trail is the most popular route through Hoover Wilderness and into the Yosemite North Country, and justifiably so. This short, scenic trail leads quickly into breathtaking subalpine terrain, and glittering Peeler Lake, surrounded by frost-shattered and glaciated granite and windswept conifers, mirrors the region's grandeur. Intimate campsites beside its shore more than compensate for the day's tough climb.

Trailhead

From Highway 395 near the west side of Bridgeport, take paved Twin Lakes Road south 13.6 miles to Mono Village at the west end of upper Twin Lake. You must pay to park in the private campground here.

Description

Mono Village, a private resort sprawling across the alluvial fan of Robinson Creek at the head of upper Twin Lake, is such a maze of dirt roads that the Robinson Creek trailhead, on the campground's western frontier, is almost impossible for the uninitiated to find on the first try. The solution: walk south from the portalled Mono Village entrance, past the store, cafe, and marina facilities to the campground entrance station, and ask directions. These should point you just south of west for 0.5 mile to a cable across a dirt road that leads west along the north margin of a lodgepole- and willow-encroached meadow.

It would be a mistake, however, to start up the Robinson Creek Trail without first spending a few minutes at the head of Twin Lakes, especially in the fall when the Kokanee salmon run and hillside aspens turn first amber, then red. Twin Lakes lie behind curving recessional moraines of the Tioga glaciation, the most recent of the Ice Age glaciations. Tioga lateral moraines form obvious bouldery, sagebrush-dotted benches high above both the north and south shores of Twin Lakes, indicating that these last glaciers filled the canyon here to a depth of about 1000 feet! Summits to the north of Twin Lakes, as well as Crater Crest and Monument Ridge to the south, are composed of sediments deposited when this part of the Sierra was near or just under a shallow sea about 180–135 million years ago. Subsequently, these rocks underwent metamorphism, caused in part by an upwelling of magma underneath them—now existing as the quartz monzonite that forms the four spectacular flatirons on Robinson Peak and the rest of the basin above Twin Lakes.

From the cable-gated dirt road at the west end of the Mono Village complex, tread the road 300 feet west to reach the indistinct start of the Robinson Creek Trail, branching right, away from the pretty meadow. The level path strikes west, entangled in a braid of jeep trails that wind north of Robinson Creek under a canopy of white fir, Jeffrey pine, Fremont cottonwood, and aspen. But presently, under the scarp of a small *roche moutonnée,* where Basque shepherds carved their names on aspen trees early in this century, these routes coalesce and the resultant path ascends gently under mixed trees, paralleling an unusual flume. A ten-minute walk reaches a persistent stream, chortling down through wild-rose shrubbery from the basin between Victoria and Eagle peaks.

Afterwards, the trail winds gently up through more-open terrain. Soon our cobbly, dusty path comes close to Robinson Creek, and here the canyon, and our vistas, open up. As our path continues on a westward course,

well above dying lodgepole pines in beaver-dammed Robinson Creek, we note the sweeping aprons of avalanche-scoured slope-wash that descend south from ruddy Victoria Peak, contrasting sharply with the spidery cliffs of light-hued quartz monzonite that form the sharper crests of Hunewill and Kettle peaks, guardians of the upper Robinson Creek basin. Here, the dry surroundings are mule ears, relieved by patches of gooseberry, turkey mullein, rabbitbrush, and some curl-leaved mountain mahogany. At 7600 feet we pass though a grove of aspens, to a sign proclaiming the Hoover Wilderness. From here a use trail cuts south to the mouth of Little Slide Canyon, up which can be seen the smooth granite buttress called the Incredible Hulk, as well as other incredible, but unnamed, rock-climbing goals.

Now ready to assault the canyon headwall, we gear down to accommodate more

Up the Robinson Creek Trail

Crown Point over Barney Lake

than a dozen well-graded switchbacks that
lead north through head-high jungles of
aspen, bitter cherry, serviceberry, snowberry
and tobacco brush, always within earshot of
invisible Robinson Creek. Above 8000 feet
we step across a rivulet merrily draining the
slopes of Hunewill Peak, a welcome respite
that furnishes flowers of creek dogwood,
giant Indian paintbrush, Parish's yampah,
Labrador tea, fireweed, asters, and ligusticum to delight the eye. Still climbing, we
return momentarily to the creekside, where
industrious beavers have created a small
pond, then climb rockily, bending south, in a
gully under aspen shade. Half our ascent is
behind us when we level out to step across a
branch of Robinson Creek that drains the
10,700-foot saddle to our west. Just a yard
beyond this creek, the easily-missed South
Fork Buckeye Creek cutoff trail branches
west through a tangle of aspens and creek
dogwoods. Just a few yards later, where
Robinson Creek is repeatedly plugged by
small beaver dams, a level use trail branches
south along the outlet stream of Barney Lake,

reaching numerous good, sandy campsites.
This spur trail joins the paralleling main trail
at the northwest corner of Barney Lake,
where prevailing southerly winds have
created a sandy swimming beach, a fine spot
for a lunch break.

Fourteen-acre Barney Lake, at 8290
feet, is nestled in a narrow, glaciated trough,
rimmed on the east by the broken, lichen-
mottled north spur of Kettle Peak. The
western shoreline, which our trail follows, is
a dry talus slope mixed with glacial debris.
Here, a pair of switchbacks elevate the trail
to an easy upgrade some 100 feet above
Barney Lake's inlet. Below, golden beavers
have dammed meandering Robinson Creek,
drowning the meadow and a grove of lodgepole pines. Farther southwest, cirque-girdled
Crown Point dominates the horizon, with
Slide Mountain behind its east shoulder.

A short descent comes in a few minutes,
after which the path winds through broken
rock and avalance-twisted aspens, over two
freshets draining Cirque Mountain, then
comes to a ford of Robinson Creek. This

crossing requires one to doff boots in early season, because industrious beavers have widened the ford by damming Robinson Creek in the soggy meadow just downstream. Rainbow and brook trout of handy pan size abound here, as in Barney Lake. After drying our feet, we climb easily south in a pleasant forest of lodgepole, red fir, western white pine, and a new addition—mountain hemlock—reflecting our higher altitude. The route soon leads back to the west bank of Robinson Creek via a 40-foot log, then crosses the steep, cascading stream from Peeler Lake, where we rest in anticipation of a long series of switchbacks just ahead. The first set of gentle, well-engineered switchbacks traverses a till-covered slope to about 8800 feet, where we level off momentarily for a breather before darting north for another, steeper and more eroded ascent. Eventually, we come to a small saddle at 9195 feet, where signs indicate the Rock Island Pass/Slide Canyon trail.

Those bound for Peeler Lake now turn northwest, walking moderately up to a small, shaded glade beside Peeler Lake creek. We step across this stream twice before switchbacking south moderately up into a narrow gully. The wind picks up as we ascend this ravine, a sure sign that we're nearing the ridgetop, and sure enough, Peeler Lake's windswept waters soon heave into view, behind automobile-sized quartz monzonite blocks that dam its outlet. Dynamited trail treads the lake's north shore, where its startling blue lake waters foreground rounded Acker and Wells peaks. Most of the good campsites, under mixed conifers, are found as we undulate rockily into forest pockets along the north shore. The lake margin, mostly rock, does have a few stretches of meadowy beach, where one can fly-cast for rainbows and brookies to 14 inches.

Leaving Peeler Lake near its northwest end, the path climbs slightly to a granite bench dotted with bonsai-stunted lodgepoles, where views back across the outlet show serrated Peak 11581 rising east of Kettle Peak. Now a short descent leads to a profusion of signs designating the Yosemite National Park boundary, beyond which pocket meadows covered with bilberry and short-hair sedge gradually coalesce into the northeastern arm of Kerrick Meadow. Soon our path ends at a 5-foot lodgepole post, indicating the Buckeye Pass Trail, north, and the Kerrick Canyon Trail, branching south.

Kerrick Meadow is named for an early sheepman. Covering a vast ground moraine at the head of Rancheria Creek, it is a frost-hummocked expanse of short-hair sedge, rice-grass, Brewer's reed-grass and dwarf bilberry, quite typical of Sierran subalpine meadows. Note the numerous young lodgepole pines here, encroaching upon the grassland downwind from taller, fringing lodgepoles.

Turn down-canyon along the path, in a rut cut sometimes two feet deep in the delicate turf, and soon cross the seasonal headwaters of Rancheria Creek to its west side. Descending easily, we amble along the west margin of the meadow, over slabs and dry terraces, typical habitat of short-hair sedge. A profusion of birds seasonally flit among the open lodgepoles near our route: Audubon's warblers, robins, mountain bluebirds, white-crowned sparrows, flickers, juncos and Brewer's blackbirds.

Soon afterward we come to the well-signed Rock Island Pass Trail. Still gently descending, we pass through a lodgepole grove, then emerge at the northern end of an even larger meadowed expanse, rimmed on the west by 400-foot-high glacier-quarried bluffs. Long views south down upper Kerrick Canyon are topped by Piute Mountain. After 1½ miles of rolling, sandy trail, our trail crosses a trio of lateral moraines, then cuts close to an oxbow in 20-foot-wide Rancheria Creek where the broad canyon pinches off above a low hillock. In this area you'll find the north-flowing outlet creek of Arndt Lake. This lake, ¾ mile south, has good campsites. Presently Rancheria Creek's banks become a broken gorge, and we drop rockily down, only to strike another sandy meadow, this one with a flanking cluster of steep domes. Our path soon leads out of this lupine-flecked flat, down through a bouldery salient of lodgepoles to yet another meadow. Down this we amble south, soon to walk muddily right along the bank of meandering Rancheria Creek. At the next curve, we cross, following a vague trail to a clump of lodgepoles on the east bank, where good trail resumes. Presently a master joint in the Cathedral Peak granodiorite bedrock forces Rancheria Creek east, and we follow its splashing course down over broken, porphyritic slabs, then back west (another master joint) for ½ mile on a cool, shaded hillside to the signed Seavey Pass Trail (Pacific Crest Trail)— (Route YP-2).

Peeler Lake and tarns above it

YP-2

Pacific Crest Trail: Tuolumne Meadows to Sonora Pass

Distances

6.0 miles to Glen Aulin
14.0 miles to Virginia Canyon Trail
17.6 miles to Miller Lake
19.8 miles to Matterhorn Canyon Trail
24.3 miles to Benson Pass
26.2 miles to Smedberg lake
30.8 miles to Benson lake
33.9 miles to Seavey Pass
38.3 miles to Lower Kerrick Canyon-Bear Valley Trail
45.7 miles to Wilma Lake
54.7 miles to Bond Pass Trail
56.2 miles to Dorothy Lake Pass

Introduction

Deep, spectacular glaciated canyons, crossed one after another, characterize this hike. The backpacker here sometimes feels he's doing more vertical climbing than horizontal walking. Nearing the north end of this hike, you leave the expansive granitic domain behind and enter Vulcan's realm—thick floods of volcanic flows and sediments that buried most of the northern Sierra Nevada before it rose to its present height. By hiking these 76.4 miles you will have completed almost 3% of the entire Pacific Crest Trail, which extends from the Mexican border north to the Canadian border.

Trailhead

At the base of Lembert Dome, at the east end of Tuolumne Meadows, leave Highway 120 and drive ⅓ mile west on a dirt road to a gate that bars it. If no space is available here, park at the base of Lembert Dome.

Description

From the locked gate we continue west along the lodgepole-dotted flank of Tuolumne Meadows, with fine views south across the meadows of Unicorn Peak, Cathedral Peak and some of the knobby Echo Peaks. Approaching a boulder-rimmed old parking loop, we veer right and climb slightly past the old Soda Springs Campground, which once surrounded the still-bubbling natural soda

springs. From here the sandy trail undulates through a forest of sparse, small lodgepole pines, and then descends to a boulder ford of Delaney Creek. Just before the ford, the stock trail from the stables back in the meadows comes in on the right. Immediately beyond the ford we hop a branch of Delaney Creek, hop another in 1/6 mile, and in 1/6 mile more pass the Young Lakes Trail.

At this junction our route goes left, and after more winding through scattered lodgepoles, it descends some bare granite slabs and enters level, cool forest. A half mile's pleasant walking brings us to the bank of the Tuolumne River, just before three branches of Dingley Creek, near the west end of the huge meadows. From here, the nearly level trail often runs along the river, and in these stretches by the stream, there are numerous glacier-smoothed granite slabs on which to take a sunny break.

After a mile-long winding contour, we climb briefly up a granite outcrop to get around the river's gorge. On the south side of the gorge below you is Little Devils Postpile, a dark plug of basalt that was forced up through the adjacent Cathedral Peak granodiorite 9.4 million years ago. Despite repeated attacks by glaciers, this intrusion remains. Now we descend on individual stones carefully fitted together, down toward a sturdy bridge over the river. The campsites on the south side of the river here are illegal, since they are within 4 trail miles of Tuolumne Meadows.

Immediately beyond the bridge we can look north up long Cold Canyon to Matterhorn Peak and Whorl Mountain, and, to their right, Mt. Conness. The trail then dips through several glades brightened by Labrador-tea flowers and corn lilies. As the river approaches Tuolumne Falls, it flows down a series of sparkling rapids separated by large pools and wide sheets of water spread out across slightly inclined granite slopes. Be-

The White Cascade at Glen Aulin

yond this beautiful stretch of river the trail descends, steeply at times, past Tuolumne Falls and White Cascade to a junction with the trail to May Lake. From here it is only a few minutes' walk to Glen Aulin Camp, reached by crossing the river on a bridge below roaring White Cascade and the great green pool it plunges into.

Just north of the camp is the heavily used Glen Aulin backpackers' campground. Only 15 yards beyond the spur trail across Conness Creek to Glen Aulin High Sierra Camp is the Tuolumne Canyon Trail, going left, and ⅓ mile down it are less-used campsites. Bears, however, can be more of a problem there, since it is easier to protect your food at the Glen Aulin site, because for a fee the High Sierra Camp will store your food.

Leaving Glen Aulin, the Pacific Crest Trail climbs north, sometimes along Cold Canyon creek, 3 miles to a forested gap, then descends ½ mile to the south edge of a large, usually soggy meadow. Midway across it

you'll notice a huge boulder, just west. Its overhanging sides have been used as an emergency shelter, but in a lightning storm it is a prime strike target. Beyond it our multi-tracked route continues north, first for a mile through meadow, then on a gradual ascent through forest to a crest junction with the McCabe Lakes trail. A long-half-mile walk northeast up it will get you to a small campsite just above McCabe Creek; an hour's walk up it will get you to larger, better campsites at scenic Lower McCabe Lake.

Now we switchback down to Virginia Canyon's floor, cross McCabe Creek—a wet ford before July—and quickly come to a junction. A spur trail continues briefly up-canyon past campsites, but we turn left to ford powerful Return Creek, which is usually a wet ford and in early season can be a dangerous ford if you're unroped. If you must rope up, hang on to the rope rather than tie into it. Yosemite hikers, slipping in a fast creek, have been known to drown before they could untie their rope (which will pull you underwater once you've slipped).

On the west bank we walk but a few steps southwest before our trail veers right and meets the Virginia Canyon Trail. On the PCT we start down-canyon, climb west up into Spiller Creek canyon, and then, halfway to a pass, cross the canyon's high-volume creek.

Beyond Spiller Creek we soon start up two dozen switchbacks that transport us 2 miles up to a forested pass, which offers fair, reasonably bear-free camps when there is enough snow to provide drinking water. Most hikers, however, continue 1½ miles southwest down to shallow Miller Lake, with good campsites along its forested west shore. From the lake we parallel a meadow north up to a low gap, then execute over two dozen often steep switchbacks down to a canyon floor and a junction with the northbound Matterhorn Canyon Trail. Here the PCT descends southwest, reaching this majestic canyon's broad creek in 80 yards. Immediately beyond the often-wet foot ford lies a large, lodgepole-shaded campsite with ample space to stretch out and dry your toes.

Heading down-canyon for a mile, we pass less obvious and more secluded campsites, then soon leave the glaciated canyon to begin the usual two dozen, short steep switchbacks—this time west up into Wilson Creek canyon, a typical glaciated side canyon that hangs above the main canyon partly because its smaller glacier couldn't erode the landscape as rapidly as the trunk-canyon glacier did. We twice ford Wilson Creek, then ford it a last time and start a switchbacking climb up to windy, gravelly Benson Pass, registering a breath-taking height of 10,140 feet.

As the passes have become steadily higher, so too have the canyons become deeper, and our multistage descent to and then ascent up from Benson Lake can best be described as "Whew!" We begin uneventfully with an easy descent to a large meadow, reaching its peaceful creeklet just before a dropoff. Veering away from the creeklet, we soon begin a switchbacking descent that in 2 miles ends at a south-shore peninsula on Smedberg Lake, named for a cavalry lieutenant.

From the lake's south-shore peninsula—below the steep-walled sentinel, Volunteer Peak—we continue west, passing a spur trail to the west-shore campsites before winding southwest up a poorly defined slab-rock trail to a close-by, well-defined gap. From it the trail switchbacks down joint-controlled granite slabs, only to climb south high up to a meadowy junction with a trail to Rodgers Lake (Route YP-3)

From this junction the PCT starts southwest, crosses a low moraine and briefly descends northwest to a junction with a trail climbing southwest to a broad saddle that harbors shallow, mosquito-haunted Murdock Lake, and thence down Rodgers Canyon. Our next step down to Benson Lake (named for another cavalry lieutenant, and past Yosemite superintendent), is a typical two-dozen-short-switchbacks descent to a ford of Smedberg Lake's outlet creek.

Now on the creek's north bank, we pass a small pond before commencing a steady, moderate creekside descent to a second ford—a slight problem in early season. Back on the south bank, we make a winding, switchbacking descent over metamorphic rock down to our last, sometimes tricky ford of the creek. The next ⅓ mile sees us climbing up to a brushy saddle just east of a conspicuous knoll, then descending into a shady forest of giant firs before crossing wide Piute Creek and reaching the Benson Lake spur trail. Piute Creek can usually be crossed via one or more large, fallen logs. No one—but no one—makes this long descent from Benson Pass without visiting the "Benson Riviera"—the long, sandy beach along the north shore of Benson Lake. Our spur trail winds southwest along the shady, often damp forest floor a short ½ mile to a section of beach near Piute Creek's inlet. *Remember this spot,* for otherwise this route back can be hard to locate. Numerous campsites just within the forest's edge testify to the popularity of this broad, sandy beach. And if you've brought in a portable folding boat or raft, you'll probably have the whole lake to

Smedberg Lake

yourself. Swimming in this large, deep lake is brisk at best, but sunning on the beach is often superb. Anglers can anticipate a meal of rainbow or brook trout.

After your stay, return to the PCT and prepare for a gruelling climb north to Seavey Pass. At first brushy, the ascent northwest provides views of pointed Volunteer Peak and closer, two-crowned Peak 10060. We cross the creek, continue switchbacking northwest along the base of spectacular Peak 10368, then climb north briefly, only to be confronted with a steep 400-foot climb east. On it we are eventually funneled through a narrow, steep-walled, minor gap which rewards our climbing efforts with the sight of a relatively wind-free, sparkling pond. Just past its outlet you'll find a trailside rock from which you can dive into its reasonably warm waters. The PCT parallels the pond's shore, curves east around a miniscule pond, then climbs northeast through wet meadows before switchbacking up to a second gap. At its north base lies a shallow, rockbound pond, immediately beyond which we meet gap No. 3—signed Seavey Pass. A small meadow

separates it from gap No. 4, beyond which we reach a more noteworthy—and the highest—gap. Now we bend northwest, travel past the head of a linear lake to gap No. 6, and switchback quickly down into a southwest-trending trough. We turn right and immediately top our last gap, from which we descend northeast ¼ mile to a junction in Kerrick Canyon with the Kerrick Meadow trail (Route YP-1).

A cursory glance at the map suggests to the hiker that he now has an easy 3-mile down-canyon walk to the Bear Valley trail junction. Closer scrutiny, however, reveals a longer, winding, too-often-ascending route.

A short northward jog of our Kerrick Canyon trail segment ends at the Bear Valley trail junction. From it Route YP-4 climbs south to Bear Valley before starting its long descent to Hetch Hetchy Reservoir. Immediately beyond this junction we cross voluminous Kerrick Canyon's erratic-coursed Rancheria Creek. Major joints cut across this area's canyons and this creek has eroded along some of them, so that today it too cuts across several major canyons. After crossing this creek, which can be a rough ford through mid-July, we find a north-bank spur trail striking east up to campsites that are popular with both backpackers and black bears. The PCT, however, climbs west, affording dramatic cross-canyon views of Bear Valley peak and Piute Mountain. The PCT eventually climbs north to a shallow gap, and just east of it you'll find a generally bear-free campsite near the west end of a small lakelet. Proceeding north from the gap, we have the usual knee-shocking descent on a multitude of short, steep switchbacks down to the mouth of Thompson Canyon. Here we make a shady, easy descent west to a large camp beside Stubblefield Canyon creek. The main trail meets the creek just below the camp, and across from it a spur trail up the opposite bank quickly meets the main trail. Cross where you will, locate the main trail near the opposite bank, and start down-canyon. In ¼ mile we leave the shady floor for slabs and slopes, in an hour arriving at a false

pass. A short, steep descent west drops us into a corn-lily meadow, from which we wind ¼ mile northwest up to the true Macomb Ridge pass.

With the deep canyons at last behind us, the 500-foot descent northwest into Tilden Canyon seems like child's play. Just beyond the west bank of Tilden Canyon Creek we meet the Tilden Canyon Trail (Route YP-8). From this junction we hike up-canyon north on the Tilden Lake Trail just 110 yards to a second junction. From here the PCT heads west to Wilma Lake and then goes up Jack Main Canyon. A much prettier and slightly longer alternate (Route YP-9) continues north gently up to huge, linear Tilden Lake, which has lots of shoreline campsites and has been stocked with rainbow trout.

Our route, however, adheres to the PCT, which goes left at this junction and winds northwest past several ponds, nestled on a broad gap, before descending west to large, shallow Wilma Lake, stocked—like so many

Benson Lake

of Yosemite's High Sierra lakes—with rainbow trout. Good campsites are found just beyond it, along broad, tantalizing Falls Creek. A few minutes' walk northwest up-canyon takes us to a shallow, broad ford of the creek, then past spacious campsites to a junction with the Jack Main Canyon Trail (Route YP-5).

From our junction, just east of and below a snow-survey shelter, the PCT winds northward up-canyon, touching the west bank of Falls Creek only several times before reaching a junction with a trail east to Tilden Lake (Route YP-9). Chittenden Peak and its north satellite serve as impressive reference points as we gauge our progress northward, passing two substantial meadows both littered now with the log debris of massive avalanches from the winter of 1985–86, before arriving at the south end of even larger Grace Meadow. Here the upper canyon explodes into plain view, with—east to west—Forsyth Peak, Dorothy Lake Pass and Bond Pass being our guiding landmarks. Under lodgepole cover along the meadow's edge you can set up camp.

Leaving Grace Meadow, we soon pass through another large stretch of avalanche blowdown that has filled a small meadow with stumps and logs. The ever-increasing gradient soon becomes noticeable. People have camped at small sites along this stretch, perhaps hoping to avoid bears, which are usually found lower down, but alas, no such luck. Our upward climb meets the first of two branches of Route KM-2, the Brown Bear Pass Trail, which unite to climb to nearby Bond Pass, on the Park's boundary. Just beyond these junctions volcanic sediments and exposures are noticed in ever-increasing amounts—a taste of what's to come—before we reach large, exposed Dorothy Lake. Clumps of lodgepoles here provide minimal campsite protection from the winds that often rush up-canyon. A short climb above the lake's east end takes us up to Dorothy Lake Pass, with our last good view of the perennial snowfields that grace the north slopes of Forsyth Peak.

To reach Sonora Pass, continue north on the PCT, described in reverse in Route SP-1.

YP-3   Maps main, 6, 3, 6, 7, 4

Hetch-Hetchy Reservoir to Rancheria Falls, Pleasant Valley, and Table, Neall, Rodgers and Murdock Lakes

Distances
6.3 miles to Rancheria Falls
16.3 miles to Bear Valley trail junction
19.0 miles to Table Lake
21.4 miles to Pate Valley Trail
27.2 miles to Neall lake
27.8 miles to Rodgers Lake
29.3 miles to Pacific Crest Trail near Smedberg Lake

Introduction
This long trail, paralleling the awesome Grand Canyon of the Tuolumne River, defines the southern boundary of Yosemite's remote North Country. Along the way, it visits the greatest variety of subalpine set-tings to be found anywhere in the Park. The first 6½ miles, to Rancheria Falls, make a fine, easy Spring or Fall overnighter, but its real rewards are inspirational vistas of the awesome cliffs and early-season waterfalls which line our precipitous path along the north wall of unique Hetch Hetchy Reservoir. Beyond, our little-traveled path across the broad, conifer-robed massif of Rancheria Mountain affords a snow-free early-summer route into the Yosemite North Country. Hikers who don't demand a spectacular, high-level trail will find it is a nice alternative to using the Pacific Crest Trail to reach the Benson Lake region.

Trailhead

Just 1.1 miles outside the Park's Big Oak Flat entrance station, leave Highway 120 and drive north 7.4 miles on Evergreen Road to its junction with the Hetch Hetchy Road. Turn right and go 9.1 miles to the large parking area at O'Shaughnessy Dam.

Description

This hike is best started early in the morning, before the sun heats the ½-mile-high south-facing slopes ahead. Walk down to chain-gated Lake Eleanor Road, atop O'Shaughnessy Dam (3814 feet) at Hetch Hetchy Reservoir. Halfway across this curving monolith, named for the Hetch Hetchy Project's chief engineer, we find a water fountain where the City of San Francisco graciously "shares" some of its precious drinking water, and we fill our canteens. Bronze plaques posted here commemorate the back-room politicos who made possible this blasphemous inroad on a national park, back in 1914, along with similar structures on Lake Eleanor and Cherry Lake. Visitors today can look, but not touch (to protect San Francisco's hygiene, one must assume), so we can only gaze east over the choppy, 8-mile-long reservoir. The soaring canyon walls that remain standing above the inundation are good reminders of what Hetch Hetchy Valley once was—a less-spectacular sibling of Yosemite Valley. On the south wall, the prow of Kolana Rock soars 2000 feet up from the water, while to the north, tiered Hetch Hetchy Dome rises about 400 feet higher. In a shaded cleft on the dome's west flank, two-stepped Wapama Falls plunges an aggregate 1400 feet. In early summer its gossamer companion, Tueeulala Falls, glides down steep slabs farther west.

Across the 600-foot-long dam, we enter a 500-foot-tunnel blasted through solid granite when the original dam was raised 85 feet in 1938. Emerging from this bat haven, the potholed, discontinuously paved road climbs steadily above the rocky west shore of Hetch Hetchy Reservoir in a pleasant grove of Douglas-fir, digger pine, big-leaf maple, and bay trees. Sour, blue-blushed California grape, shiny poison oak, and palmlike giant chain ferns grow in the trees' shadows. Each one of these plants was utilized by the Miwok Indians that visited Hetch Hetchy. Soon we reach the signed junction with our route, the Rancheria Falls Trail, at the road's first switchback. Lake Eleanor road is described in Route YP-5. From here we descend gently across an exfoliating granitic nose, then switchback once down to a broad, sloping ledge, sparingly shaded by Digger pines and mountain mahogany. Odd-appearing bird's beak and lavender Sierra lessingia grow here, amid boulders splotched with mosslike selaginella, actually a relative of ferns. We follow this shelf ½ mile to an unnamed stream that cascades hundreds of feet down some brushy slabs as Tueeulala Falls—but only in the spring and early summer. Beyond its step-across ford, we wind down along the

Hetch Hetchy Reservoir

north shore of Hetch Hetchy Reservoir to a bridge over a steep ravine, where our views east to the lake's head expand impressively. On the north wall stands multifaceted Hetch Hetchy Dome, guarding thundering, split-level Wapama Falls. Opposite this monolith towers the warshiplike prow of Kolana Rock, which forces a constriction in the 8-mile-long reservoir's tadpole shape.

A few minutes of easy traverse east from here end at a steep, dynamited descent through a field of huge talus blocks under a tremendous unnamed precipice. Soon, if we're passing this way in early summer, flecks of spray dampen our cobbly path, as we come to the first of four bridges under two-stepped Wapama Falls. During some high-runoff years, even these high, sturdy steel bridges are inundated by tumultuous Falls Creek.

East of Wapama Falls, our rocky path leads up around the base of a steep bulge of glacier-polished and striated granite under a fly-infested canopy of gold-cup oak and California laurel, or bay tree. Four switchbacks eventually raise our route 500 feet to a 100-foot-wide ledge, formed along a master joint, that slopes across the mind-boggling face of Hetch Hetchy Dome. Looking south across the lake to Kolana Rock, we see that an extension of the same joint plane has formed a similar terrace, with the same shady collection of Digger pines, scrub and gold-cup oaks, laurel, poison oak and wild-grape vines. Huge flakes of shattered granite also dot this bench, spalled from the walls above. After the terrace we're on tapers off, our frequently dynamited trail undulates along a steep hillside in a hot, open chaparral of yerba santa and mountain mahogany, making switchbacks on occasion to circumvent some cliffy spots.

Eventually our path descends to the oak-and-pine-shaded gorge cut by Tiltill Creek and crosses two steel bridges, the second over the named stream's 60-foot-deep, inaccessible cleft. Beyond the second span, our route climbs the canyon's east slope via a set of tight switchbacks to emerge 250 feet higher on a gentle hillside. Soon our way

levels off, and we spy Rancheria Creek as it slides invitingly over a broad rock trough, superb for skinny-dipping. Just a minute later we pass the first of dozens of good campsites along the cobbly north bank of wide Rancheria Creek. The duff-floored forest stretches to within 100 yards of 25-foot-high Rancheria Falls, which shoot off a ledge of resistant dark intrusive rock. Fishing below the falls might yield pan-sized rainbow trout. Be warned that these popular camps are often shared with marauding black bears, and bearbag your provisions accordingly.

The next morning, ascend easily past the Tiltill Valley Trail (Route YP-7) to a 40-foot-long bridge over Rancheria Creek, which bumps and slides frothily below us through a series of well-worn potholes and slabs, inviting divers and sun-bathers. Tank up on water here—your next source will be a hot 3000 feet higher, on the west slope of Rancheria Mountain. Marching south from the streamside, we contour under shadeless, bedraggled Digger pines into a broad ravine draining the north slope of brushy LeConte Point.

Now we start the first, 1400-foot leg of our 4000-foot climb over Rancheria Mountain. The trail switchbacks methodically up on a moderate ascent under some forest cover. As we progress higher, vistas west over the reservoir and Kolana Rock improve. We finally top a sandy nose at 6225 feet, east of a saddle on LeConte Point, then lose a bit of elevation while traversing east along a sandy chaparral hillside. The ascent resumes, on dusty switchbacks up past some fire-cleared forest openings that now support a thriving population of deer, flickers and chickarees. At 6800 feet we swing onto a south-facing chaparral slope and can look south across the Grand Canyon of the Tuolumne River to the rolling upland region around the Tioga Pass Road. From this bench our path climbs northeast, then resolves to switchbacks, so we tediously zigzag up on the dusty, dry forest litter to our first honest respite, at 7700 feet. Here, near an adequate camp, an unnamed tributary of the Tuolumne River cuts a sandy swath through

Lower cascade at Rancheria Falls

a dry flat and offers the first almost-permanent water source since Rancheria Creek.

After quenching our thirst and topping off our canteens, we continue up the duff-treaded path, now under sun-dappled lodge-poles and red firs, to another creek draining the west flank of Rancheria Mountain. In a pleasant glade on its north bank we find a small, ruined log cabin, constructed, like the one in Tiltill Meadow, by pioneer fish-propagator H. G. Kibbe. Beyond this relict angle northeast, ascending up over a morainal divide back to the first creek that we met. A fallen lodgepole here facilitates our crossing to the north bank, where we may linger for some time to observe the shoulder-to-shoulder ranks of wildflowers spread under the scattered timber here. Standing almost head-high are stalks of blue-bonnet larkspur, slender lupine, umbrella-leaved cow parsnip, red elderberry and four-petalled

green gentian. Reaching our waists are lacy meadow rue, purple asters, white yarrow, yellow senecio, aromatic pennyroyal, and sunflowery mule ears. Under them all is a mat of deep-blue-flowered Jacob's ladder, rarely seen in such large numbers.

From this flower garden, our path turns northeast up the shallow canyon and soon climbs easily along a dry volcanic hillside. This volcanic-mud-flow material and the overlying darker cap layer of harder andesite (it forms the summits of Peaks 8772 and 8995) are one of the most southern remnants of the lava flows that inundated the entire northern Sierra area during and just before the present-day Sierra's upheaval. After a mile our way becomes a ridgetop amble, eventually bringing us to our high point (8650 feet) on Rancheria Mountain. To reach the 8015-foot saddle north of us, our path makes five switchbacks which spare our knees on the steep hillside. The trees disperse momentarily, and we look northeast to the Sawtooth Ridge and closer Volunteer Peak. A short distance later, we reach a signed junction with the Bear Valley Trail (Route YP-4). Here we branch southeast, then head more eastward down a shallow draw to the rim of Piute Creek canyon's 1200-foot western scarp. Emerging from a thick stand of young aspens, we are treated with superb vistas northeast over sparsely forested Pleasant Valley to a rolling landscape of dark exfoliating domes and hillsides above Piute Creek, terminating this side of spiry Sawtooth Ridge. A part of little-visited Irwin Bright Lake, one of several shallow, granite-rimmed lakes arcing around Pleasant Valley, can be seen on a forested bench below. As we switchback down moderately-to-steeply east, we can also look southeast across the Grand Canyon of the Tuolumne River to the flying buttresses on Double Rock and Colby Mountain. Below 7500 feet our path swings northeast. Soon we reach a hanging-valley aspen grove and walk in the seasonal creekbed that drains it, then descend down along the stream in a narrow chute. A few short switchbacks lead us north from this ravine down to the floor of Pleasant Valley, at 6860 feet. Here we find an interesting forest of red and white firs, Jeffrey pines, incense-cedars, junipers, and dominant lodgepoles pines, growing on a sparsely meadowed alluvial floor. A few minutes' amble through these woods brings us to a signed trail branching northeast 0.2 mile to large packer camps beside a pool on Piute Creek. Campers should beware of persistent black bears that forage there seasonally.

From the Pleasant Valley camping spur trail, our path veers south to momentarily reach shaded Piute Creek. This ford could be a 50-foot-long wade in early summer. On the east bank another spur trail heads upstream to more camps, but we turn downstream. Just past a stock-drift fence our route leaves shading conifers and begins to ascend moderately on an open hillside of friable dark diorite. The rocky climb does have one very steep pitch, to reach the south shoulder of a low ridge, and then it dips easily to a log

crossing of Table Lake's outlet stream. The best campsites on Table Lake are reached by ascending north along the open bench just before crossing this stream. A dry peninsula, sparsely forested with Jeffrey pines, lies between the main lake, which is ringed with low, broken bluffs and shrubbery, and its southern arm, which is shallow and dotted with pond lilies. This rocky peninsula holds the best campsites. Angling for rainbow trout in Table, Irwin Bright and Saddle Horse lakes is good due to a scarcity of fisherman.

Now we pass south of Table Lake under a canopy of aspens. The herbaceous understory of this damp-floored flat is so dense that it has obliterated the mapped trail that once started here, bound north for Irwin Bright Lake. Near this old junction we hop a stream, and then ascend rapidly out of the shade and mosquitos onto a brushy hillside. Soon we pant up the inevitable rocky switchbacks and are partly consoled by an improving picture of Pleasant Valley. Our zigzag course persists until 7600 feet, where we top a bench to find, in another stand of aspens, the stream we crossed lower down. Now our climb moderates, proceeding southeast to a ridgetop just under 8000 feet. This open spot lets us look south down Piute Creek's gorge to Double Rock, and marks the start of the path's undulating traverse south to the Pate Valley Trail. A mile later we find a sloping glade, some clustered, quivering aspens, and a sign pointing out the Pate Valley Trail, which descends southwest. For a description of this trail, see Jeffrey Schaffer's guide, *Yosemite National Park.*

Our route curves southeast from the trail junction and climbs across an open volcanic hillside where a small spring trickles across the path. Excellent views and myriad wildflowers recommend this spot for a lunch break. Afterward, we gear down for a short but steep ascent east to the crest of a bouldery medial moraine robed in dark conifers. Our way descends east from the ridge crest across a hillside on rich volcanic tread. Twenty minutes later we reach our low point along the north rim of the Grand Canyon of the Tuolumne River. Just a few minutes later we enter Rodgers Canyon, then abruptly turn uphill.

The trail ascends a series of well-forested glacial steps to come alongside seasonally large Rodgers Canyon creek just under 8000 feet, then actually follows its bed for a moment. For the next 1½ miles our gentle-to-moderate climbing trail keeps on Rodgers Canyon's west side, passing through pockets of lodgepoles that cluster near the cascading stream. After one cobbly pitch, we find a stock-drift fence, then emerge moments later on the south edge of Rodgers Meadow. Here Rodgers Canyon creek cuts a broad, lazy snake through the sedge turf, overshadowed by a small dome near Neall Lake. Staying near the forest that demarcates the west side of Rodgers Meadow, we amble north to find a very good campsite, complete with stumptables. A few yards north of this camp we leave the meadow and walk over a log to the east bank of Rodgers Canyon creek, only to cross back moments later, this time via a long boulder-hop. Now we come abruptly to a

trail junction. By continuing north you can take a shorter route to the PCT, via Murdock Lake, to be described later.

Most hikers will branch right on the longer, far more scenic trail to Neall and Rodgers lakes. This route heads east to Neall Lake's unnamed outlet creek, then climbs pleasantly east along its north bank. Less than a mile from the Murdock Lake junction, we find a short spur trail going south to Neall Lake, which has fine campsites nestled by its outlet. Cupped by a terminal-moraine loop under the sharp crest of West Peak, small Neall Lake reflects surrounding cliffs, blue sky, fringing conifers and willowy fellfields. Fishing for rainbow trout to 14 inches is excellent.

Pushing on toward Rodgers Lake, our trail steeply ascends a cobbly ridge under a western outlier of Regulation Peak. Soon we swing north, wind over terraced short-hairsedge flats, and come to the south shore of long, subalpine Rodgers Lake. Named for the second Superintendent of Yosemite Park, it is

Rodgers Lake

divided into two bodies by a low granitic isthmus; the larger, eastern portion is more open and rockier. Our way rounds Rodgers Lake to a handsome grove of lodgepoles and hemlocks on the north shore. Here lie some good camps that afford excellent panoramas over the shallow waters to the ruddy north faces of Regulation and West peaks. Farther east we switchback north over platy diorite that has been intruded by a netlike swarm of quartz veins.

Presently we arrive atop a grassy saddle at 9790 feet, where the stunning sheer profile of nearby Volunteer Peak completely dominates a horizon of greater summits throughout the north country—Piute Mountain, Price and Tower peaks, and Crown Point. Descending north from this gap via short switchbacks, we soon re-enter timber and wind to a well-signed junction with the Pacific Crest Trail (Route YP-2). Here, under the brooding face of Volunteer Peak, which has been frost-riven into thousands of vertically oriented flakes, we may decide to

strike northeast one mile on the PCT to Smedberg Lake, or continue west 3.6 miles along the PCT to spend the night at large Benson Lake. Within ⅓ mile along our way to Benson Lake, we strike the Murdock Lake Trail, the shortcut from upper Rodgers Canyon.

From the trail junction at 8800 feet in Rodgers Canyon, the Murdock Lake Trail heads up along a morainal hillside, quickly leaving behind the canyon-floor lodgepole forest. Soon we tackle a set of very steep, sandy switchbacks, then angle once again northeast. Ascent ends abruptly on a level subalpine meadow at 9530 feet. Shallow Murdock Lake is cupped in a depression in this rolling grassland. Some adequate camps lie in lodgepoles above its west shore and have interesting views of Volunteer Peak, Matterhorn Peak and Sawtooth Ridge. Leaving the ridgetop meadowland, our trail descends back into mixed conifers and soon reaches the Pacific Crest Trail (Route YP-2).

YP-4

Maps main, 6, 3

Bear Valley Trail: Rancheria Mountain to Bear Valley Lake and Kerrick Canyon

Distances
5.6 miles to Bear Valley Lake
7.6 miles to Pacific Crest Trail in Lower Kerrick Canyon

Introduction
A long distance from anywhere, Bear Valley gives the diligent hiker well-deserved solitude in secluded hemlock-bower camps beside a lovely subalpine lake. In addition, the trail in affords fast access to lower Kerrick Canyon, at the hub of some of northern Yosemite's longest canyon cross-country hikes.

Trailhead
Same as the Route YP-3 trailhead.

Description
Ascend Rancheria Mountain via the Rancheria Mountain Trail, Route YP-3, 16.2 miles from O'Shaughnessy Dam to a well-signed trail junction on the broad, timbered, 8015-foot saddle north of Rancheria Mountain. The Pleasant Valley—Rodgers Canyon Trail (Route YP-3) branches right here.

The Bear Valley Trail drops north across the timbered saddle, then climbs up a steep, shaded pitch to a small, grassy pond. Climb gently north from this pond along a sandy ridge to the willowy east bank of an unnamed creek. In ½ mile, a big leap takes us across this stream so that we can climb northwest through a meadow of dry wheat-grass and squirrel-tail barley to top a lateral moraine and find yet another creek. After jumping to its west bank we ascend gently north on a hard gruss tread. Soon our little-traveled trail fades to a faint depression in the meadow turf. Small cairns and ducks guide us, however, right on course to a windy saddle, flanked by huddled whitebark pines, lying just under 9500 feet. Below us is pastoral Bear Valley, overshadowed by knife-edged Bear Valley peak. Farther north, the Yosemite North Country rears its shining ivory summits and red-volcanic Relief Peak, near Sonora Pass, touches the horizon.

Raucous Clark's nutcrackers supervise our knee-jarring plummet north down the cirque wall of Bear Valley. At first our path is contorted into short, tight, rocky switchbacks, but later the legs lengthen as we descend a wet route through a lush thicket of willows, mountain maple, meadow-rue and seasonal forbs. After rapidly losing 500 feet of altitude, the descent becomes gentler and turns northwest down to the south side of meadowed Bear Valley. The path is lost for some 150 yards north across the hummocky, frequently soggy grassland, but we can pick it up again easily enough beside a metal sign. We then climb over a forested medial moraine and drop to the east end of a small, hospitable lakelet nestled in mixed lodgepoles and western white pines. Just a minute north of this tarn we hop across Breeze Creek, then ascend northeast along it. Soon the trail levels off through a delightful open stand of pines and hemlocks and arrives at the outlet of long-awaited Bear Valley lake. This shallow gem sits in a washboard-bottomed glacial trough, and numerous reefs of polished quartz-monzonite push up through the lake's mirror-surface. These picturesque islets, combined with a shore line of closely cropped grasses, red heather, and dwarf bilberry, provide a stunning foreground for soaring Bear Valley Peak. The total scene will send even the most jaded photographer scrambling for his wide-angled lens. Excellent camps are found in conifers back from the north shore.

The next morning we walk a short distance northwest from the lake's outlet to a small gap between two low domes. Here we gird ourselves for a 1200-foot descent north into Kerrick Canyon, involving the better part of 100 moderate-to-steep switchbacks. For the first 400 feet of this direct descent, we can pause to gaze north over intervening ridges to Snow Peak and ragged Tower Peak. Lower down, however, the views are hidden by a rising horizon and a thick growth of hemlocks and lodgepoles. Finally reaching morainal till rearranged by sometimes-raging Rancheria Creek, our descent abates and we turn east through dry lodgepole flats to join the Pacific Crest Trail (Route YP-2) where it bends north at an over-signed junction to cross Rancheria Creek.

YP-5

Laurel Lake Loop

Distances

6.2 miles to Beehive
7.7 miles to Laurel Lake
12.8 miles to Miguel Ranger Station
18.3 miles to Hetch Hetchy via Eleanor Lake Road

Introduction

Large, forest-nestled Laurel Lake sits somewhat off the beaten path to Jack Main Canyon. Its 6485-foot elevation, lowest of any large natural lake in Yosemite, places it in the hospitable fir belt, providing warm swimming and secluded camping. It's a great early- or late-season overnighter.

Trailhead

Same as the Route YP-3 trailhead.

Description

First, follow Route YP-3 to the Rancheria Falls-Lake Eleanor junction. Here we keep to the road and attack the steep north-canyon wall. Eight cobble-paved switch-backs take our route inexorably north to better views up the reservoir of LeConte Point and the Grand Canyon of the Tuolumne River.

Our switchbacking road finally swings north to a trail junction on a small flat. The road curves west, but we continue north, climbing briefly to a small meadow, by which we spy this hike's first sugar pines, with their long, pendulous cones. Beyond, our generally viewless trail climbs in earnest, ascending 1000 feet of forest slope—steep at times—to the low crest of a moraine that dams a linear, knee-deep pond. Past it, we exit over a low morainal crest, then climb easily north, being thoroughly shaded by a dense white-fir canopy in our half-mile hike up to a trail junction. Laurel Lake, though only ¾ mile northwest of us, is at least 2½ *trail* miles away by either trail we can take, and one wonders why a trail was not built directly to it. On our return from Laurel Lake, we may choose to hike up the narrow, little-used trail that descends southwest from this junction. If your throat is really parched, you can de-scend ¼ mile on it to everflowing Frog Creek.

From the junction we follow the shady trail northeast, dip to cross a bracken-bordered creeklet, then soon hike alongside a linear meadow that in season is profuse with arrowhead butterweed and Bigelow's sneeze-weed, two kinds of sunflowers. The meadow pinches off at a low pass, beyond which we quickly find ourselves in the southwest corner of a triangular meadow. Staying within the shady cover of white firs and lodgepole pines, we parallel the meadow's edge past snow-survey equipment, over to its east corner, called Beehive, where there is a signed trail junction. Here the Laurel Lake Trail veers northwest, while the Jack Main Canyon Trail starts east, described as Route YP-6. Beehive was the site of an 1880s cattlemen's camp, and a log cabin once stood north of the trail junction, where a popular camp is now found. A small spring lies 20 yards west of the junction, protected by a wooden box.

By walking north only a minute on the Laurel Lake Trail, we reach another trail junction. Here a signed path that loops around Laurel Lake's north shore branches north, while a shorter trail to Laurel Lake's outlet strikes west. Following this latter route, we drop easily down to cross 40-foot-wide Frog Creek via large cobbles. On its west bank, we pantingly ascend to a heavily forested ridge before gently dropping to good camps at Laurel Lake's outlet. Another frac-tion of a mile brings us to a signed junction with the north-shore loop trail, branching northwest to the best campsites. At shallow

Eventide at Laurel Lake

60-acre Laurel Lake, western azalea grows thickly just back of the grassy lakeshore, a fragrant accompaniment to huckleberry and thimbleberry.

By continuing north around Laurel Lake, one will encounter a large campsite on the northwest shore. There the trail turns east through a bracken-overgrown deadfall to a camp beside Frog Creek, here running through cobbles and tall creek dogwood shrubs. Across that stream, our way turns southeast, ascending easily to a junction with the southern Laurel Lake Trail, just north of Beehive.

Leaving Laurel Lake near its outlet, we pick up the Frog Creek Trail, heading southwest, and wind under a dense canopy of white fir. Within ½ mile this walk becomes a gradually steepening descent, down an open nose. A trail junction is reached midway down the nose, where we must make a choice of return routes. The first contours 1¼ miles east to Frog Creek, then another ¼ mile up to the trail we came in on, leaving us with 5.3 miles of backtracking to Hetch Hetchy. The second—straight ahead—descends to Miguel Meadow.

Should we choose the longer route via Miguel Meadow, we head west from the trail junction and drop steeply to Frog Creek. We easily hop cobbles to the south bank and climb a short switchback. Now a traverse leads southwest through dry forest to a saddle. We turn south from this saddle, gently descending into the basin of Miguel Creek, where we walk under a pleasant canopy of Jeffrey pines and black oaks where flickers and white-headed woodpeckers dwell. Lower down, we pass north of unseen Gravel Pit Lake, then traverse southwest to an intersection with dirt Lake Eleanor Road.

From this junction, Miguel Meadow, with a NPS ranger and pleasant camping under large black oaks, is just ⅓ mile southwest along the road. However, to return to Hetch Hetchy, turn southeast on Lake Eleanor Road, cross nearby Miguel Creek, wind east for 3.2 miles up a shallow, open-floored canyon, top a mile-high saddle, drop a few hundred yards to the Laurel Lake trail, which we climbed the first morning, and finally descend the switchbacking road back to O'Shaughnessy Dam.

YP-6

Jack Main Canyon Trail: Branigan Lakes and Wilma Lake

Distances
6.2 miles to Beehive-Laurel Lake Trail
11.8 miles to Jack Main Canyon
15.1 miles to Branigan Lakes trail junction
18.4 miles to Pacific Crest Trail near Wilma Lake

Introduction
Following a route used around the turn of the century by both illegal sheepherders and their US Army pursuers, the Jack Main Canyon trail (named for one of the early sheepmen) visits a succession of small subalpine meadows along the course of delightful, cascading Falls Creek. Wilma Lake, the gem of Jack Main Canyon, marks our northernmost point in that glacier-scoured trough, and offers pastoral camping with the opportunity to visit over 20 fishing and swimming lakes or climb to more than a dozen viewful mountaintops, each within an easy day's hiking!

Trailhead
Same as the Route YP-3 trailhead.

Description
Follow the Laurel Lake Trail (Route YP-5) from Hetch Hetchy Reservoir up to Beehive, then west 1.3 miles to Laurel Lake, and camp there the first night. The next morning, retrace your steps to Beehive and pick up the Jack Main Canyon Trail, which ascends gently northeast through a forested glade. Soon we bend northeast on a more moderate forested ascent, which later be-

comes rocky and dusty on more open slopes, to reach a morainal crest, where we pass the Lake Vernon Trail (Route YP-7).

Here our Jack Main Canyon Trail veers north to begin a long, sandy, dry ascent of Moraine Ridge. Aptly named, Moraine Ridge was formed as the medial moraine between the broad, 500-foot-deep Frog Creek glacier on the north and the 1200-foot-deep Falls Creek glacier south of the ridge. Knowing this, we can easily predict the nature of our surroundings along this 3-mile, gentle-to-moderate ascent: our trail is mostly in deep, glacial sand, paralleled by narrow ridges topped with large, rounded boulders. A sparse ground cover of drought-tolerant species includes silver-hairy Brewer's lupine, pussy paws, snow bush, squirrel-tail barley and delicate whisker-brush. Overhead, sun-loving Jeffrey pines dominate the conifers until supplanted above 7500 feet by wind-damaged red firs. Higher still, we can look down into Falls Creek's cirque to the lily-padded tarns above shallow Lake Vernon, and glimpse the outlet of rockbound Branigan Lake. When we finally reach the sandy 8110-foot crest of Moraine Ridge, panoramas explode to the north and east, stretching from the broken, water-streaked summits of Richardson, Mahan and Andrews peaks in the foreground to distant Saurian Crest, Piute Mountain, Sawtooth Ridge and Mount Conness.

Leaving this viewful height, our path begins a descent of the "Golden Stairs" northeast toward Falls Creek. Moderate switchbacks lead to a dogleg in a seasonal stream, where a pleasant campsite has views to the east. Beyond this flat, our staircase is more demanding—very steep, tight switchbacks of riprapped and dynamited granite plunge down along a joint-controlled ravine amid a sundrenched tangle of western choke-cherry, mountain maple and Indian hemp. After hopping the small creek that drains this gorge, we come alongside pooling Falls Creek and begin our ascent of Jack Main Canyon.

Our first mile of walking along Falls Creek sets the tone for the rest of our jour-ney: the trail undulates moderately, alternately visiting benches of sunny, glaciated granite dotted with huckleberry-oak thickets and precariously rooted western junipers, and pocket stands of lodgepoles and stately red firs, their canopy shading twinberry, mountain ash and red elderberry. We pass above a triad of sand-banked pools, then descend slightly to a horseshoe bend in Falls Creek. East of this bend our still-undulating trail winds among open slabs and up to a piney bench. Here one may choose to leave the trail and strike south across Falls Creek and up through a gap west of striated Andrews Peak to Andrews and Branigan lakes. Our path turns north, dropping to the largest and most beautiful of a number of unnamed lakelets in lower Jack Main Canyon. Shaped somewhat like a horseshoe, this shallow lakelet reflects the broken south face of Mahan Peak while supporting a shoreline garden of Parish's yampah and Bigelow's sneezeweed. Our route skirts its north shore, then veers south around another pond following "T" blazes back to the north bank of slow-moving, tepid Falls Creek. Here we turn east, on a 30-foot-wide isthmus between the stream and an aspen-bordered pond that lies just north of the trail, fed only by ground water.

From the head of this pond, we climb north to a gap, then drop easily to a large meadow known as Paradise Valley. Here our path keeps near the screen of infringing lodgepole pines, leaps the outlet stream of Mahan Lake, and comes to a large complex of streamside campsites surrounding a signed junction with a cut-off east to Tilden Canyon. This hot, unworthy route is recommended only for those headed for the Branigan Lakes. To take it, wade across sandy Falls Creek and find the vague trail as it swings east around the south side of a grassy mosquito pond. The route then climbs tortuously southeast through pockets of lodgepole pines to a viewful knoll. Next, this route drops east, then turns southwest up a narrow rock corridor. Near the head of this ravine, where further progress seems blocked by ladyfern and rare baneberry near a talus slide, the path turns abruptly and steeply up to the east. Then the trail bends back to the northeast and climbs easily to a tarn-dotted flat. From here you switchback steeply east over gneissic-banded intrusive rocks into a forested canyon. Lodgepoles and hemlocks shade the way as the drainage heads northeast, then south, to 8575 feet, where the route tops out in a narrow gap. From this pass you drop southeast to find the signed Tilden Canyon Trail.

To finish our hike up Jack Main Canyon to Wilma Lake, we slog through sand beyond the Tilden Canyon cutoff, quickly reaching the shores of a glacial lake that is picturesquely backdropped by a lichen-covered cliff. Beyond it, we're led back through a gap to Falls Creek, and we walk north near its meadows, which are hidden by tall willows. Above us, the ancient Falls Creek glacier sculptured the resistant rock of Peak 8280 into some fantastic fins which today provide excellent multipitch rock climbs. Later, Sybol Lake, now reduced to a seasonal lily pond by a fast-encroaching meadow, is passed with only a glimpse of it through a screen of lodgepoles and aspens.

North of Sybol Lake, Falls Creek, true to its name, tumbles through a narrow gorge of mafic rock and slides over some smooth slabs that are ideal for bathers, and our path takes some rocky, dynamited switchbacks up along it. Above the gorge our streamside way is more gentle. Note that many of the lodgepoles hereabouts have prominent "witches brooms"—bizarrely twisted branches of too-dense needles—that are caused by a virus which disrupts their growth pattern. Presently we spy turf-bounded Wilma Lake lying across the stream, in a pleasant mixed-conifer forest. Now our route ascends a final shoulder and drops to a large, dry flat from where the signed Pacific Crest Trail (Route YP-2) is intersected. It leads both north, up Jack Main Canyon, and east, across broad Falls Creek, to some heavily used camps. Pastoral Wilma Lake, named for the daughter of Clyde Seavey, is just a moment farther. It is a recommended stopover.

Wilma Lake

YP-7

Lake Vernon-Tiltill Valley Trail

Distances
1.9 miles to Lake Vernon
8.4 miles to Tiltill Meadow
11.5 miles to Rancheria Falls

Introduction

This relatively low-country route, a good early-summer conditioner, winds through gently rolling forest stands to large Lake Vernon—a good rainbow-trout fishery, then visits meadowed Tiltill Valley, an interesting pocket of spring wildflowers and grasses. For the finale, choose the Rancheria Falls Trail, so that your return route undulates among the cliffs and waterfalls surrounding the magnificent Hetch Hetchy gorge.

Trailhead

Same as the Route YP-3 trailhead.

Description

Follow the Laurel Lake-Jack Main Canyon Trails (route YP-5 and YP-6) 7.7 miles up through a forest of white firs and lodgepole pines to a moraine-crest junction with the Jack Main Canyon Trail, just below the higher crest of Moraine Ridge. From the junction we descend to an open, granite bench. Now on bedrock, we follow a well-ducked trail past excellent examples of glacier-smoothed rock—glacial polish—and glacier-transported boulders—glacial erratics. Scattered Jeffrey pines lend occasional shade along our northeast traverse, their roots seeking out cracks in the granite in which they might take hold and help form a soil. On drier, more inhospitable sites grow rugged western junipers, which manage to survive where the Jeffreys don't because their scalelike leaves lose less water to the atmosphere than do the Jeffrey's long needles.

Along this section we can look across the far wall of Falls Creek canyon until a nearby granitic outlier, Point 6800 on the topo map, obstructs our view. Just after this happens, we angle southeast and follow a winding, ducked route up toward the point, but cross a low ridge just north of it. Now below us lies large but shallow Lake Vernon, flooding part of a broad, flat-floored canyon.

From this view-packed ridge we descend generally northeast—the trend of this area's master joints—and in ⅓ mile reach a junction with the Lake Vernon Trail. Leaving a small flat, this trail shoots northeast, at first staying close to the base of a similar-trending wall. After ¼ mile of walking, you'll be close to the shore of the unseen lake, and you can head southeast to it. A popular horsemen's campsite lies by the lodgepole-lined lakeshore, just out of sight. More campsites will be found as you approach Lake Vernon's north corner. Just beyond that corner, the trail quickly fades into the bedrock landscape.

After your stay at shallow, fairly warm Lake Vernon, backtrack to the main trail, head southeast to a quick bridging of Falls Creek, then round a bedrock slope back to the lake's southwest corner. More campsites will be found along the lake's south shore. Our next objective, a descent to Tiltill Valley, *first* involves a thousand-foot climb, accomplished with the aid of about three dozen short switchbacks. The view improves as we climb higher, and the spreading panorama gives us good excuses to take plenty of rests. The views disappear when we enter a tiny hanging valley. Now under a cover of firs, we make a short climb up past several moraines until we top the last of them.

With easy hiking ahead, we first dip into a gully, then contour south, passing above two small meadows before crossing another moraine and gently descending to the lower end of a long meadow. Leaving the meadow, we arc southwest up to the crest of a nearby moraine. This vantage point, though only a low ridge, stands a full 4,000 feet above the inundated floor of the Grand Canyon of the

Falls Creek below Lake Vernon

Tuolumne River. While Neanderthal Man roamed Europe, roughly 50,000 years ago, this canyon was completely buried by a tremendously large glacier—a glacier so thick that it overflowed the canyon in several places. Smith Peak, the high point of the canyon wall south of us, stood only 800 feet above the glacier back then.

The moraine we stand on is littered with red-fir snags, their destruction probably due to violent winds along this exposed ridge. After the forest canopy was downed, the soil was once again exposed to sunlight, and thorny snow bushes now crowd the moraine, making it "deer heaven." Indeed, this area is one of the best browsing areas for deer in the entire Park. In addition to snow bush—a favorite food—deer have nearby supplies of aspen, huckleberry oak, scrubby black oak, gooseberry and willow. Our descent along the brushy hillside provides grand views, but the flanking shrubs at times present thorny problems to hikers in shorts. After an initial brief descent, our trail contours for about a

mile, then steepens and on well-built switchbacks descends southeast toward distant Tiltill Valley.

Our descent ends where thirst-quenching Tiltill Creek spills out onto flat-floored Tiltill Valley. On its west bank is a small campsite under incense-cedars and pines, which is enjoyable once the mosquitoes abate, usually after mid-July. A cluster of Miwok Indian bedrock mortars lies nearby, under some large black oaks. Our trail leaves the creek and hugs the base of the valley's towering north wall. At times the trail seems too close to it, for it wanders among large blocks of rockfall-deposited talus; however, a trail built in the meadow would often be waterlogged. We soon pass an unmarked junction with the Tiltill Canyon Trail (route YP-8) and head south across the seasonally boggy meadow, our trail being protected by levees and ditches. The thigh-high bunchgrasses forming the meadow teem with life— grasshoppers and Brewer's and red winged blackbirds are constantly active by daylight hours, while mule deer and black bears forage timidly in the morning and evening. The meadow's dry hummocks and sodden drainage channels themselves offer an ever-changing display of a unique Transition Zone meadow flora, including 8-foot high mountain helenium, a close relative of sneeze-weed, giant umbrella-topped cow-parsnip, elephant's heads, yellow evening primrose, square-stemmed horse mint and fireweed, to name but a few of the showier blooms. Presently we strike an old signed trail junction at the meadow's center. From it a disused trail heads toward the valley's east end, but fades away just yards from the Wilma Lake trail.

From this junction we continue south to the base of some steep bluffs that bound Tiltill Valley on the south and enter a lush stand of aspens, alders and willows surrounding a small spring. Both the treelike mountain dogwood and the shrubbier, red-barked creek dogwood thrive here, shading lady-fern, bracken, thimbleberry, raspberry and currant. Upon reaching the canyon wall, our path immediately begins to climb, taking some well-engineered switchbacks south-west to a large joint-controlled rift. This we follow gently up, southwest, past a small, linear pond decked with yellow pond lilies.

Fragrant western azalea is the dominant understory shrub, joined in sunnier spots by uncommon white-bugled Washington's lily. Straight as an arrow our trail zooms up through a narrow saddle and then gently down into another straight-sided canyon, this one also trending southwest.

After ½ mile we angle west out of this canyon onto open slabs, where we have views south over brushy LeConte Point to somber-cliffed Smith Peak. Now the route begins to descend in earnest, high above the forested coolness below. The trail twists itself into numerous sandy, moderate switchbacks, soon dropping to the 5300-foot level, where the hillside is too hot for Transition Zone species, and Digger pines and gold-cup oaks take over, offering meager shade. Here, too, we perceive some blue slivers of Hetch Hetchy Reservoir, bent around sentinel Kolana Rock to the west. Six hundred feet more of occasionally furnace-hot switch-backing descent follow, depositing us, finally, at a signed junction with the Rancheria Mountain Trail (Route YP-3) on a man-zanita-cloaked sandy hillside. Here we turn right, down some easy switchbacks, and soon bend south to find the cool haven of a large, thick conifer grove along the north bank of Rancheria Creek.

YP-8

Maps 3, main

Tilden Canyon Trail: Pacific Crest Trail to Tiltill Valley

Distances
3.4 miles to Tiltill Meadow
7.8 miles to Tiltill Valley—Rancheria Falls Trail

Introduction
This little-used but highly scenic path leads from the vicinity of northern Yosemite's two prettiest lakes—Wilma Lake and Tilden Lake—on a wild plunge down to unusual Tiltill Valley, a remote pocket of flowers that has been, in years past, both a summertime Miwok village and a turn-of-the-century homestead. The author recommends using this trail in a downhill direction only.

Trailhead
Same as the Route YP-2 or YP-3 trail-head.

Description
Follow the Pacific Crest Trail (or the Jack Main Canyon Trail and then climb east on the PCT above Wilma Lake) to find a signed junction with the Tilden Canyon Trail, in lodgepole-pine forest, just 110 yards south of the PCT's junction with the Tilden Lake Trail (Route YP-9).

Turn southwest down along Tilden Canyon Creek under a mosquitoey lodgepole canopy. This shady walk soon reaches a pear-shaped, grassy tarn rimmed with Labrador tea and bilberry. From its west end, we bend south, following blazes and ducks in open lodgepole stands interspersed with erratics and glaciated slabs. In about a mile we again come close to Tilden Canyon Creek—here a wide lagoon cut deep through meadow turf—where one might disturb a family of mallard ducks. Pressing on, we ascend via steep, eroded, rocky switchbacks, past a junction with the cut-off route to Paradise Valley, described in Route YP-6. The grind abates minutes later, when we level off just below the summit of Peak 8778. The summit of this small *roche moutonnée* is well worth the minute it takes to reach it, for it presents sweeping panoramas of northern Yosemite. We can look all the way up Jack Main Canyon to Bond Pass; then, swinging our gaze east, we spot Tower Peak, Matterhorn Peak, Piute Mountain, and the Cathedral Range from Fairview Dome to Mt. Lyell.

Upon returning to our packs, we walk south along Bailey Ridge, on an easy traverse that is well-shaded by red firs, hemlocks and western white pines. Uncommon bleeding-heart and pine-woods lousewort grow in the shade here. Presently we ascend gently to a broad, forested saddle, then descend on duff to a diminishing lakelet, our last permanent water source for almost 8 miles. Below it, we walk, on again, off again, beside the meadowed outlet stream under moderate forest cover, to small Tiltill Meadow, where a cabin built by H. G. Kibbe lies ruined by a fallen lodgepole.

South of Tiltill Meadow, we continue in the same easy manner for ½ mile, then turn southwest down a dry slope to a small meadow drained by a step-across branch of Rancheria Creek. Now begins a 2300-foot descent to Tiltill Valley, Chaparral areas allow views south and east over the bluffs of Smith Peak and Rancheria Mountain. Moderate switchbacks ease our descent to 7300 feet, and then we drop more gently southwest down a sandy canyon and look west to a brush-covered Mount Gibson. Next we work south along a bouldery, brushy bench, and

then begin the final 1300-foot plunge. At first, we stay on the north side of a small ridge, descending steeply on sand in the relative shade of high huckleberry-oak brush and scattered Jeffrey pines. But below 6600 feet we swing onto the ridge's south face, which allows our first views of lush Tiltill Valley and, beyond it, Hetch Hetchy Reservoir, but also subjects us to the full heat of the midday sun. Woe betide anyone climbing *up* this slope! Eventually, at 6330 feet, we reach a gap on the ridge, which affords some shade and a good spot to study the effects that the mammoth Rancheria Creek and Tuolumne River glaciers had on the country below us. At this elevation, during the Ice Age's height, we would have been buried under about 1200 feet of glacier ice, since the Tiltill Creek glacier had a trimline near 7500 feet on Mount Gibson and the Rancheria Creek glacier rose to the level of the last small meadow that we passed at 7900 feet, at the start of this steep descent! At Hetch Hetchy, the Tuolumne glacier filled the 2-mile-wide canyon to well over the 7500-foot elevation.

Below this instructional rest stop, more steep, rocky, exposed switchbacks ensue, this time leading east through gold-cup-oak scrub. Eventually the trail bends south and lowers us to the long-awaited shade of a grove of incense-cedars, black oaks and Jeffrey pines at the eastern corner of Tiltill Valley. We turn west onto the flats and emerge into a hummocky, open grassland, then follow its edge to join the Lake Vernon Trail (Route YP-7), which turns south across the meadow.

YP-9

Tilden Lake

Distances

3.1 miles to Tilden Lake southeast shore
4.0 miles to Mary Lake Trail
5.8 miles to Pacific Crest Trail in Jack Main
Canyon

Introduction

Tilden Lake epitomizes the shining pastoral beauty of northern Yosemite. Its 2-mile sweep of quiet water reflects blue skies, soaring granite peaks and dark stands of cool forest. Its campsites are superb, the fishing usually excellent. It is the ultimate base camp—dozens of exciting lakes, peaks and meadows lie within easy reach.

Trailhead

Same as the Route YP-2 or YP-6 trailhead.

Description

Follow the Pacific Crest Trail or the Jack Main Canyon Trail to reach Tilden Canyon. Here, at the south end of a lovely tarn, just yards from Tilden Canyon Creek, a well-signed intersection denotes our trail, branching east. We quickly ascend, with the aid of a few switchbacks, out of the dark, damp flats of lodgepole pines that surround the junction, onto a more open hillside. We curve north to follow the axis of Tilden Canyon, and then occupy the next hour in a gentle upstream amble. Pleasant lodgepole-pine forest is our overstory, with purple aster and lacy meadow-rue beneath. We stay always within earshot of burbling Tilden Canyon Creek; later, we step across it twice. As we proceed up-canyon, pockets of grass coalesce into rolling, hummocky grasslands. By the time the path nears a quartet of shallow tarns that lie astride the broad saddle which separates Tilden Canyon from Tilden Lake, we are walking in a broad meadow swale carpeted with sedges, paintbrush and lupine.

Now descend just a bit to the first of many first-class campsites on the southeast shore of long, narrow Tilden Lake. Horse-packer use of these sites is heavy, as indicated by log tables, benches and big fire-pits. But no one can fault their choice—early morning reflections in Tilden Lake's still waters of Saurian Crest and Tower Peak are among the most sublime in Yosemite. The camps are populated enough to make them a favored dinner spot for local bears as well—secure your food accordingly.

Our trail bends southwest along the forest-pocketed south shore of Tilden Lake, passing quite a number of good camps and granitic promontories from which to angle for a breakfast of rainbow trout. Tilden Lake narrows into a rocky bay under the impressive dome-face of Chittenden Peak, at its outlet. There we find a trail that crosses Tilden Creek to traverse the much-less-visited west shore of Tilden Lake. Beyond, it ascends to Mary Lake, as described in Route WB-1—a highly recommended day trip.

From the outlet of Tilden Lake, the cobbly trail drops west along the slabby, south banks of frolicking Tilden Creek, where a profusion of shrubs and herbs line our path. Chittenden Peak's south face looms well above us, and we gain views west across the wooded trough of Jack Main Canyon to Schofield and Haystack peaks. Soon switchbacks appear to smooth our way down into thickening forest, always near now-cart-wheeling, sometimes free-falling Tilden Creek. Below 8400 feet we turn south through sandy lodgepole forest and trace Jack Main Canyon downstream for ½ mile before stepping through a fringe of Labrador tea to the 70-foot-wide, shallow ford of Falls Creek. This horse ford will confer wet feet most of the year. On the west bank, we find a pleasant camp and 80 yards later reach the signed Pacific Crest Trail (Route YP-2).

Ch. 14: Cherry Lake

CL-1

Kibbie Ridge Trail: Cherry Dam to Huckleberry Lake

Distances

1.7 miles to Lake Eleanor Trail
4.1 miles to Shingle Spring
5.3 miles to Kibbie Lake Trail
13.1 miles to Styx Pass
15.1 miles to Lord Meadow
19.3 miles to Huckleberry Lake (south end)
22.0 miles to Huckleberry Lake (north end)

Introduction

The lower, less-trammeled Kibbie Ridge region of Yosemite is the favorite among knowledgeable backpackers for early- and late-season weekenders. Deep forests and some little-fished subalpine lakes are their rewards. For the more adventuresome, the Kibbie Ridge Trail is the fastest way in to Huckleberry Lake, in the Emigrant's heartland.

Trailhead

From Groveland drive east 13.6 miles on Highway 120 to paved Cherry Oil Road 1N07, just beyond the highway bridge over South Fork Tuolumne River. Follow it 5.3 miles to a junction with paved Hetch Hetchy Road, then go left along potholed pavement 17.6 more miles to dirt Cottonwood Road 1N04. The signed Cherry Dam parking area is just yards down Road 1N04 to the east.

Description

As of 1988 there were *two* possible trailheads for the Kibbie Ridge Trail, one part way up the old trail. The entire original path, beginning at Cherry Dam, will be described below.

But first, thoughtless action by Stanislaus National Forest authorities to allow logging on the west slopes of Kibbie Ridge has resulted in construction of a logging road—now seasonally open to public travel—essentially all the way to Shingle Spring. The unfortunate outcome of this road's construction will be to do away with a buffer zone (4.3 trail miles and 1200 feet of hot ascent) that previously existed for Kibbie Lake and Many Island Lake—increased overuse, litter and pollution are inevitable. To reach the new roadend, drive across Cherry Valley Dam, then ½ mile up old oiled Road 1N14 to a T, where the left (north) branch, Road 1N45Y, is signed WILDERNESS VISITOR PARKING. Drive up this good dirt road, then down 2 miles to a succession of signed trailhead parking areas, for the Lake Eleanor, Kibbie Creek-Flora Lake, and old Kibbie Ridge trails, respectively. Now the road begins to climb alongside Kibbie Ridge. Three switchbacks and 2¼ miles eventually lead up to an abrupt deadend at 5880 feet. Here a green metal corral is found, and a gray sign indicating the Kibbie Ridge Trail. This short, rough spur trail leads east-northeast uphill to strike the main trail, which gently traverses the hillside. Shingle Spring, with excellent water, beautiful dogwoods and nearby camps, is found just a minute back down the trail to the south.

In early season, late fall, and times of high fire danger, the logging spur to Shingle

Cherry Reservoir (Lake Lloyd)

Spring will probably be closed by the gate at Cherry Dam. Then, as in years past, park at Cherry Lake and follow the old Kibbie Ridge Trail. From the parking area, located in a dusty forest at 4780 feet just west of the south end of Lake Lloyd, popularly known as Cherry Lake, we follow the short parking spur back to Road 1N07, which winds down past USFS and City of San Francisco houses to 2600-foot-long Cherry Valley Dam. Walking northeast along a road topping the 330-foot impoundment, we gaze north over the clear blue waters of this 268,000-acre-foot reservoir to the granite domes dimpling Cherry Creek Canyon. After turning north on a dirt road at Cherry Dam's east end, we stroll through a dry Transition Zone forest that is floored with fragrant mountain misery, abundant shield-leaved streptanthus, and dainty purple and yellow mimulus. Our road contours just above a trail coming from the horse stables west of the dam via a ledge on the upstream dam face. Soon, this trail crosses our road, and we take it, to wind

above the lakeshore in denser forest. Later, our route turns northeast to a thick stand of young incense-cedar, where the Lake Eleanor/Kibbie Creek Trail branches southeast. After crossing an oiled gravel road and a spring-fed rivulet and ascending a small granite knoll, we hit wide, gravelled logging road 1N45Y. The trail's crossing of this road is marked by small signs, and a trailhead parking area is seen just up the road.

We now switchback on a northward course over bouldery till along the west slope of Kibbie Ridge, sometimes perceiving blue fragments of Cherry Lake through a now-thicker forest of Jeffrey pine and white fir. These infrequent vistas are only partial consolation for the steep, dusty ascent, often in deep sand, with ample evidence of past logging operations.

We do have one respite from our monotonous climb—at 5920 feet we halt to sample the pleasures of Shingle Spring, situated in a ravine shaded by white fir, Jeffrey pine and dogwood, and giving water from a wooden horse-trough. (Best to treat the water.) Continuing on, our feet lead us up to a ridgetop, then gently down into cool, forested Deadhorse Gulch. Soon we reach the well-marked Kibbie Lake Trail in a fine duff-floored conifer grove beside a small grass-choked pond. Dropping past signed Sand Canyon, we pass, in quick succession, a marshy flat, a mapped creek with a good camp (at the Emigrant Wilderness boundary) and a switchback that leads up onto sparsely forested granite slabs covered with "grus," or rotten granite. Note how the massive roots of the Jeffrey pines loosen and crush the peeling rock, hastening the development of soil.

Soon re-entering red-fir forest, we climb steadily to signed Lookout Point, with vistas west of the deep cleft of Cherry Creek Canyon. Next, we pass Swede's Camp—a corn-lily-filled meadow—and ascend to a large, warm, shallow pond. After skirting its sandy north shore, we climb under sparse mixed trees, often at a steep incline, to an open-ridgetop sand flat where we find the Yosemite National Park boundary. A steep, vague path straight up the sandy ridge, blessed with fine panoramas southeast to Mount Conness, leads to the muddy, marsh-marigold-dotted vicinity of Sachse Spring, where there is a good camp.

East of Sachse Spring, the trail undulates on morainal material in well-spaced western white pine and red fir. A large lakelet almost 0.2 mile north of the trail affords very good, but littered, camping on its south side. Beyond a seasonal creek, our route begins to descend onto open granite slabs, a harbinger of typical Emigrant Basin terrain to come. Mercur Peak, 8080+, a prominent granite dome in the northeast, is a good showpiece of the two dominant erosional processes in this part of the Sierra—exfoliation ("onion-skin" rock peeling) and glaciation. Coming off the slabs into a small lodgepole forest surrounding a brown tarn, we keep right following blazed trees and ducks, then continue on a bearing straight for Mercur Peak over sandy slabs. Mercur Peak, an easy scrambling ascent via the south slope, provides a fine vantage point for examining the southern Emigrant Basin. South of Mercur Peak, in lodgepole forest, we pass a large tarn, quite wet in early season around the camps on its north side, which marks the turnoff point for Many Island Lake.

To reach this aptly named lake, proceed due south from this tarn through lodgepoles and around numerous early-season ponds to low-angle slabs bounding the north part of the cirque that contains this glacial lake. By keeping one's feet flat on the sloping rock and pointed downhill, one should have no difficulty descending to the campsites flanking its warm, shallow waters, which harbor rainbow trout.

East of the junction with the Many Island Lake cross-country route, the Kibbie Ridge Trail passes through a narrow, joint-controlled gully to unsigned Styx Pass, where we leave Yosemite National Park. We descend to better views of the North and East Fork Cherry Creek drainages, flanked by soaring domes. Eight tight, rocky switchbacks decorated by clumps of sedge and red Sierra onion bring us to a long traverse east to the Boundary Lake Trail, 0.6 mile from Styx Pass. The unsigned Boundary Lake Trail (Route CL-4) can be readily identified by its proximity to a double-trunked lodgepole snag. A long switchback leg completes our downgrade to Cherry Creek, where we enter a dense forest of lodgepole flanked on the north by very wide, green Cherry Creek. A fine technical climbing dome, Peak 7604, lies north of the creek.

In Lord Meadow, the soggy lowland east of the confluence of the two forks of Cherry Creek, we encounter lodgepoles, mosquitoes, muddy early-season detours, deer tracks, one good camp, one packer camp, and an easy, 80-foot-long crotch-deep (in early season) wade of East Fork Cherry Creek on sand and cobbles. About 150 feet after Cherry Creek, we come to an unmarked junction with the North Fork Cherry Creek Trail (Route CL-5). The ducked North Fork Trail here begins north, then goes west around a 40-foot granite outcrop, while our route along the East

Many Island Lake

Fork has a bearing of due east.

Walking off the slabs, we climb gently, alternating through wooded and open stretches, often near the cascading creek and its streamside accompaniment of lupine, bitter cherry, spiraea, serviceberry and willow, to a tricky ford to the south side of East Fork Cherry Creek. Poorly situated just below a series of cascades, the 15-foot crossing is deep and fast over large, slick boulders. Hikers should avoid this crossing at high water by using the Cross-Country alternate along the north side of Cherry Creek.

North Side Cherry Creek Cross-Country Alternate Route: West to East:

In times of high water it is better to avoid the second and third fords of Cherry Creek. You can do so by taking a cross-country route that leaves the trail about 75 yards before the second crossing. Bear left, northeast, to enter a bare glaciated bowl, the lip of which overlooks rapids above the second ford. A short pitch of scrambling to the top of a broad, flat dome finishes the difficulties, from which the Huckleberry Lake Trail is rejoined a few hundred yards to one's east.

While taking a few minutes on the south side to dry your feet, one might keep an eye out for juncos and violet-green swallows—the most common birds in this area. Dynamited switchbacks amid a riot of wildflowers lead us above foaming white cascades; then we contour back to the creekside, just above a large pool where we tread waterworn exfoliation shells to yet another crossing of East Fork Cherry Creek. Here the sliding stream is gentler, allowing an easy but slippery ford. Our route then cuts cross-slope under a fine dome, on slabs covered with exfoliation debris from across the canyon. This debris is ample evidence that avalanches can cross creeks and even move uphill. Ending the traverse, we come to a steep, gravelly climb on switchbacks to a small nose where we meet the North Side Cross-Country Alternate Route. Now in a broad glacial hanging valley, we climb more gently past mauve, shreddy-barked Sierra junipers, and come to a barren, glacially polished exfoliation surface, sprinkled with rounded erratic boulders and dimpled by smooth solution pockets. This bowl precedes the low saddle just west of Pruitt Lake creek.

To reach Pruitt Lake, bear north from this saddle for about 200 feet of gain before swinging away to avoid huckleberry-oak thickets. Near Pruitt Lake's outlet it is possible to return to the creek. The deep, blue, rough rectangle of Pruitt Lake is nestled in groves of lodgepole and western white pines. Rainbow trout to 8" are numerous.

From the glaciated col marking the way to Pruitt Lake, the East Fork Trail hops across Pruitt Lake creek, then ascends close to the rocky banks of dancing Cherry Creek, with violet-green swallows swooping and gliding overhead to capture dinner—mostly mosquitoes in June and July. Our way skirts the south side of a glaringly polished dome, returning to the chuting rock trough of Cherry Creek, and comes into pastoral groves of mat manzanita and lodgepole pine under an awesome cliff face on the 400-foot dome to our northwest.

A winding, imperceptible ascent soon brings us to a snow-survey cabin, good campsites, and a junction with the Horse Meadow Trail, all of these beside broad, smooth-running Cherry Creek. Now we can follow either of two good trails levelly up-canyon a short distance to Huckleberry Lake. The better path crosses near the cabin to the south bank, while the northside trail makes a very muddy ford south, after striking Huckleberry Lake at the terminus of the Bell Meadow Trail (Route PC-10). Huckleberry Lake is a surprisingly clear 200-acre expanse of granite- and lodgepole-rimmed blue water, with camping possibilities on duff and mat manzanita around much of its shore. The generally shallow lagoons at its south end offer pleasant swimming, and abundant rainbow and brook trout live here.

Continue northeast along the shore of this largest of Emigrant Wilderness' lakes. Our trail is essentially level in pleasant lodgepole forest with an understory of bilberry and blueberry, and small pockets of meadow dotted with white gentian. However, if you come here before the mosquitoes burn off in summer's heat, beware: the environs of Huckleberry Lake, with its shallow embayments and tiny ponds, are a veritable mosquito hell! Presently, we note a good, but unsigned trail branching left, northwest. It leads to signed "Anderson Camp—Established 1941"—a delightful spot on a small peninsula near the south end of Huckleberry Lake. The Anderson Camp turnoff is also about the right place to begin a cross-country hike up to Fawn and Peninsula lakes: Scramble east up the obvious, bouldery gully just south of a domelike cliff to top the low, open divide between Cherry and Kendrick creeks. Now walk southeast down to diminutive, linear Fawn Lake—which, though secluded, has nothing else to recommend it. One could continue from here to Peninsula Lake, via Route KM-4.

Back on the Huckleberry Trail, continue levelly northeast, soon passing large, picturesque lakelets that connect with the main lake in early season. Later, near the largest northern arm of Huckleberry Lake, we traverse rockily, right on the shore. Now rounding above the head of Huckleberry Lake, we enter drier, open forest, pass a spur west to a horse-packer camp, and then strike wide, shallow East Fork Cherry Creek at a willow-lined cut-bank. Make a 20–30' wade (in early season), then walk briefly north into forest to find an unsigned intersection with the Huckleberry Trail (Route KM-1) and the Bell Meadow Trail (Route PC-10) at a large, dry camping area.

CL-2

Kibbie Lake Trail

Distances
2.7 miles to Kibbie Lake
4.1 miles to Flora Lake trail junction

Introduction
Large, rock-girdled Kibbie Lake, named for Tuolumne County pioneer H. G. Kibbe, is the terminus of this pleasant trail, and the recommended spot to spend the first night for those entering the Emigrant Basin via Kibbie Ridge Trail (Route CL-1).

Trailhead
Same as the Route CL-1 trailhead. Note the possibility of driving to near Shingle Spring to begin the hike.

Description
The well-marked Kibbie Lake Trail junction, 5½ miles up the Kibbie Ridge Trail (Route CL-1), stands in a fine duff-floored conifer grove. Skirting a tarn, we near a ridgetop open space dominated by silver-haired dwarf lupine, pretty face, used by the Miwok Indians for food, shield-leaved streptanthus, and buckwheat. This area is an ancient glacial erosion surface, as can be seen from the smooth rock surfaces and large erratic boulders scattered abut. Presently our route enters Yosemite National Park and drops on rocky tread surrounded by chaparral, lightly treed with Jeffrey pines, into a small canyon. We amble north through sodden bottom land, passing the first lodgepole pines of our trip, which here, accompanied by white fir, form a dense canopy. Indian-hemp, false Solomon's seal, bracken fern, Queen Anne's-lace, violets, shooting stars and the delicate but deadly blooms of bleeding heart nod in the shadows, inviting the traveler to linger in coolness. But mosquitoes, far and away the most numerous

Kibbie Lake

inhabitant of damp early-season forests, will no doubt urge you on!

The trail leaves the forest, climbing northeast onto granite slabs mottled by huckleberry oak, to a 6500-foot-high saddle. An observant naturalist will possibly encounter white, greenish-spotted explorer's gentian, discovered by John Newberry, physician for the transcontinental railroad surveys in the 1850's. The rocky route here descends to cross a tributary of Kibbie Creek under a south-facing dome that offers good rock climbing on its peeling skin. After the step-across ford, we closely parallel smooth green pools on Kibbie Creek, which is shaded by western azaleas, willows and tall conifers. We pass a good camp on the right, then, just yards later, before a poorer trail climbs up amid huckleberry oak to the right of a granitic outcrop to continue over slabs to the west shore of Kibbie Lake, our route angles down to a 30-foot rock-hop of Kibbie Creek. A very good meadowed camp is found across the ford amid lodgepoles, before we turn up the creek over blasted granite ledges, our way copiously indicated by ducks.

Passing ice-scoured lagoons presaging Kibbie Lake, we reach its south shore, where camps are found in a lodgepole-and-lab-rador-tea fringe. One hundred-six acre Kibbie Lake is bounded on the west by gently sloping granite, while the east shore is characterized by steep, broken bluffs and polished bosses. The waters themselves are shallow, with an algae-coated sandy bottom, where distinctively orange-colored California newts may take your bait if a rainbow trout (to 12″) doesn't.

A little-used trail, well-ducked but now fallen into disrepair, ascends south from Kibbie Lake's outlet to meet the Kibbie Creek Trail (Route CL-3) on a high ridge. Following it could enable hikers to make a loop trip out of the walk to Kibbie Lake. This route begins at camps on the south shore, then turns south, winding gently up along the steeper hillside via a rather circuitous link of forest patches, slabs and brushy, joint-controlled ravines. Eventually, we attack the slope no-holds-barred: small, eroded switchbacks rapidly gain over 300 feet, yielding somewhat oblique views back over Kibbie Lake. Abruptly cresting the rise at a series of narrow ridges of lateral moraine cloaked in deep litter of downed red firs, we find the obvious Kibbie Creek Trail (Route CL-3) to Flora Lake, paralleling the ridgetop.

CL-3

Kibbie Creek Trail to Flora Lake

Distances
   1.7 miles to Lake Eleanor Trail
   2.6 miles to Flora Lake Trail Junction
   4.1 miles to Kibbie Creek Ford
   7.2 miles to Kibbie Lake Trail
10.6 miles to Flora Lake

Introduction

Flora Lake was once proposed as the site of a cavalry outpost, as an alternative to the one eventually built at Miguel Meadow, east of Lake Eleanor. At the time, this was proposed because Flora Lake was centrally located for day-long horse patrol forays by U.S. Army guardians of the new Yosemite National Park, against encroaching sheepherders. Today, Flora Lake makes a good base camp for the same reasons—one-to-two easy walking hours through open country can lead to Kibbie, Many Island, Boundary, Little Bear, Spotted Fawn or Inferno Lake; all are prime producers of rainbow trout.

Trailhead

Same as the Route CL-1 trailhead.

Description

Round the east shore of Cherry Lake on the Kibbie Ridge Trail (Route CL-1), then head inland a few minutes to the signed Lake

Eleanor Trail, 1.7 miles from the roadend on Cherry Lake. Follow this later path gently east, up alongside dirt road 1N40Y to its well-signed crossing of that road. Alternatively, if roads to the east side of Cherry Lake are open, one can drive to this point and park nearby, as described for the Route CL-1 trailhead. In either case, a large gray wooden sign shows where the Lake Eleanor Trail branches right, southeast, from dirt road 1N40Y, just downhill from a signed wilderness visitor parking area. The trail climbs easily and rockily up in live oak and Jeffrey pine, quickly reaching the signed Yosemite boundary, and then, a moment later, a signed junction. From here the right trail branch drops to a short spur to camps on a peninsula on the west shore of Lake Eleanor, then continues south to Lake Eleanor's dam. But our route forks left, northeast, signed for Kibbie Lake (though this is neither the most direct nor the easiest route to get there). Staying just within the Park boundary, our path ascends gently near the morainal ridgetop, in a sunny open conifer-and-oak woodland, with delightful harlequin lupine, colored magenta and yellow, under foot. Presently the climb turns northeast, and enters ponderosa-pine and incense-cedar forest, here and there giving glimpses of Lake Eleanor below. Eventually, the way levels out to find Kibbie Creek. Camping is illegal here. Mounds of earth scattered here are the work of curio hunters, illegally sifting for Miwok Indian artifacts. This was a Miwok village site, as shown by mortar holes in rocks at the lip of the cascades.

Ford Kibbie Creek by a rock-hop just above a small cascade. Across it, begin to climb rather steeply on a duff-covered, fire-scarred hillside. Soon enough, the climb moderates and bends northward, first to round under the steep gray nose of a small ridge, then to hop across an east branch of Kibbie Creek. Tank up on water here—a hot grind lies ahead. Now work fairly directly up a cobbly ridge northwest of the stream, alternating between coniferous shade and hot, open benches with huckleberry oak and pinemat manzanita. Eventually, the path almost levels out near the ridgetop—a narrow moraine—and enters open red-fir forest. Almost as soon as we top the ridge, we merge with the unsigned Kibbie Lake Trail (Route CL-2), which drops vaguely north. Fallen trees obscure the route through a series of sandy flats, but the route is easy enough to follow—just keep trending toward the north side of the ridge, following ducks. Where the ridgecrest broadens, the grade levels into a denser forest of fir and lodgepole. With fallen trees across one's way, the path—now an indistinct rut—is very easy to lose. If you do get off-route, simply continue to walk east— soon enough, the track will be found as it crosses a trickling early-season creeklet that drains a small, swampy meadow just north of the trail. Now, fairly well-marked by ducks, the trail to Flora Lake heads directly uphill, into a small ravine just under the crest of the Kibbie Creek/Eleanor Creek divide. Here, again, the path peters out in scattered logs and forest litter in a dark forest stand. Continue up along the left side of the streambank to find the path as it arcs up a final rise to a sandy divide. The trail there is more conspicuous, as it traverses fairly levelly northeastward, soon yielding vistas southeast to the Clark Range, to the uplands south of Hetch Hetchy and over a sea of granitic domes to the dark parapets of Piute Mountain.

Beyond this summit vista, the path descends back to denser forest, where again, in spite of ducks, the route will most likely be lost. At this point, walk east to vantage points from where you can probably choose a fairly brush-free route east, down over broken white granitic slabs and small steps. Most of the easier routes lead first to a small, pretty, horseshoe-shaped lakelet on a bench overlooking Flora Lake. Beyond, descend easy glacially polished slabs to Flora Lake's southwest shore. Nice camps are found in stands of lodgepole above the west side, overlooked by low cliffs. Similar but damper accommodations may be had east of Flora Lake, in denser forest with an understory of fallen timber and knee-high bracken ferns. The waters here are warmish, and angling for rainbow trout to 16 inches is fair.

Easy day hikes, mostly over open, slabby terrain, are possible to any of the lakes north and east of Flora Lake. However, I recommend against attempting to descend Bartlett Creek below the confluence of the streams from Flora and Spotted Fawn lakes—it is a narrow, brush-choked gorge. For the same reasons, the Eleanor-Kendrick Creek drainages are also not recommended, though they offer total seclusion, magnificent virgin mixed-conifer forest, and truly stupendous sheer, clean granite walls and small domes.

CL-4

Boundary Lake Trail to Little Bear Lake and Spotted Fawn Lake

Distances
0.6 mile to Boundary Lake
2.5 miles to Little Bear Lake
2.9 miles to Spotted Fawn Lake

Introduction
The Boundary Lake Trail opens up the rugged splendor of northwest Yosemite National Park's Eleanor Creek country to exploration by the competent cross-country adventurer. Awesome rock cliffs, hewn by massive Ice Age glaciers, and numerous lakes, also the result of glacial action, are found in this lonely region, offering challenging rock-climbing, virginal fisheries, or days of wild solitude.

Trailhead
Same as the Route CL-1 trailhead.

Description
The unsigned Boundary Lake Trail begins on the Kibbie Ridge Trail (Route CL-1) 0.6 mile east of Styx Pass, at 7320 feet on a steep, broken slope of exfoliating granite. Just before one makes two small switchbacks and starts a traverse northwest down to Lord Meadow, a double-trunked lodgepole snag is seen south of the Kibbie Ridge Trail, marking the junction. A vaguely ducked switchbacking trail leads us steeply south toward Boundary Lake, presently becoming less steep through a jumble of lodgepoles and rocks to a forested tarn. From it, a final rise passes the limits of Yosemite National Park to a pair of seasonal ponds that connect with Boundary Lake's north side. Sandy flats softened by red Sierra onion and sparse conifers make for good camping at this side of the lake; the east shore is composed of high bluffs. The trail around Boundary Lake's west side winds over granite outcrops, through patches of huckleberry oak and stands of fir and pine. Our undulating path keeps generally away from the irregular rocky shore, but sometimes we near the shore to find a snug camp in protective clumps of Labrador tea or willows. Campers will find good fishing for rainbow trout.

At Boundary Lake's south end, we steer through a notched dome, to a step-across ford of the outlet. On the south bank for a moment, we have telescoped views across the lake's slate-gray entirety before we turn south down a joint gully to the marshy north end of Little Bear Lake. Heading east of this islet-speckled expanse, we pass a fine packer camp in the north shore, then turn south behind a red-fir-and-lodgepole grove entangled in a marshy maze of brake fern and manzanita. At the south end of Little Bear Lake we have the option of descending south to granite-cupped Spotted Fawn Lake, which has camping in its northshore lodgepole curtain. Spotted Fawn Lake, with its large rainbow trout, gives the adventuresome explorer access to the Inferno Lakes, Nance Peak, Edyth Lake, and the unnamed lakes of Kendrick Creek by rough but rewarding cross-country routes.

Spotted Fawn Lake

CL-5

North Fork Cherry Creek Trail: Lord Meadow to Cow Meadow Lake and Emigrant Lake

Distances
4.9 miles to Cow Meadow Lake
6.6 miles to Starr Jordan Lake
8.2 miles to Crabtree Trail at Emigrant Lake

Introduction
The North Fork Trail, now fallen into disuse, still provides a quick, scenic way from Lord Meadow to Cow Meadow and Emigrant lakes, as well as access to Yellow-hammer Lake.

Trailhead
Same as the Route CL-1 trailhead.

Description
The North Fork Cherry Creek Trail has its vague beginnings in a sand flat, about 150 feet north of the crossing of East Fork Cherry

Creek in Lord Meadow (see the Kibbie Ridge Trail, Route CL-1). Here, where the Kibbie Ridge Trail can be seen to head east, following ducks, our route begins to curve north, then northwest, along the margin of a bracken-floored lodgepole stand to our left, while skirting a 40-foot rock wall to our right. Following ducks, we ascend gently along this outcrop, pass through a litter of downed lodgepoles, and emerge beside a wide, emerald-green pool in the otherwise roaring North Fork Cherry Creek. One might see a mallard duck, a summer transient, and its clutch of marbled ducklings dabbling here. A red-fir grove here, with sandy underfooting, provides restful shelter, but the through traveler walks behind the trees to ascend gently before returning to the stream's east bank. A few hundred yards later we spot a blazed lodgepole bending over the far shore, marking our route's crossing. This ford could be chest-deep and very swift in high water, magnifying the poor footing provided by slippery boulders, so it should be treated with proper respect. Later, it's a cake walk.

After toweling dry, ascend straight up the west bank of Cherry Creek for a bit, following ducks, to find the trail beside blazed Sierra junipers. Then parallel the stream on a forested bench below a tall cliff. Returning to the creekside from this essentially level traverse, the route peters out in a stand of red fir, so we stay near the slowly moving stream to find a ducked sand-and-slab route when we emerge from the trees. The next leg of our journey keeps us within 100 feet of the frothing white water, rarely presenting a true trail tread, but ducks are plentiful and the route obvious. Soon an incredibly blank unjointed friction face, 500 feet high, is seen on the North Fork's northwest wall, and we pass the Big Lake Trail (Route PC-11), which, in its last leg from Yellowhammer Lake, is a cross-country walk down a prominent gully extending from the south ridge of Peak 8206. A cascade at 7480 feet precedes more meadowy walking to come. At 7680 feet a 60-foot-high double waterfall is encountered, which we skirt to the left. Hikers proceeding down canyon won't have any trouble finding the way around, but those going northeast will want to begin ascending around the falls 100 yards below them.

Thin white petals of western serviceberry catch the eye as the forest opens up dramatically near the outlet of Cow Meadow Lake. Just in sight of the low stream-flow-maintenance dam that impounds this lake, we pass a packer camp, then hug the base of a 60-foot cliff along the western lake's north shore. Cow Meadow Lake is in reality a series of lakes and marshes which, with the help of the check dam, run together in high water. For this reason, the lake's size fluctuates widely, and, although its maximum depth is 36 feet, much of the lake doesn't attain more than a 3-foot depth. While the seasonal inundation of meadowland does kill many of the lodgepole pines that rim the shore, it also sweeps much food into the water, as well as providing good spawning areas, so Cow Meadow Lake's rainbow trout are big (to 15") and numerous. Pleasant lodgepole forest is the site for many packer campsites as we wind north along the meadowed fringes of first Cow Meadow Lake, then North Fork Cherry Creek. Unfortunately, inconsiderate horsemen have marred the splendor with a plethora of cans and bottles. Soon we arrive at a four-way unsigned intersection with the Bell Meadow–Huckleberry Lake Trail (Route PC-10).

Now in heavy lodgepole forest, our obvious path continues north right alongside wide, slow North Fork Cherry Creek, which itself harbors many rainbow and brook trout. Soon, however, the little used trail, which is *not* recommended for stock, alternately hops fallen logs and meanders vaguely through tiny, corn-lily meadows to the base of the brushy canyon wall. After a time we are led away from the stream bed, and then, abruptly, the well-ducked but very rocky trail turns steeply uphill in a narrow gully choked with huckleberry oak. Tight, eroded switchbacks and poor shade are the order of the day, to eventually gain the seasonal outlet stream of Starr-Jordan Lake. Momentarily losing the path in a small bog, we nonetheless easily reach camps at the south end of small, shallow Starr-Jordan Lake, which commemorates an early advocate of Yosemite's conservation. This lake was planted with a few rainbows in past years. The trail skirts its east shore, then climbs briskly in a stand of mountain hemlocks. The understory here is primarily mat manzanita, but look for rare, red-brown coralroot orchids, as well. We may also glimpse a clean dome face to the north, and from here one can wind cross-country northwest to Estella Lake, also stocked with rainbow trout. The next important flower we encounter is *Senecio triangularis*—a waist-high sunflower relative. We lose the trail for a moment in a patch of it, then wind over a sandy ridge to once again

Cascade on North Fork Cherry Creek

encounter North Fork Cherry Creek. Now look north, where cascades on the horizon mark the outlet of Emigrant Lake. We pass them, going up easy switchbacks alongside dancing water, to find an 8-foot-high rock-and-concrete dam at Emigrant Lake's outlet. Here a cross-country route (KM-5), to Fraser and Shallow lakes leads east. Our trail heads along Emigrant Lake's west shore, through thickets of Labrador-tea, over downed logs, and sometimes ankle-deep in wet lakeside meadows. Halfway along, at a fair camp, a faint use-trail in a small gully climbs west over to the three tiny Maxine Lakes. As we proceed north, views improve up the length of the lake to the Emigrant Pass area. A final scramble over rocky ledges leads to a meadow beside the northwest shore. Hop a small stream and join the obvious but unsigned Crabtree Trail (Route PC-4).

CL-6

Cherry Creek Canyon: Cross Country From Lord Meadow to Cherry Lake

Distances
 8.9 miles to campsite in Lower Cherry
       Creek
13.8 miles to Shingle Springs Roadend

Introduction

Without a doubt the finest trek within the bounds of Emigrant Wilderness, the rugged traverse of Cherry Creek Canyon can be summed up in one word—granite. Granite boulders, slabs, talus and sand, spawned from soaring Yosemite-like cliffs and buttresses, broken from sensuously curving arches and exfoliating aprons, or ground by frothing whirlpools in spray-flecked, water-polished granite gorges—granite makes Cherry Creek Canyon the most exciting chasm north of Yosemite National Park. This route is not for the inexperienced, however. Frequent rock-scrambling and taxing route-finding problems make Cherry Creek Canyon a world accessible only to the mountain-wise explorer, and sometimes high water will hamper even the most resourceful of these. For safety and ease of travel, this hike should be undertaken only in good weather and only when water is low, but the intrepid few who navigate Cherry Creek Canyon when the water is high and wild will be treated to an unforgettable experience. The rewards for all are total solitude, unclimbed domes and faces of Yosemite-like proportions, deep, clear swimming pools, virgin fisheries, and unspoiled forest camping. The hike is described here from Lord Meadow out to Cherry Reservoir; it is demanding enough without going uphill!

Trailhead

Same as the Route CL-1 trailhead.

Description

The start of our exciting trip through pristine Cherry Creek Canyon is found just after the last switchback into Lord Meadow from Styx Pass, at 7200 feet. Here we veer north from the Kibbie Ridge Trail (Route CL-1) and traverse slabs to Cherry Creek, which is pooled wide and deep over green, sandy gravels. A short scramble brings us to the first of many precariously angled traverses on water-polished exfoliation slabs, 25–50 feet above white, cartwheeling cascades in the creek, which during spring runoff is more appropriately likened to a river. The cascades end at a small conifer grove, where

there is a fair camp, and our rate of descent becomes negligible along the alternately pooling and rushing stream.

Turning west, we begin a long ramble down sandy, water-worn slabs under the brow of two spectacular multi-pitch rock towers which loom from the north flanks of Mercur Peak. Near the influx of Yellowhammer Lake creek, the canyon floor is alive with plants—paintbrush, phlox, Bridges' penstemon, serviceberry, pretty face, wallflower, hulsea and onion are among the notables. But later, as the 1000-foot-deep canyon bends north, the slick granite is devoid of life except for a few bonsai-like miniature lodgepoles managing an existence in seemingly sterile cracks.

Beyond the Big Lake stream, we re-enter a forest of sorts, finding Jeffrey pines. Walking through sand flats where Cherry Creek Canyon begins to turn southwest, following the master-joint system which defines most northern Yosemite drainages, we gaze all around at the nearly unlimited rock-climbing possibilities presented on nearby granitic bluffs. Passing, at 6400 feet, into another slickened chute of exfoliation flakes, we note that our route along the water's edge is pinched off ahead, along even steeper slabs, so we climb south to round east of a low dome. Since our way back to the riverside would be thwarted by horrendous cliffs in a chute between two remarkably striated domes, we stay high, scrambling through a tangle of huckleberry oak and mountain maple 100 feet up, to the backside of the next ridge south. Expansive panoramas of the terrain down-canyon can be had by walking to the high point of this dome. Rattlesnakes make the shrubbery-dotted slabs atop this rock their home, so walk with care.

After descending this dome's sloping south side, we once again choose to remain away from the creek and the steep rocks that border it. The sandy Jeffrey-pine-shaded flats on the east side of the next dome afford hospitable camping, if you decide to lay over. If not, saunter south, then southwest, over lustrous glacial slabs to a large swimming

Cherry Creek in the upper part of the cross-country route

hole where Cherry Creek momentarily eases its raucous descent. A fine campsite graces the sandy banks here, where Jeffrey pines and hunched junipers foreground a roiling, potholed chute notched deeply in the monolithic granite. Highshooting torrents of white froth, enveloping the hiker in cooling, rainbow-generating spindrift, complete the scene, but to the through traveler, it means another detour. After a short thrash around a small dioritic dome, we rejoin the stream in a stand of conifers fragrant with the lilting aroma of white, yellow and rose-colored western azalea. For the next few minutes, we stay just under the 5600-foot level on rotting ledges of diorite cut by multitudes of lighter dikes, well above the cleft of Cherry Creek, which has weathered oddly-shaped potholes in the surrounding rock.

Nearing the north shoulder of an impressive cliff, follow a series of ledges that lead down to a sloping ramp covered with manzanita. Soon we find ourselves at the base of a fine waterfall. Inspirational views of the stupendous 700-foot dihedral-cut cliff to the east repeatedly draw our eyes from our

footing as we scramble around a rocky nose east of the stream that drains a tiny lake on Cherry Ridge. Presently, a mature mixed-conifer forest closes around us at the most idyllic spot in the entire Cherry Creek Canyon, and possibly in Emigrant Wilderness. Here Cherry Creek runs up to 70 feet wide and 7 feet deep over foot-soothing sand and gravel, cutting 2–3 feet into the dark alluvium of this pristine lowland. Mammoth specimens of Jeffrey and sugar pine, incense-cedar and white fir, possibly of record proportions, shade a mattresslike pine-needle-strewn floor—a virginal site for a memorable camp. Bigleaf maple and flowering dogwood reflect the diffuse yellow light of the understory. Travelers whose desire for strenuous activity is not overcome by the delicious lethargy of this quiet locale will no doubt challenge the rarely-climbed cliffs that loom over the camp. Truly confirmed masochists, however, will try the swimming.

All good things must end, as this restful forest soon does, giving way to rocky bluffs up which one must scramble, to traverse under some cliffs that give the hiker feelings similar to those that the discoverers of Yosemite must have experienced. Near the east edge of a swimming hole complete with sand-bar beach, the rocks above close in, forcing us down slabs and ledges to a little forest south of that pool. From this lagoon, it is best to remain near the stream, with some deviations to avoid bluffs, huge down logs, side creeks, and the odd morass, until you emerge from the forest at another, very deep basin located ¼ mile below the influx of West Fork Cherry Creek. Turning south from the nice camp beside it, we traverse slabby granodioritic rock showing prominent red and orange weathering of iron from the rock's dark mafic minerals.

Once more our way is barred down the creek, forcing us to climb south on the crumbling slopes of a southwest-jutting rib, to find a poorly ducked path that leads down a gully on its lower side, then vanishes. Bulling our way through a thicketed forest of ponderosa pine and white fir, we soon regain Cherry Creek. Now descending east, we reach an unnamed creek coming down from Kibbie Ridge.

Hikers intent on reaching Cherry Lake should note that the way down canyon to the reservoir's head is blocked by slabs on Peak 5319, so one must follow the unnamed creek, or more open terrain to its south, 400 feet up to a saddle to the east of that peak. Here the hiker should continue climbing southeast through forested shrubbery to the Kibbie Ridge Trail (Route CL-1) somewhere in the vicinity of Shingle Spring, 700 feet above. Now that a logging road extends almost to Shingle Spring, this is the fastest way home.

Dome about halfway down the cross-country route

Ch. 15: Bourland Creek

BC-1

Box Spring Trail: Weed Meadow Road to Pine Valley and Dutch Lake via Skeleton Pass

Distances
0.9 mile to Mud Lake Trail
2.1 miles to Skeleton Pass
2.9 miles to Dutch Lake
3.4 miles to Grouse Lake-Bell Meadow Trail

Introduction
The little-used Box Spring Trail affords a quick, uneventful route to Pine Valley and is the quickest path to Dutch Lake and other members of the quiet, forested Chain Lakes.

Trailhead
Leave Sonora Pass Highway 108 at the second (east) Long Barn exit. Follow Long Barn Road (Old Highway 108) 0.1 mile to paved Merril Springs Road 3N01, signed for the North Fork Tuolumne River and Cherry Reservoir. Go left on 3N01, 0.8 miles to paved North Fork Road, and take the latter over the Tuolumne River, passing Hull Creek Campground in another 8.8 miles. Beyond, 3N01's surface deteriorates to dirt. Bridge the Clavey River and, 3.8 miles later (20.2 miles from Highway 108), turn left (north) on dirt Bourland Creek Road 3N16. Follow it, ignoring similar, branching roads, to signed Weed Meadow Road 3N20Y, in 5.4 miles. Now go left (north) on Road 3N20Y, across Bourland Creek and up to a ridgetop road junction. Continue right, east-northeast on 3N20Y. A descending contour leads above and south of Weed Meadow to an abrupt switchback where our road turns down (southwest). Park here on the shoulder.

Description
From the abrupt switchback on the Weed Meadow Road, situated in a logged-over forest of fir and pine, we find the Box Spring Trail by dropping steeply north down the embankment for about 40 vertical feet to a blazed red fir. Here the well-defined path is marked by deep blazes highlighted by yellow paint. Proceeding northeast over a small rib, we drop to the base of a hillside stripe of corn-lily and stickseed meadow. In early season, a profusion of wildflowers grows here on gravelly, cinder-strewn volcanic soil. From this meadow a short descent finds Box Spring, emerging from brown clay soil just below the trail in an eroded corn-lily flat. A poor camp lies nearby.

The next few minutes pass in a gentle ascent through lodgepole, western-white-pine and red-fir forest, culminating in a short drop to the meadowed upper end of a shallow, pear-shaped lake, ablaze with yellow pond lilies. Sharp-eyed hikers will spot two old USFS signs tacked to a lodgepole left (north) of the trail, marking a lateral that continues prominently around the lake's southern shore to Skeleton Pass and Dutch Lake, as described below.

The Pine Valley lateral trail, continuing north to link up with the Bell Meadow Trail, makes its way around this frog-infested lake's west shore, then, more easily followed, continues past a smaller pond to a ravine. Our path descends this incipient canyon, soon leaving open slopes behind for quiet groves of yellow pine. A small creek is forded twice in quick succession, then, keeping on its west bank, we drop gently through muddy lodgepole-aspen forest. Beyond a few smaller streams, negotiate the east branch of Lily Creek, then change course for a westward traverse out of the soggy lowland. A gentle descent over duck-marked slabs leaves us in a pleasant meadowed grove of lodgepoles beside a 15-foot-wide sandy ford of Lily Creek. Now on Lily Creek's west bank, our trail remains near it under a conifer canopy, soon arriving at a fine campsite. Only yards later we step out onto a large pasture blotched with the yellows of buttercups and clover. Here the trail vanishes, so we follow a compass bearing of 340° across this sometimes damp grassland to the point where a meadowed arm extends west, the Mud Lake Trail's rut cutting a prominent line up its center. Instead of following this route to unappetizing Mud Lake, we cut 40 yards straight north over a few downed lodgepoles to a continuation of duff trail tread. Climbing gently, this route then ascends a granodiorite bench. Dropping to enter Pine Valley—true to its name a dense assembly of lodgepoles—our way soon arrives at a signed T with the broad Bell Meadow Trail (Route PC-10).

From the poorly signed junction with the Pine Valley lateral, the Dutch Lake Trail heads around the forested east shore of an unnamed shallow pond, passing under chartreuse-lichened cliffs to descend gently along an intermittent creek. Hounded by mosquitos, we turn east up steep, rocky tread. Further moderate ascent brings us to a branch of Lily Creek, here hardly more than a trickle. Rocky climbing ensues—right up Lily Creek's bed—with a shiny-leaved shrub with odd, double-tube-shaped flowers called twinberry growing thickly beside us. The ascent ends in a sandy-floored gully named Skeleton Pass. Dutch Lake's lodgepole-decked west end is reached a minute later. Our trail continues around its forested southwest shore, reaching an excellent campsite on a rocky peninsula. Dutch Lake's grass-and-granite shoreline bounds 4 acres of fair rainbow-trout fishing and is the best base for exploration of the other Chain Lakes.

BC-2

Chain Lakes Trail: Bourland Meadow Roadend to Chain Lakes and Grouse Lake

Distances
3.8 miles to Upper Chain Lake
4.5 miles to Dutch Lake

Introduction
The Chain Lakes have nothing special to offer. Their pleasant but unspectacular scenery, fair fishing and difficult-to-follow pathway keep away the crowds—this could be your destination for an easy overnighter with solitude.

Trailhead
Follow Bourland Creek Road, as described for Route BC-1, up to its boulder-blocked end at 7200 feet, 0.7 mile beyond the Road 3N20Y junction. Park on the shoulder.

Description
Seventy-five feet after the mammoth boulders blocking farther passage along the Bourland Creek Road, the Chain Lakes Trail—actually a jeep track at this point—veers, unmarked, from this soon-deadending logging road, to drop down through lodgepole pines to the green, Bigelow-sneezeweed-lined trough of Bourland Creek. Now on the northwest side of the canyon, our obvious path leads gently up to Bourland Meadow. Closely cropped vegetation and a sluggish, Indian-pond-lily-decked creek are the hallmarks of this half-mile-long grassland. Skirting the meadow's north side on sometimes-trail, we pass a sign indicating the now-

defunct Weed Meadow and Hells Mountain trails. From it, we cut east across the trickling stream to find a faint trail leading northeast past a campsite at the meadow's head. More clearly now, the well-used path ascends gently along the south bank of Bourland Creek, while the forest cover, initially red fir, gives way to lodgepole pines. A small meadow might pose momentary route-finding problems, but the trail is found by blazed trees at meadow's edge. Soon we swing east, then southeast, to cross a branch of Cherry Creek in a thick lodgepole forest. Climbing imperceptibly, the route presently re-fords, to parallel the northern branch of that stream. Near 7600 feet the trees give way to an open granitic basin. No tread marks our way, but ducks are easily followed northeast to the obvious saddle. From this divide it is only a short distance to Upper Chain Lake, situated amid thick lodgepoles. Considering better overnight possibilities at the other Chain Lakes, the only possible attraction here is poor angling for small brook trout. To reach the northern lakes of this group, we walk north, then follow Upper Chain Lake's outlet stream, soon discovering ducks that lead down. Wind north, down along the margin of an immature stand of lodgepoles to the circular west bay of Middle Chain Lake. Good trail rounds the north shore of this barren (only 4 feet deep) lake, passing a good camp and a ducked side trail before swinging north to a fine packer camp on the east end of Dutch Lake, largest and prettiest of the Chain Lakes. A use trail runs around the southern perimeter of Dutch Lake to meet the Box Spring Trail (Route BC-1) and there passes the nicest camp for miles.

From the packer camp on Dutch Lake's east end a ducked route to Grouse Lake leads north around the lake shore to a lakeside meadow. This lush swale is a good example of siltation-caused lake destruction, the even-

Grouse Lake

tual fate of many Sierran lakes, but with a twist—here sphagnum, grasses, sedges and shooting star have gradually grown out from shore to form a thick carpet of organic material that actually floats like an Aztec garden in early season! Sooner or later, the meadow will become anchored. With the help of more detritus, Dutch Lake's fate will be sealed. Leaving the lake, pass northeast through a gap, then follow ducks gently down to bluffs overlooking Grouse Lake. Here the ducks end, but it is simple enough to wind down through the broken rock and huckleberry oak to Grouse Lake's lower end and the Bell Meadow Trail (Route PC-10).

Those who desire to sample Lower Chain Lake might follow a variant route. From the north shore of Middle Chain Lake, follow the outlet creek northeast. The volcanic slopes here are crowded with lovely mule ears, a large-leaved member of the sunflower family, so named for the striking resemblance of its leaves to the ears of familiar Sierran pack animals. Lower Chain Lake is undistinguished, but pleasing. Shallow water and winter kill prevent fish life, but swimming is excellent. From the lower lake's west shore, we can walk north along the outlet stream, following ducks to join the aforementioned route down to Grouse Lake.

BC-3

Studhorse Meadow Trail: Groundhog Meadow to Chain Lakes

Distances
1.4 miles to Studhorse Meadow
4.1 miles to Upper Chain Lake

Introduction
Overgrown and little-used, the lateral from Groundhog Meadow to Chain Lakes is nonetheless a worthwhile route for adventuresome hikers who want to explore the rarely seen West Fork Cherry Creek country. The route is not recommended for pack stock.

Trailhead
Same as the Route PC-10 trailhead.

Description
The Studhorse Meadow Trail is found just west of Groundhog Meadow and east of Piute Creek, 6.7 miles up the Bell Meadow Trail. From a sandy-floored grove of lodgepoles, the signed trail crosses a low rock outcrop on a southeastward bearing, reaching the old stream-course of Piute Creek a few yards later. A log crossing of this small creek leads to a winding traverse southwest. Presently, the trail climbs slightly under a granitic nose, then drops back to the level of Piute Creek over rough switchbacks in

masses of gabbroic and peridotitic rock. We see good campsites to our east just before we come upon a 6–10-foot-wide ford at a sandy crook in Piute Creek. Our way along the west bank wends through meadows and willow thickets to an abrupt left turn in the quiet stream's trench.

One-tenth mile later, we make a long jump to Piute Creek's forested north side, then step east into very wet Studhorse Meadow. We round a small tarn in this grassland, then climb east, along a low boss. No longer following any visible trail tread, we now proceed southwest atop this outcrop to a thin rib at 7370 feet, where talus in the stream bed allows us to ford Piute Creek. Now begins a long cross-country traverse. It will serve you well to stay as high as possible along the west wall of this canyon, to avoid frustrating dropoffs and interminable barriers of huckleberry oak and bitter cherry. By staying high among the solitary junipers and stunted pines one will also perceive how the rock's jointing pattern aided, or hindered, West Fork Cherry Creek's glacier in plucking and smoothing the landscape. Once we're west of Peak 7750, a large *roche moutonnee*, we have panoramas of the lower West Fork, including Hell's Mountain and the scoured shoulders of Cherry Ridge. Turning northwest, following ducks above a rounded knob, we leave slabs behind to enter a rocky gully which ends at a pinhead tarn. Now skirt north of a second pond to a saddle. Following a 345° bearing, an easy one-third-mile duff-softened descent in dense red fir brings us finally to the south end of Upper Chain Lake and the Bourland Meadow Trail (Route BC-2).

Largest Chain Lake

Ch. 16: Hoofing It
Horsepack Trips into the Emigrant Basin

Horsepack trips are the traditional way to visit Emigrant Wilderness and the Walker Basin. These areas were first explored on horseback, and their trails were developed by horsemen. Unlike other areas of the High Sierra, where horsepacking is on the decline, pack trips are still very popular here, and excellent pack outfits still offer a range of services. Deer-hunting season, in the autumn, sees a peak in horsepacking activity, so be sure to reserve your trip early.

With the capacity to carry 150 pounds of food and equipment, a pack animal opens up a range of wilderness opportunities that would be almost unthinkable if on foot. Children and large, comfortable tents are easily transported, and basecamps can be stocked. Since the average one-day trip length (one-way) for a loaded horse or mule is 16–20 miles, almost any spot mentioned in this guide can be reached by a two-day horse trip.

Four pack stations offer trips into the Emigrant-Yosemite Sierra and Walker Basin.

From Gianelli Cabin, Crabtree or Bell Meadow trailheads into the western Emigrant Wilderness:

Reno Sardella's Pack Station
Summer: P.O. Box 1435
 Pinecrest, CA 95364
 (209) 965-3402
Winter: P.O. Box 159
 Jamestown, CA
 (209) 984-5727

The station is located on Crabtree Road 6.5 miles from Highway 108, as described for the Route PC-3 trailhead.

From Kennedy Meadows into the northern Emigrant Basin:

Kennedy Meadows Resort
Summer: Star Route Box 1490
 Sonora, CA 95370
 (209) 965-3900
Winter: P.O. Box 4010
 Sonora, CA 95370
 (209) 532-9096

The station is located at Kennedy Meadows roadend, as described for the Route KM-1 trailhead.

For the Walker Basin, use:

Leavitt Meadows Pack Station
P.O. Box 124, Bridgeport, CA 93517
 (916) 495-2257

The pack station is located on Highway 108 in Leavitt Meadow, 7.4 miles east of Sonora Pass and 7.7 miles west of the Highway 108-Highway 395 junction.

From Cherry Lake trailheads into the southwestern Emigrant Wilderness:

Cherry Valley Pack Station
4033 N. Thornton Road, Merced, CA 95340
 Summer: (209) 723-9538
 Winter: (209) 921-3988

Find the pack station just before the Cherry Lake roadend, as described for the Route CL-1 trailhead.

Horsepackers in the western Emigrant Wilderness should note that horse grazing and picketing are forbidden within ¼ mile of Rosasco, Pingree, Piute, Gem, Jewelry, Long and Maxwell lakes.

Ch. 17: Kick and Glide
Winter Travel in Emigrant Wilderness

Winter sees the High Sierra enveloped in a thick, quiet blanket of shining white snow. Knowledgeable winter campers know that this quiet season—December through mid-May in most years—is the prime time to enjoy the Emigrant Wilderness.

The most popular area for nordic skiers is the Aspen Meadow-Crabtree Road area near Pinecrest, accessible via Dodge Ridge Road during winter months. Here the Forest Service has laid out marked but ungroomed ski trails, mostly along dirt roads. Trailhead information signs show the routes, or consult Marcus Libkind's comprehensive guide *Ski Tours in the Sierra Nevada, Volume 2* for descriptions of these tours.

The following are suggestions for some longer trips into and across the Emigrant high country.

1. Follow Sonora Pass Highway 108, which is closed in winter, over Sonora Pass to Pickel Meadow. Gates close the road at Cow Creek on the west and near the Mountain Warfare Training Center on the east. The route is fun and fast. Beware of areas of moderate avalanche hazard west of Clark Fork, between Kennedy Meadows and Chipmunk Flat, and along Leavitt Creek. Snowmobilers may share your way in to Kennedy Meadows.

2. Leavitt Peak and Blue Canyon afford great late-spring telemarking, when the highway first opens.

3. Eagle Meadow Road: This gently undulating road becomes an ideal skinny skiing trail in winter. A fine long overnighter or 3-day trip could reach the rolling hills and delightful vistas of Sardine Meadow, near the Bennett Juniper.

4. The most northern route across Emigrant Wilderness entails skiing up Herring Creek Road to Coyote Meadows. Then follow the line of Route HC-1 to Cooper Meadow, then ski over to Upper Relief Valley via Cooper Pocket. From there, ski in bowls on the west slopes of Granite Dome. If you're planning a trans-Sierra trip, continue on to Emigrant Pass via the rolling summit ridge from Granite Dome to Blackhawk Mountain, then past Mosquito Lake (this way is cold and windy, but prettiest), or (easier) swing south as described in Route PC-3 to Deer Lake, then follow Route PC-4 over frozen Buck, Emigrant and Middle Emigrant lakes, to gain Emigrant Pass.

5. The most-often skied trans-Sierra route from Pinecrest climbs from the environs of Dodge Ridge Ski Area to Gianelli Cabin. Then, Route PC-3 is generally followed to Deer Lake. Now, as in the previous route, ski down to Buck Lakes, then up and across frozen Emigrant and Middle Emigrant lakes to Emigrant Pass or Grizzly Meadow. Traverse southeast now, across an open highland above the line of the Bond Pass High Trail to a large slope above Dorothy Lake—this often yields some fine skiing. Cross Dorothy Lake Pass and traverse east across the head of Cascade Creek's cirque, as described in Route WB-10. Some fine skiing leads down into Tower Canyon, which can be crossed at about 8,800 feet to gain Rainbow Canyon. Easy skiing leads up Rainbow Canyon (see Route WB-9) and across the head of Thompson Canyon. Now, more fine skiing eastward reaches Route YP-1 at Kerrick Meadow. Follow this trail, in

reverse, down to Twin Lakes. This last section is quite exposed to numerous large avalanche releases in late spring.

Possibly most important to skiers unfamiliar with Emigrant Wilderness is a list of places to avoid:

1. The Bell Meadow Area—Snow quality is usually poor.
2. South Fork Stanislaus River above Pinecrest Lake—Slick slabs under the snow create extreme avalanche hazard.
3. Slopes north of Burst Rock, Powell Lake and Lake Valley also have high danger of slab avalanche.
4. Upper Herring Creek Area—Generally overrun with snowmobiles.
5. Summit Creek/Relief Creek area between Granite Dome and Kennedy Meadows—Has high avalanche danger and treacherous stream crossings.
6. Lower reaches of West Walker River Basin—Below Fremont Lake, the snow is often poor, routes are brushy and river fords are very dangerous.

Boulder Peak seen from the north

Ch. 18: Fat-Tire Fun
Mountain Biking Around the Sonora Pass Country

Mountain bikers have no place in Emigrant Wilderness, Hoover Wilderness Addition, or on the trails of Yosemite Park. In fact, their use there is illegal.

That being said, there is no denying the sheer thrill of piloting a bicycle along high mountain roads and trails, and thankfully, opportunities abound on the perimeters of our high-country preserves to experience the excitement of mountain biking.

Single-track trail rides are uncommon here, since most good foot trails are on Wilderness or Park Service lands. There are three notable exceptions. The Eagle Meadow Trail is the best and the most difficult ride in the area—definitely only for expert riders. Its continuation, the Eagle Pass Trail, is a very steep, narrow trail, which can be traced up to Eagle Pass (you'll probably have to push in a few places). Do not enter Emigrant Wilderness, south of Eagle Pass. The third option for trail riding is a decrepit jeep road that connects Coyote Meadow roadend with Pinecrest Peak Road at the roadend for Waterhouse Lake. It is hard, steep, and very scenic.

While single-tracks are rare, fun dirt roads abound. Look at the map—any road can give hours of good riding. My recommendations include:

1. Leavitt Lake Road—Short, scenic, and a lung-searing uphill. Make sure your brakes can stand the rollercoaster stream-splashing return trip!

2. Eagle Meadow Road—The best long day-tour. Be sure to go as far as the wide-open vistas and fields of mule ears at Sardine Meadow, where you can have lunch beside the Bennett Juniper. Hot-shots will continue on some technical double-track to Silvermine Creek roadend. To lengthen your ride, ride up Long Valley as far as you can, or take a myriad of logging roads north to Double Dome Rock.

3. Herring Creek Loop Road—Paved at first, but later fast dirt, a good half-day workout. Do it counterclockwise for the best hills; detour to Pinecrest Peak for views. To make it tougher, include the third single-track option mentioned above.

4. Crabtree-Gooseberry Loop—A 3000-foot hill climb from "downtown" Pinecrest. Hammer up paved Dodge Ridge Road to the entrance to Dodge Ridge Ski Area. Here, turn right on Road 4N06Y, signed for Aspen Meadow. In ½ mile, it intersects Crabtree Road. Take this steeply uphill to Aspen Meadow, where the road becomes dirt. Continue up to Gianelli Cabin roadend. Add another 600 feet of elevation workout, and superlative views, by hiking up to Burst Rock for lunch. On the return trip, continue to your right (northwest) from Gianelli Cabin on less-used, narrow Gooseberry Road. It allows you to scream down the ridge, back to Dodge Ridge Road at the ski-area parking lot.

5. Bell Mountain—A killer hill, with killer views. Ride to Aspen Meadow, then turn south on poorly paved Dodge Ridge Road 4N25. Follow this 3.1 miles southwest, under Dodge Ridge to signed Dodge Meadow Road 4N09. Turn left (east), leaving behind pavement, to reach sunny Dodge Meadow in 0.7 mile. In 1.6 miles bridge the Clavey River. Climb 1.0 mile east to north-branching Bell Mountain Road 4N50Y. It immediately fords Lily Creek, then steeply attacks the southwest flank of Bell Mountain. Stay right at a junction in 2.4 miles, then grind up a final very steep, dusty double track to the summit, 1.7 miles beyond. The summit is an ideal picnic spot—a meadow of mule ears with panoramas east and southeast to Tower Peak, Haystack Peak, the Cathedral Range and Mount Lyell.

Ch. 19: Aiming High
Climbing in the Emigrant-Yosemite Sierra

Tower Peak, the most prominent mountain in northern Yosemite, sees 20 or 30 ascents each summer. With that exception, unlike the true High Sierra to the south, the Emigrant Basin-North Boundary Country is not a target for mountaineers. In fact, few prominent peaks of any kind are found in Emigrant Wilderness proper. The great Ice Age was responsible for the Emigrant Basin's rolling character: its glaciers completely overrode the land, shearing away any sharp ridges and smoothing away all the sky-scraping peaks. So ambitious mountaineers tend to shun Emigrant Wilderness, setting their sights farther south.

Unfortunately, in doing so, climbers miss out on the best and largest rock-climbing area in the Sierra north of Yosemite, and the only almost unclimbed region in all of California. Throughout the region, 400- and 800-foot-high walls, slabby aprons, and domes abound, all boasting exceptionally clean rock untouched by rock-climbers. Cherry Creek Canyon, the South Fork Stanislaus River canyon above Pinecrest Lake, the south face of Nance Peak, Tower Peak's incredible "Watchtower", and Hawksbeak Peak all offer outstanding high-angle rock. The rock's quality is much like that in Yosemite Valley, but without the attendant crowds, noise, air pollution, and scarred rock. Easy access to the summits and bases of most walls without rappelling makes it particularly easy to climb more than one route in a day.

These precipitous climbs are not for the casual mountaineer. Special equipment is required for safety, but even more important is rigorous and extensive training in the proper safety techniques. Those interested in learning to rock-climb should contact the Sierra Club or some other mountaineering organization for classes.

Steep volcanic summits, such as the Three Chimneys, East Flange Rock and Molo Mountain, along the northern boundary of Emigrant Wilderness should, in general, be avoided. These cliffs are composed of poorly cemented volcanic debris which affords no anchoring points and will break apart almost without provocation. Other, gentler summits, such as Relief Peak, Kennedy Peak and Leavitt Peak, are safe and exhilarating.

Climbing a glacial erratic

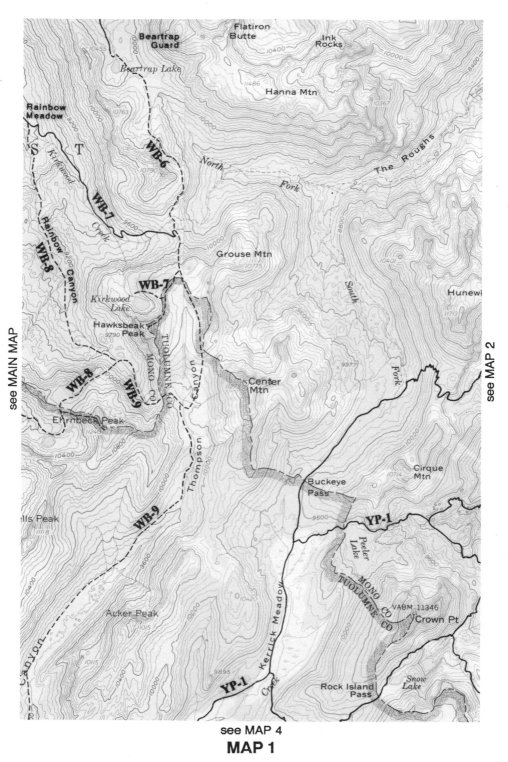

see MAIN MAP

see MAP 2

see MAP 4

MAP 1

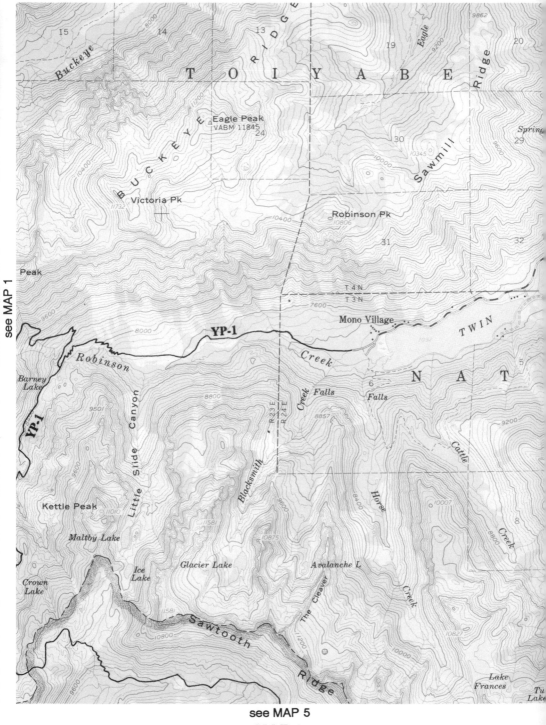

see MAP 5

MAP 2

see MAIN MAP

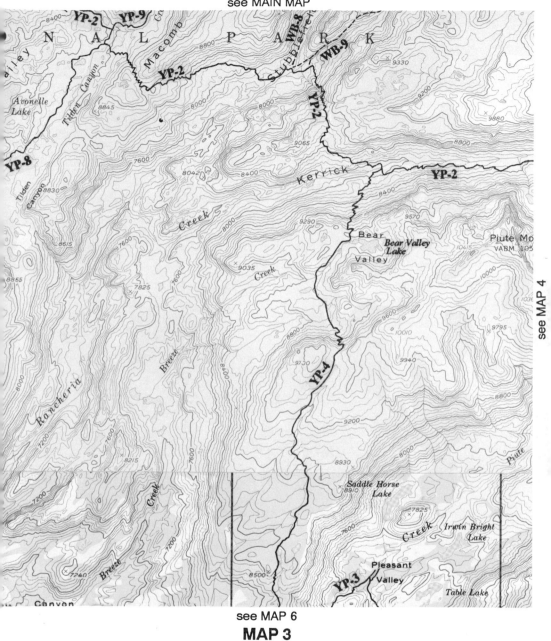

see MAP 6

MAP 3

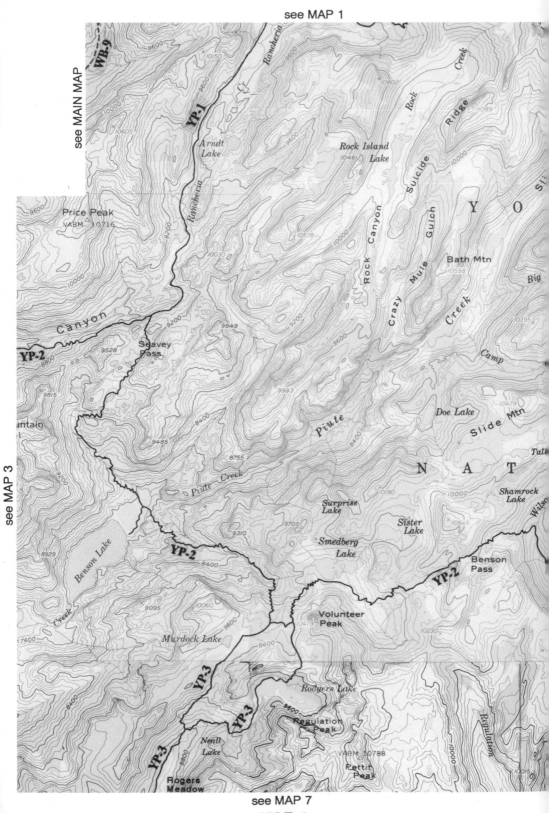

WB-9

YP-1

Rancheria Cr

Rancheria

Arndt
Lake

Rock Island
Lake

Rock

Suicide

Ridge

Rock
Canyon

Crazy
Mule
Gulch

Creek

Y O

Camp

Price Peak
VABM 10716

YP-2

Canyon

Seavey
Pass

Bath Mtn

Big

Doe Lake

Slide Mtn

Tal

Piute

N   A   T

Piute Creek

Shamrock
Lake

Surprise
Lake

Sister
Lake

Wilso

Benson Lake

YP-2

Smedberg
Lake

Benson
Pass

YP-2

Volunteer
Peak

Murdock Lake

YP-3

Rodgers Lake

YP-3

Neall
Lake

Regulation
Peak

Regulation

YP-3

Rogers
Meadow

Pettit
Peak

VABM 10788

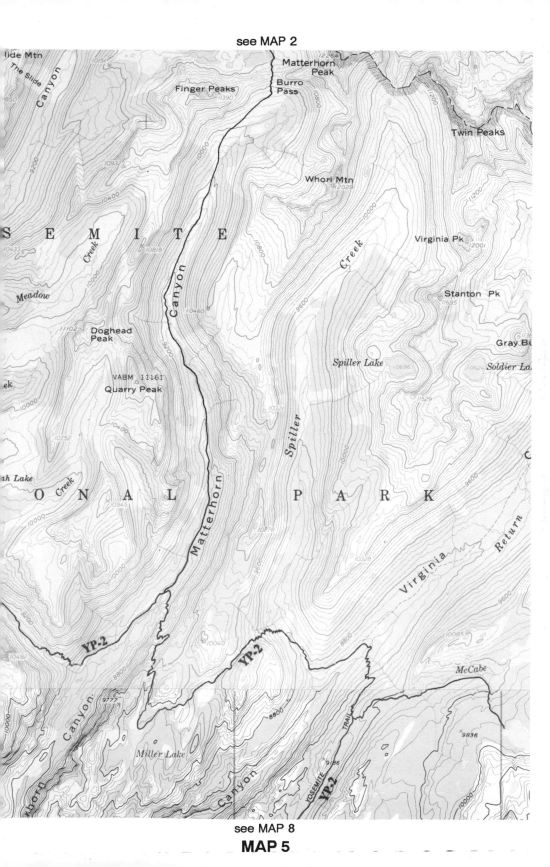

see MAP 3

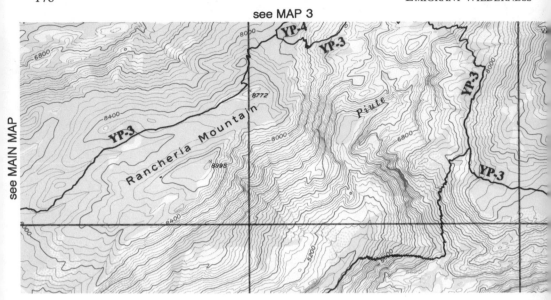

MAP 6

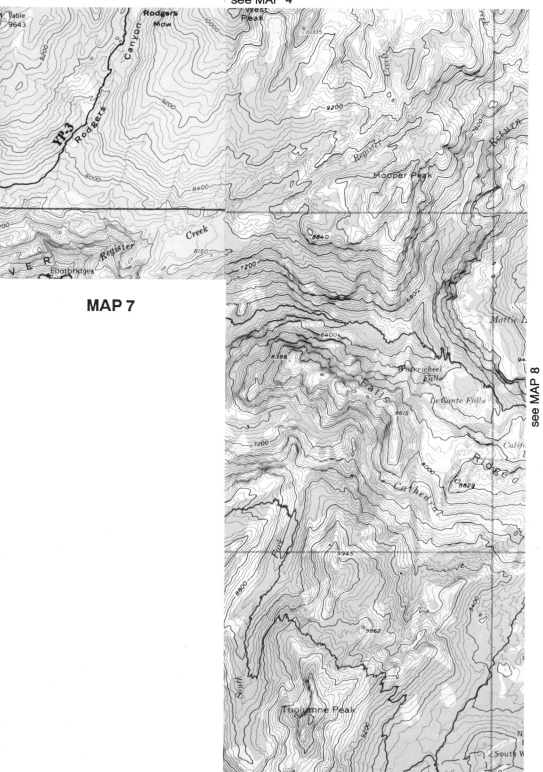

see MAP 4

MAP 7

see MAP 8

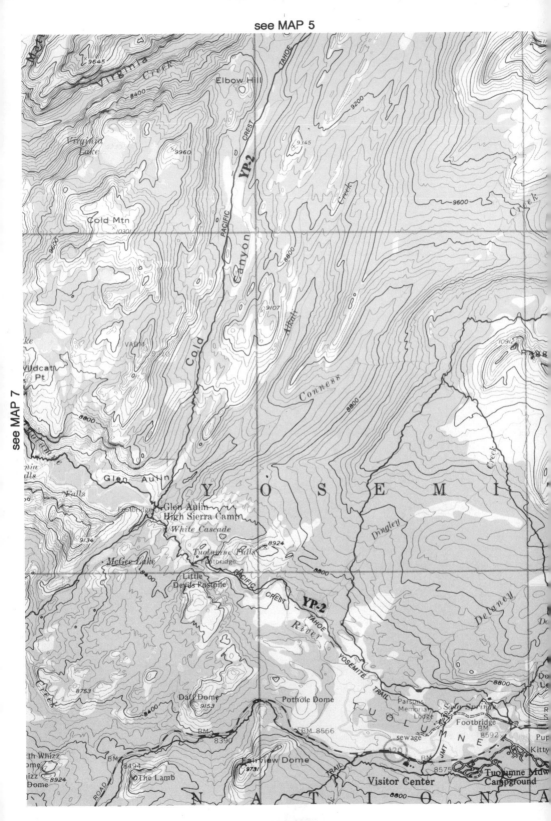

see MAP 7

MAP 8

INDEX

Most of the trips in this book are shown in their entirety on the large foldout map that comes with the book. But some trips are shown in whole or in part on separate pages at the end of the book. The maps for these trips, in the order needed, are listed at the beginning of the trips that need them. (The term "main" refers to the large, foldout map in the back of the book.)